VITTORIA COLONNA

Hanfstaengl

Cardinal Reginald Pole.
by Sebastiano del Piombo.
(The Hermitage. Petersburg.)

VITTORIA COLONNA

WITH SOME ACCOUNT OF
HER FRIENDS AND HER TIMES

BY

MAUD F. JERROLD

Select Bibliographies Reprint Series

BOOKS FOR LIBRARIES PRESS
FREEPORT, NEW YORK

First Published 1906
Reprinted 1969

STANDARD BOOK NUMBER:
8369-5153-0

LIBRARY OF CONGRESS CATALOG CARD NUMBER:
72-103653

PRINTED IN THE UNITED STATES OF AMERICA

TO

MY HUSBAND

THIS is the Harvest-month, the blades are bent
   With weight of golden corn fast ripening.
   Soon will be heard the voice of them that bring
Their sheaves rejoicing.   Sadly forth they went
Till labour found its due accomplishment;
   At evening they will come again and sing
   According to the joy of harvesting,
Voices of sower and of reaper blent.

This is the Harvest-month, the golden tide
   Of golden grain and ruddy golden leaf.
   Then take as first-fruits my one garnered sheaf
(No golden gift, Belovèd, worthy you);
   Be Love the sower and the reaper too,
   For is not Love, like Wisdom, justified?

August 4, 1906

PREFACE

It must always be with diffidence that anyone puts
forth a volume on such a well-worn epoch as that of
the Renaissance, and this must be doubly felt in the
case of a work like the present, which makes no claim
to any sort of original research, but is simply a selection of materials more or less generally accessible.
Whether the fascination of selecting be a sufficient
excuse for adding to the world of books must be a
matter of opinion, but it is not, perhaps, presumptuous
to hope that a small part of the pleasure experienced
in the writing may be felt in the reading.

I wish to thank my brother, the Reverend Lionel
Goodrich, most gratefully for all the help and interest
and advice he has given me in my work, and still more
for the help and guidance of years.

Also my warmest thanks are due to my friend, Mr.
Edmund Gardner, for most substantial assistance
throughout, especially in the laborious task of correct-
ing the translations; for truly invaluable encouragement and advice; and for such unfailing kindness as
no words of gratitude can repay.

London, *August* 4, 1906.

CONTENTS

CHAPTER   PAGE

I.   From Child to Woman   .   .   .   I

II.   Choice and Circumstance   .   .   . 32

III.   Early Poems   .   .   . 63

IV.   A Chronicle of Friendships   .   . 86

V.   The Love of Friendship   .   . 119

VI.   A Sister Poet, Veronica Gambara   . 139

VII.   Gaspara Stampa   .   . 169

VIII.   The Beginning of a Tragedy   .   . 198

IX.   In the Storm   .   .   . 225

X.   Viterbo   253

XI.   Later Writings   .   .   . 283

XII.   Out of the World   .   .   . 298

Genealogical Tables   .   .   . 318

Bibliography   322

Index   327

ILLUSTRATIONS

CARDINAL REGINALD POLE. By Sebastiano del Piombo ('The Hermitage, Petersburg) . . . *Frontispiece*

Facing page

GIOVANNA D'ARAGONA. By Raphael (The Louvre) . . 61

MICHELANGELO BUONARROTI (Portrait in the Gallery of the Capitol, Rome) 128

VITTORIA COLONNA. By Girolamo Muziano (Palazzo Colonna, Rome) 198

PAUL III AND THE FARNESE. By Titian (Picture Gallery, Naples) 235

VITERBO FROM THE GIARDINO PUBBLICO . . . 280

VITTORIA COLONNA

CHAPTER I

FROM CHILD TO WOMAN

Es bildet ein Talent sich in der Stille,
Sich ein Charakter in dem Strom der Welt.

GOETHE.

THERE is an endless fascination to be found in that
flowering time of the world's history which we call
the Renaissance.   It was a period of eagerness, activity,
and restlessness, of unprecedented sharpening of wits,
when the head dominated the heart.   It brought forth
a profusion of rich and beautiful growths, and was as
remarkable for its women as for everything else ; but
they are jewels rather than flowers, and, if they are as
brilliant as the diamond, they have also something of
its hardness.   They come before us adorned with that
wonderful fifteenth-century teaching of which we, in
these days when education is our most popular fetish,
have no adequate conception, because we do not choose
to cast our eyes back on the nobler past and see what
it has to teach us.   It is pitiful to hear women exult in
the liberal training now provided for them, and yet to
know that the curriculum of the High School, chiefly

B

directed to the passing of examinations, would have
been absolute intellectual starvation to the women of
five centuries ago.

Certainly, in reading the lives of such illustrious
ladies as the Princesses of the House of Este, who
seem to have been dowered with all the arts and
sciences, we may wonder whether they were as accomplished in all ways as contemporary historians would
have us believe, and we can hardly help allowing something for the language of flatterers ; but, on the other
hand, how much was normal to them which would be
exceptional to us ! To begin with, they were all
classical scholars, which means starting in life with the
equipment of a trained mind ; and, furthermore, just
as one can hardly live in a library without imbibing
something from it, some acquaintance with its contents,
or at least some atmosphere of literature, so we can
hardly conceive the denizens of that fortunate period
being untouched by the wealth of culture around them.
They must have drunk in, almost unconsciously, an
apprehension of the relative value of things, an appreciation of those high lights which surrounded them,
so that, if not artists and poets themselves, they were
at least artistic and poetic. There is that vast difference
between the education of their age and ours, that theirs
was humanistic, ours utilitarian ; and, in that alone,
theirs would be the more excellent.

It is perhaps disappointing that, though the Renaissance is the time of all others when we might expect
to find literary women of the first order, they are not
forthcoming. Women were splendidly educated, highly
cultured, accomplished in many ways ; they must,

indeed, have been charming companions, gifted, intellectual, and, besides that, their minds were well-balanced, they had a fine judgment, a great courage ; but the creative faculty in them is no more developed than it has been at any other time in human history. And, surely, it is profoundly unimportant; so that high ideals are conceived by the race, and great works brought forth, it matters little who is the doer in the last resort: men and women are never really independent of each other, and whenever any worthy thing is done, anyone with true insight knows that it is not due to one or to two, but that the hidden forces of many lives and loves have been required to perfect the work.

Born in 1490, Vittoria Colonna, the central figure of the present volume,

> " Che tra bella e buona
> Non so qual fosse più,"

may fairly be called a child of the Renaissance, but she is characteristic of it only in its very best developments. She was in no sense a type, because she had that interesting peculiarity of combining contrary traits. By birth, beauty, talent, and culture, she seemed destined to take her rank among the typical stars ; but there was another vein running through her nature—a sense of the value of retirement, a love rather of wisdom than of mere knowledge, and a thread of mysticism. Though the details of her childhood and girlhood are disappointingly meagre, in later life she holds a prominent place in the history, the art, and the literature of her time.

Daughter of one of the great Roman Houses (she is described in her marriage-contract as *illustris domicella Romana*), her father, Fabrizio Colonna, lives for us no less in the pages of Machiavelli as one of the foremost authorities in the art of war, than in the troubled history of those conflicts in which he played so conspicuous a part; while her mother, Agnese da Montefeltro, younger daughter of the Duke Federigo of Urbino, and sister of the celebrated Guidobaldo whose court was second to none as a centre of learning, must certainly have been imbued with all the best traditions of the intellectual life.

Marino, one of the ancient castles of the Colonna family, stands upon the wooded slope of the Alban Hills; it was there that Vittoria was born, and, if early surroundings can affect the character, we may well think that the influence of that marvellous nature counted for much in her life. For Albano is not merely lovely, it is the quintessence of loveliness; it is one of those places where Beauty unveils herself before us, and ever afterwards we say: Here I met with Beauty; I may meet her again, for she has many shrines, but here at least I saw her face to face; I have had my revelation and I am satisfied.

It is unfortunate that we know almost nothing of the upbringing of Vittoria, of the way in which she passed her days, her course of study, her proficiency in accomplishments; but we know that her early, no less than her later, life was disturbed by the unhappy struggles from which Italy was never free, and it was directly in consequence of these that her fate was decided so soon. It is difficult to follow out, still

harder to account for, the political point of view of the
Roman nobles, and this is complicated in the case of
the Colonna in that they were also feudatories of the
King of Naples, and Vittoria's father was Constable of
Naples. In 1482, we find the family siding with the
Neapolitans against the Pope; a little later, their sym-
pathies seem to be with France; but we see them
deserting the French cause and rallying to Ferdinand II
when he regained possession of Naples on the departure
of Charles VIII. Ferdinand, no doubt desiring to
bind the Colonna still closer to the furtherance of
Aragonese interests, induced Fabrizio to betroth his
little daughter to Ferrante Francesco d'Avalos, Marchese
di Pescara, the descendant and representative of the
noblest Spanish and Neapolitan families, though Paolo
Giovio, the historian, somewhat unkindly remarks that
his race was more ancient than illustrious; the fiancés
were only five years of age.

It does not appear that the agreement was actually
signed before 1507, nor did the marriage take place
until 1509. Meanwhile, Ferdinand, dying suddenly,
was succeeded by his uncle, Federigo, who made a
gallant stand against the French invasion, but finding
himself betrayed and abandoned by Spain, his natural
ally, gave up the hopeless struggle and escaped to
Ischia, giving himself up to France, and dying an
exile, almost a prisoner, in Anjou. Fabrizio and his
cousin, Prospero, fought for him bravely, the one holding Capua and the other Naples; but both places fell
before the superior numbers of the French, and
Fabrizio was taken prisoner, but was quickly set at
liberty. The two cousins then joined Federigo at

Ischia, but on his surrender they espoused the Spanish cause, uniting themselves to Gonsalvo di Cordova, and bearing their part in his brilliant campaign, which resulted in the expulsion of the French from Southern Italy. Meanwhile, the Colonna seem to have been in bad odour in Rome, where the Pope, Alexander VI, desiring their lands for the aggrandizement of his own family, issued a decree banishing them from their hereditary estates, and ordering their castle of Marino to be razed to the ground. Before this edict was carried out, however, Alexander died, and the mushroom power of the Borgias crumbled away as suddenly as it had sprung up.

Where was Vittoria during these troublous times? We have no record whatever of her movements; we do not know if she and her mother remained at Marino (no very safe residence, as we have seen), or whether they went south and were partakers in the tragedies that were overwhelming the kingdom of Naples: the veil is never lifted for us until we read of the marriage contract being signed at Marino in 1507 before many distinguished witnesses, among others Costanza d'Avalos, Duchessa di Francavilla, aunt of the Marchese di Pescara, who had educated and cared for him all through his orphaned childhood, a woman of much charm and strength of character, at whose castle in Ischia the marriage subsequently took place with great pomp on 29 December, 1509.

Both nineteen years of age, endowed with remarkable gifts of mind and body, with intellectual tastes in common, life must have seemed to open brilliantly before this pair; and, in the beginning of their married

life, we may hope that Vittoria had some golden days
of happiness. Married at Ischia, they proceeded to
Naples, where great receptions and rejoicings were held
in their honour, and they then settled at the villa of
Pietralba on Monte Sant' Ermo. Congenial society
would not have been wanting to them there : Jacopo
Sannazzaro was then living at his villa at Mergellina,
and it seems to have been the habit of the young
Marchese di Pescara to pass a good deal of time with
him. A fascinating personality his must have been,
combining poetic gifts with an exquisite loyalty to
a fallen house and a lost cause. He had been attached
to the Aragonese party in Naples and had followed the
exiled King into France, continuing there with him
until his death, when he returned to Mergellina, remaining equally hostile to French and Spaniards, and
making no secret of his political opinions, even to the
much-feared Gonsalvo di Cordova, who is said to have
felt a profound respect for him. He made many
literary friendships, and was looked up to by all the
authorities of his time.

If these tranquil two years seem something like
a prolonged honeymoon, the rest of Vittoria's married
life was certainly akin to widowhood, as after this time,
until her husband's death in 1525, they were scarcely
together at all. One would give much to know what
was the real interior history of this marriage. One
visible sorrow it had : it was childless. For other
lights upon it we must turn chiefly to Vittoria's own
works, about half of which are devoted to celebrating
the memory of her husband—" *il mio bel sole*," as she
loves to call him. With some hundred sonnets before

us, it would seem that we ought to gain some real
knowledge of the relations that existed between them,
and yet the tone is so artificial, so conventional, that
they really convey little to us. The same metaphors
are repeated again and again, and they certainly strike
but coldly on our ears. There is no trace of union,
sympathy, interdependence. It is most noticeable that
Pescara's glory, his fame as a warrior, his loss to his
country, is the main theme ; that this should be dwelt
upon is all that is most natural when the subject was
one of the great generals of a warlike age, but verily
these are not love-sonnets, and we confess to growing
weary of the reiterated exploits of a warrior whom we
picture to ourselves as but an indifferent lover.

The very year after Vittoria's marriage, we find her
father leaving Naples as second in command of the
Spanish army in Italy, to assist the Pope, Julius II, and
the Spaniards against the French, who, since their con-
quest of the Duchy of Milan in 1500, disputed with
Spain and the Pope the hegemony of the Italian penin-
sula, and found their chief supporter and ally in Duke
Alfonso of Ferrara. The history of the succeeding
years is, as usual, one of leagues and counter-leagues,
jealousies and betrayals ; Italy was no less a curse to her
conquerors than to her natural rulers. Fired with the
desire of military glory, Pescara soon followed his
father-in-law, and to him was given the command of
the light-armed cavalry. Whatever may have been the
defects of Ferrante d'Avalos, there was no lack of
courage in his character, and he seems also to have
been endowed with the qualities of a leader, to judge
from the high posts to which he was preferred, and

from his popularity with the army. No woman worthy of the name ever lived who wished to withhold her husband from his country's service and the obligations of honour, and we are sure that the Marchesa must have incited and encouraged Pescara to set forth, and would have bid him good-bye with a smile upon her lips, keeping all her tears to shed them in the long loneliness that was to follow on his departure.

She remained behind at Ischia, and it was at this time that she undertook the charge of her husband's young orphaned cousin, Alfonso d'Avalos, Marchese del Vasto, who became to her like a child of her own, though at first his education seems to have been no easy task, and for a long time the boy was a source of great anxiety to her. Wild, headstrong, and intractable, devoid of gentleness, with no bent but for war, Vittoria yet seems after some years, and with infinite care and patience, to have instilled into him a love of learning, together with a real taste for letters, and to have trained him in true chivalry, of which things he was to give abundant proof during his eventful life. His career, albeit it ended in misfortune, certainly counted as one of the bright lights in Vittoria's life— one of those apparent failures where the real end has yet been surely reached.

Costanza d'Avalos must have been a great comfort to her young niece by marriage at this time, and the Marchesa passed much time with her, no doubt in those intellectual pursuits in which both took so much pleasure. There is a story told that, in the stormy, threatening springtime of 1512, Vittoria felt a foreboding of coming disaster, but that her aunt, with that hopefulness so much more characteristic of age than of youth, assured her that no ill-fortune could await such an army under such leaders. Close on this followed the news of their overwhelming defeat. Ravenna was a fatal field for the combatants on both sides. It seems possible that, but for jealousy between the leaders of the Spanish and Italian troops, the victory might have remained with their allied armies. The Viceroy, Cardona, was in command of the Spaniards, Fabrizio Colonna of the Italians; the former was entirely under the influence of Pedro Navarro, whose reputation as an engineer had procured him a high command. Navarro's advice was that the allies should remain within their entrenchments and trust solely to their artillery. Colonna was for attacking the French, who, having to cross a small river, made a somewhat broken advance; but the advice of the Spaniards prevailed, the French were suffered to take up their position unmolested, and then the contending armies cannonaded each other with immense loss on both sides. At length the Duke of Ferrara, seeing that the French were beginning to fall back, brought his artillery to their assistance and cleverly attacked the enemy on the flank with terrible slaughter of men and horses. Fabrizio could no longer be withheld from making the sortie he had always advocated, and, breaking through the entrenchments, he threw himself on the enemy. His indomitable courage and the valour of the Spanish infantry bid fair to turn the fortune of the day, and again and again the issue seemed doubtful. Pescara made an impetuous attack with his light cavalry, but was beaten back, and the allies were at length com-

pelled to give way, their artillery, baggage, and stan-
dards falling into the hands of the enemy. Besides
Colonna and Pescara, Navarro was made prisoner and
also the Cardinal de' Medici, the future Leo X. Bayard's chronicler, from whom we get one of the most
spirited accounts of the battle, thus sums it up :
"There have been many battles since God created
heaven and earth, but never was one seen, for the
numbers engaged in it, so cruel, so furious, and so well
fought on both sides, as the battle of Ravenna."[1]
Indeed the day was less fatal to the allies than to the
victorious French, for, besides other generals, they lost
their valiant young commander, Gaston de Foix, and
with no available leaders they retired in disorder, and
from that time their success in Italy was over. Fabrizio
Colonna had surrendered to Alfonso, Duke of Ferrara,
and received the most gracious treatment from his
adversary, who refused to give him up to France, and
shortly released him without ransom. Ariosto thus
mentions Alfonso's illustrious prisoner :—

> "The great Colonna of the Roman name,
> Whom your own hand made prisoner, and whom
> You wholly guarded, more shall swell your fame
> Than if your arm had driven to their doom
> Those fierce battalions, even as many of them
> As fed Ravenna's field, or fled therefrom,
> Their arms found vain, the banners overthrown
> Of proud Navarre, Castile, and Aragon."[2]

---

[1] *Le Loyal Serviteur*, chap. LIV. p. 96.
[2] " La gran Colonna del nome Romano,
    Che voi prendeste, e che servaste intera,
    Vi dà più onor, che se di vostra mano
    Fosse caduta la milizia fiera,

The Duke quickly reaped the fruits of his generosity when he set out for Rome with a safe-conduct, obtained through the mediation of the King of Spain and the Marchese of Mantua, in order to get absolution from his excommunication. This was readily given, but Julius II made it clear that the safe-conduct only referred to the Duke's person and not to his States, of which the Pope was determined to gain possession. Every means of inducing Alfonso to surrender Ferrara was tried in vain, and finally the Pope decided to arrest him. At this juncture Colonna felt bound to interfere, and, breaking through the papal guard at the Porta San Giovanni, he escorted the Duke to Marino. Colonna, of course, incurred the papal displeasure for this act, but Ferdinand plainly informed the Pope that the Colonnesi were his subjects and would be protected by him.

Pescara also regained his liberty after a short captivity, but only on payment of a very large ransom. During his imprisonment, he is said to have written a *Dialogo d'Amore* to his wife, of which no trace now remains, but Giovio assures us that it testified equally to his conjugal affection and his literary talents. Vittoria's *Epistola a suo Consorte nella Rotta di Ravenna*, of which a little is quoted in another chapter, is certainly not one of her happiest efforts.

The Marchese may have returned to Ischia now for

Quanta n' ingrassa il campo Ravegnano,
E quanta se n' andò senza bandiera
D'Aragon, di Castiglia, e di Navarra,
Veduto non giovar spiedi nè carra."

(*Orl. Fur.*, xiv. 5.)

a short time, but we have no intimation of the fact. In 1513 (the date of the accession of Leo X), we find him again in Lombardy, where the war still continued for the next two years, until the death of Ferdinand, when hostilities ceased in Italy for a brief space, and Pescara rejoined his wife at Ischia. Here our records are as scanty as before ; we know that Vittoria's brother Federigo, a youth of great promise who had already distinguished himself as a soldier, died suddenly in 1516. In the next year we have the account of two great marriages, celebrated with all the pageantry proper to the time ; first that of the sister of the Marchese del Vasto with the Duke of Amalfi, and then that of Bona, daughter of Isabella of Aragon, with Sigismund, King of Poland. It is most tantalizing that, though history has preserved for us an exact record of the dress worn by Vittoria on this second occasion (to wit, crimson and gold brocade), the trappings of her horse, and the number and attire of her ladies-in-waiting, we have not one line to give us any insight into her habitual occupations and way of life ; and, still more remarkable, though she and her husband were certainly in Rome somewhere about this time, and must have shone even among all the stars that adorned the papal court, we know nothing of their stay there, the people they met, and the impressions they received and produced.

It would be delightful if we could be sure that Vittoria had met the great Ariosto in Rome, but it does not seem likely that he was then at Leo's court. Certainly he may have been there, and as it is difficult to find any other probable time and place in which he could have met the Marchesa, it is permissible to think that the meeting may have taken place now. The vivid and well-known praises of her in the *Orlando* hardly allow us to think that their author was only cognisant by hearsay of the rare gifts of which he sang so eloquently, nor is he likely to have been content to remain unacquainted with one of the most beautiful and talented women of the time.[1]

Ariosto's first visit to the court of Leo was very brief; coming there with an assurance of patronage and advancement, he received nothing but a gracious welcome from the Pope, and left Rome speedily, disappointed but not embittered. In the end, he seems to have received some small benefits from Leo, but nothing on the scale of his expectations. Leo X, though not a commanding figure, is one who attracts our attention, and in some sort our sympathy. Without greatness, he had the great quality of esteeming talent for its own sake. He inspired the idea that genius and worth would never be unrecognised by him, and if he promised more than he was able to perform, yet the expectations that he raised were not all illusory. And that he was no mean judge was attested by the fact of his choosing for secretaries two men without interest or influence, who had risen solely by their talents. With these two, Jacopo Sadoleto and Pietro Bembo, Vittoria now formed lifelong friendships, and this brief sojourn in Rome, the date of which we cannot precisely fix, must have been a little St. Martin's summer for the Marchesa; and in 1521 the war broke out again.

---

[1] *Orl. Fur.*, xxxvii. 16–20, xlvi. 9.

The French again tried to make good their claims to Milan, and Leo X allied himself with Charles V. To Pescara was confided the command of the Imperial infantry, and this time he was accompanied by his young cousin, del Vasto. It would appear that Pescara was desirous of leaving the youth at home, but Vittoria strongly urged that the boy should devote himself to his country's cause, rightly arguing that the dying out of one line would be a small misfortune in comparison to its continuing in the person of one who had not known how to maintain its traditions.

Success waited upon the Spanish-papal troops, who now took possession of Milan and Parma. Hostilities were suspended for a short time by the death of Leo X; and the election of Clement VII, after Leo's immediate successor, Adrian VI, had later some far-reaching effects on the war. It is said that rarely had any Pope been acclaimed with such general joy as Giulio de' Medici; the Florentines, however, who knew him best, uttered sinister predictions, and a letter which Ariosto sent to the Duke of Ferrara shows that the satisfaction was not, at any rate, universal :—

"A letter came to me from Lucca which advised me that Medici had been made Pope; and when the people of Castelnovo had heard this news, it seemed to them as if their heads had all been cut off, and such a great fear fell upon them, that there were some of them who wished to persuade me to set a guard on the town that same evening; and some think of selling, and some of carrying off their possessions. I am endeavouring to reassure them, and I tell them I know that a close friendship exists between your Excellence and Medici, and that they have nothing but good to expect."[1]

Vittoria and her husband seem to have had high hopes of the new Pontiff, and we find the former writing to her friend, Giovan Matteo Giberti, who now became datary and head of the papal secretaries :—

"REVEREND AND RIGHT MAGNIFICENT LORD,

"This night I have heard the welcome news that your most reverend Cardinal has been made Pope. May Our Lord God be unceasingly thanked, and I pray Him to give to this beginning such a continuation and end that men shall see clearly that a more perfect work has never been seen, nor one so wisely carried through, and obtained by the Cardinal himself through his own prudence. I shall not presume to attempt to express the insuperable gladness that I feel at this, since it is well known to you, both because of that other time when I hoped for it, and because of the good reason that I have to be glad. I confidently affirm that I am certain it would be impossible for anyone but you to understand the greatness of my joy, because you can judge of it by your own; and I do not reckon mine in any way inferior to yours. You will kiss the feet of his Holiness for me, and you will tell him that I can do nothing but continually implore Our Lord and Our Lady for his preservation, no less necessary to us than to you and also to all the world. I beg your magnificent Lordship that this felicity may not take from you

---

[1] Letter of November 23, 1523 (cxv., Ed. Cappelli, Milan, 1887).

what the other did not take, but on the contrary write to me more than ever.

"From Naples, November 21, 1523,
"My Lord, your most obliged,
"THE MARCHESA DI PESCARA."[1]

In the light of subsequent events this reads rather sadly.

In 1522, the armies met again at Bicocca; Pescara was in command and was as usual victorious, but his glory is eclipsed by the cruelties he permitted in the sack of Como and of Genoa. It was just after the taking of the latter town that he returned to Ischia and remained three days with his wife, and this was the last time they ever met. Reumont makes this hurried visit take place just after the death of Vittoria's mother, which he believes to have occurred in the October of 1522. But the correct date of Agnese's death is established by a letter from Ascanio Colonna, Vittoria's brother, to Federigo Gonzaga, the Marchese of Mantua, of April 6, 1523, in which he announces that his mother had died on the 1st of the month. Ascanio's letter runs thus: " It happened that on the return of my most illustrious Lady-mother and Lady of blessed memory from Our Lady of Loreto, where she had gone for her devotion, she came to the Rocca half-way near Aquila. When she arrived there, she was much indisposed after the journey, which she had made quite against my will, and then, as it has pleased the Lord of all, after having made such a holy and salutary journey,

---

[1] *Carteggio*, Letter ii.

c

and confessed and communicated with the greatest devotion as a good and faithful Christian should, she departed this life on April 1. And by this death I remain overwhelmed with grief for the loss of such a mother. And (since, when people are connected either by relationship or friendship, one ought to communicate both joyful and sorrowful tidings) it has seemed to me that I ought to send word of this to your most illustrious Lordship."[1]

At this time Pescara was in Spain. Returning to Northern Italy, he held Cremona and Milan against the French, and the latter, being unable to make any impression, withdrew in the spring towards Lago Maggiore. It was at this time that Chevalier Bayard, being in command of the rear-guard, was killed in defending the passage of the Sesia. He had been set an impossible task, *dangereuse et doubteuse*, as he himself told Bonnivet, as neither his men nor his ammunition were sufficient, and, in the event, nothing but retreat was possible. The story of his death is best given in the inimitable words of his chronicler, the Loyal Serviteur. "In war there is fortune and ill-fortune more than in all other things. . . . The good Knight put his soldiers in motion, and retired slowly, as much at ease as though he had been in his own house ; and with his face always turned towards the enemy, and brandishing his sword, he kept them more in fear than a hundred others would have done. But, as God willed it, a shot was fired from an arquebus which struck him through the loins and broke his spine. When he felt the blow,

---

[1] Luzio, *Vittoria Colonna* (in the *Rivista Storica Mantovana*, I), p. 10 *n.*

he cried out, ' Jesus ! ' and then ' Alas ! my God, I am
slain.' Then he took his sword by the cross-handle
and said aloud, ' *Miserere mei, Deus, secundum magnam
misericordiam tuam*,' and immediately he became quite
pale as though he was swooning and almost fell ; but
he had still strength to grasp the saddle-bow, and
remained upright until a young gentleman, his steward,
helped him to dismount and placed him under a tree.
In a short time it was known among friends and foes
that the captain Bayart had been killed by a shot of
artillery, whereat all those who heard the news were
marvellously displeased.

"When the tidings were spread abroad among the
two armies that the good Knight had been killed, or
at least mortally wounded, even in the camp of the
Spaniards, although he was one of the men in the world
of whom they had most fear, gentlemen and soldiers
were marvellously displeased at it for many reasons.
For when during his lifetime he made assaults and took
any prisoners, he was always wont to treat them so
humanely as it was a marvel, and to ask so little ransom
that every one was content with him. They all agreed
that by his death knighthood was greatly weakened, for,
without derogating from others, he was a perfect knight
in this world. Their young nobles acquired skill in
warring with him, and one of their principal captains,
the Marquis of Pescara, who went to see him before he
rendered up his soul, said a high word in his praise,
which was this : ' Would to God, gentle seigneur de
Bayart, that it had cost me a quart of my blood (short
of dying), and that by abstaining from flesh-meat for
two years I might have kept you whole and in good

health as my prisoner ; for, by the treatment that I
would have given you, you would have known how
much I have esteemed the prowess which was in you.
. . . Since I have borne arms, I have never seen nor
heard tell of a knight who approached you in all virtues.
And though I ought to rejoice to see you in this plight,
being assured that my master, the Emperor, had in
these wars no greater or more formidable enemy than
you, yet when I consider the great loss which all chivalry
sustains to-day, God aid me never if I would not have
given the half of all I am worth that it had befallen
otherwise.' Such pitiful and tearful laments did the
gentle Marquis of Pescara and several other captains
make over the body of the good Knight, *sans paour et
sans reprouche*. . . . His poor servitors were quite
frozen with horror, among whom was his poor steward
who never left his side, and the good Knight confessed
himself to him for want of a priest. The poor gentleman burst into tears, seeing his good master so mortally
hurt that there was no hope for his life. But the good
Knight comforted him gently, saying, ' Jacques, my
friend, it is the will of God to take me from this world.
By His grace I have lived long in it, and have had
goods and honours more than I deserved. All the
regret that I have in dying is that I have not done my
devoir as well as I ought, and I well hoped, if I had
lived longer, to amend my past faults. But since it is
thus, I beg my Creator of His infinite mercy to have
pity on my poor soul, and I have hope that He will do
it and that of His great and incomprehensible goodness
He will not use the rigour of justice towards me.'
. . . He remained alive a few hours longer, and a

beautiful pavilion was placed over him by his enemies, beneath which he lay, and a priest was brought to him to whom he confessed himself devoutly, saying these words: 'My God, I know that Thou hast said that whoever shall turn to Thee with all his heart, however great a sinner he may have been, Thou art always ready to receive him to mercy and to pardon him. Alas! my God, Creator, and Redeemer, I have offended Thee grievously during my life, for which I repent with my whole heart. I know well that if I were to remain in the desert for a thousand years on bread and water, that would not give me the right to enter Thy kingdom of Paradise, except Thy great and infinite goodness were pleased to receive me into it; for no creature in this world could merit so high a reward. My Father and my Saviour, I implore Thee not to regard the faults that I have committed, but let Thy great mercy be meted out to me instead of the rigour of Thy justice.' Having said thus, the good Knight rendered up his soul to God, whereat all his enemies felt a grief not to be believed. The chiefs of the Spanish army commissioned certain gentlemen to carry him to the Church, where solemn services were held for him during two days; then he was taken into Dauphiné by his servitors. . . . The deceased was carried to the Church of Notre Dame at Grenoble where he reposed a day and a night, and a very solemn service was held for him. The next day, with the same honour with which he had been brought thither, he was taken to a religious house of the Minorites about half a league from the town (which had formerly been founded by his good uncle, Laurent Almont, bishop

of the aforesaid Grenoble), where he was honourably
buried." [1]

Chivalry, one of the world's saviours, might be in
danger of becoming a mere shadow to some of us, if
a few heroic figures here and there—a Godefroi de
Bouillon, a Bayard, a Philip Sidney—did not rise up to
witness to it and to show us, as Mr. Swinburne has
beautifully said, that their life was lovelier than aught
but their death.

All this time Vittoria seems to have been travelling
about incessantly. In May of 1523 we find her at
Arpino, and from there we have the following letter
from her to Federigo Gonzaga, Marchese di Mantova, petitioning him for the repayment of the four
thousand ducats due from him to the Marchese di
Pescara. She says :—

"Most illustrious Lord,

"I wrote to Messer Mario Equicola concerning
the four thousand ducats which your most illustrious
Lordship owes to my lord the Marchese on account
of Messer Teodoro, and I have received no answer.
I do not know if this is because he is ashamed of the
long delay, but I believe it to be because he did not
care to remind your Lordship of it, and also that the
letter was wrongly transmitted. But even if there
were no fault in the cause, it produces the same result
and much harm, on which account I am obliged to
advise your most illustrious Lordship of it. And
although it grieves me to trouble you, still, being certain that, bearing the goodwill you do towards my

---

[1] *Le Loyal Serviteur*, chap. LXV. p. 121.

Marchese, neither the letter nor the action will annoy you, I write and beg you to send the payment, because it is only with the greatest difficulty that I have stopped the sale of a castle for twenty days. And certainly if the necessity were less, although the condition and resources of your most illustrious Lordship are such that to use more courtesy towards you would be an insult to you, I should not have undertaken to write this, because I think it is more painful and disagreeable for me to seek the money than for your most illustrious Lordship to pay it. The other reasons which Messer Mario wrote about this, apart from the fact that I have answered them, are such as to make me feel sure that your most illustrious Lordship will have discounted them with your accustomed prudence, therefore I do not repeat them, but I conclude, after what has passed, your Lordship will judge that you ought to pay the money without further delay, even if you thought you were losing it. May Our Lord rejoice and favour the most illustrious person and State of your Lordship as you desire.

"From Arpino, May 8, 1523.

"Of your most illustrious Lordship
the most devoted servant,
"THE MARCHESA DI PESCARA."[1]

---

[1] *Carteggio*, Letter 1. Mario Equicola, whom we shall meet again in these pages, was the secretary of Isabella d'Este Gonzaga (the mother of Federigo), and a friend and correspondent of Ariosto. Federigo had apparently made himself responsible for the ransom due to Pescara from Teodoro Trivulzio, one of the Venetian captains, who had been taken prisoner at the capture of Milan in November, 1521.

From Arpino Vittoria probably returned to Ischia, but went in December to Aquino, and passed the winter at Arpino, going to Marino for Holy-week, where Giberti sent her a palm blessed by the Pope, in acknowledgment of which she wrote the following letter : " Your letters are always most welcome to me, but that of to-day has given me more consolation than I can possibly tell you, because those of the Prior had made me terribly anxious, as he sent me with them letters from the Marchese, who was lying ill in bed. I thank Our Lord God that he is up again, and you a thousand times for your diligence in sending me word of it. . . . I have received the palm with so much pleasure, both on account of him who blessed it, and because of its signification, and because of its being sent by you." . . .[1]

The beginning of the year 1524 must have been cheered for the Marchesa by hopes of peace, much talked of, but not destined to be realised. Clement VII did not throw himself heartily into the Spanish alliance, and as he found the Emperor getting more and more powerful, he leant rather to establishing a peace and striking a balance between the two great rivals, than allowing Spain to get the upper hand. The first reverse experienced by the Imperial troops, commanded by Bourbon and Pescara, was at the siege of Marseilles ; the town was bravely defended by its infuriated inhabitants, whose anger against Bourbon, whom they regarded as a traitor, combined with their hereditary hatred of the Spaniards, made them too formidable to be overcome, and Bourbon was obliged to return to

---

[1] Letter dated Marino, March 30, 1524. *Carteggio*, Letter IX.

Italy. Francis I followed hard on his footsteps, and, throwing a garrison into Milan, turned his attention to besieging Pavia, then held by de Leyva, the most distinguished of the Spanish generals. The French troops suffered much during the winter, and, when the Imperial army was increased by a large band of lands-knechts, the advisers of the king urged him to withdraw from the siege; but this his youthful ambition would not allow him to do, and on February 24, 1525, was fought the far-famed battle of Pavia, in which Francis was made prisoner. Pescara distinguished himself greatly; the victory was considered to be chiefly due to his valour and strategy, and, covered with wounds, he retired to Milan. There is no doubt that he had formed high and just expectations of the rewards he would receive from the Emperor in acknowledgment of his services, and we can well understand the bitterness he felt when, far from conferring any honours or territories upon him, Charles refused him even the small prizes which he demanded—namely, the duchy of Sora and the county of Carpi.

And now we come to a very dark place in Pescara's history, which is open to different interpretations; but whatever view we take of it, it is difficult to regard him as innocent.

The victory of Pavia brought no peace to the Imperial allies, all of whom quarrelled fiercely among themselves; the Emperor seems to have satisfied nobody, and Pescara least of all. Disappointed and broken in health, it is probable that the latter gave voice to his discontent; at any rate, it is clear from contemporary records that he began to be regarded as

a man who could be got hold of. "Infermo dell'
animo," "Uomo d' incerta fede," are two epithets
bestowed on him ; and Morone said of him : "Non
essere uomo in Italia nè di maggior malignità nè di minor
fede."[1] This Morone was the chancellor of Francesco
Sforza, Duke of Milan. He had opened negotiations
with the Pope, and had formed the idea of a united
Italy; Milan, Venice, Florence, and Naples were to
enter into an alliance with the Holy See, and an
attempt was made to attach Pescara to the scheme by
offering him the crown of Naples. The diplomatic
arrangements were entrusted chiefly to Giberti, who
sent his friend, Mentebuona Romano, to treat with the
Marchese. It is interesting to note that Giberti never
believed that Pescara would be induced to join the
league, as it is probable that Vittoria herself inspired
him with this idea, for we know how averse she was
from the plan.

We may imagine her through these lonely years as a
woman of somewhat severe beauty, with a dignified
reserve, and a great genius for friendship. But,
primarily, she was the wife of the man she never failed,
in whom, we think, she must have ceased to believe, but
whose honour was no less her honour, his interests hers,
his affairs notably hers. We have already noticed her
letter to Gonzaga about his debt to Pescara, and her
anxiety at Marino about his health. After Pavia we
have a very flowery letter from the Emperor to Vittoria
in which he acknowledges the great services rendered
by her husband, and writes with a magnificent vague-
ness that, besides the honour and glory that have

---

[1] Guicciardini, XVI. 4.

accrued to Pescara, there is no favour, however great, that he may not expect from the Emperor's gratitude and liberality. To this the Marchesa replied in the same strain, as no doubt the exigencies of the case required: but, with an evident desire to reap some tangible benefit, she writes at the end of her letter: "I hold the services, the faithfulness, and the sincerity of my lord the Marchese and of my House to be such that they are not unworthy of the acceptance of your Cæsarian Majesty, and I desire the promised acknowledgment more in testimony of this than because of any unwonted covetousness on my part; although your Majesty's gratitude and liberality always anticipate every just demand. I do not know which is most to be prized, a guerdon from so great a Prince, or the glory that he should say that he is in our debt."[1]

Vittoria must have felt her husband's disappointment keenly, but this could not warp her judgment, and, on the occasion of the Neapolitan scheme being divulged to her, Giovio has preserved for us the noble sentiments of this "donna d' incomparabile ingegno." "Most earnestly," he writes, "she implored her husband, who at that time was wont to communicate all his plans to her, that he would be mindful of his wonted virtue, with the reputation and renown of which he surpassed the fortune and the glory of many kings. Because not with the greatness of kingdoms and of states and of titles, but with illustrious faith and pure virtue, is acquired that honour which with ever-living praises comes down to one's descendants. And there is not anywhere a royal name of such exalted

---

[1] *Carteggio*, Letters xx. and xxi.

degree that would not be easily vanquished by a height of perfect virtue. And on this account she did not in any wise desire to be the wife of a king, wishing much rather to be the wife of that captain, who, not only in war with a valiant hand, but likewise in peace with the high honour of a just and invincible soul, had known how to conquer the greatest kings." [1]

This leaves us in no doubt of the view taken by the Marchesa, and we feel that this must have been one of those dividing pathways which are the hardest parts of life's journey. However honourable and far-sighted we may think Morone's policy as that of an Italian, it takes a different light when entered into by a man like Pescara, who was a Spaniard of the Spaniards ; by race, speech, and tradition he belonged to Spain ; his appearance was wholly Spanish, and Spanish was the only language he would ever use ; he was in the service of his hereditary sovereign, and we can see nothing but treachery in his desertion of the Imperial cause, if that was what he really meditated. The negotiations hung on for many weeks ; Pescara raised difficulty after difficulty, and finally invited Morone to come and meet him at Novara to detail the plan. It seems remarkable that Morone, having such a clear-cut impression of Pescara's character, should have acceded to this demand, but he appears to have gone in complete confidence and to have laid bare the whole scheme to the Marchese. The latter had placed the Spanish general, de Leyva, behind the arras where he could overhear all, and, the interview being concluded, Morone was arrested and conveyed to the Emperor at Pavia, whither Pescara

---

[1] *Le Vite di dicenove huomini illustri*, p. 256 *v.*

also repaired to make known the plot. It is fair to add that, in giving up Morone, Pescara specially pleaded that his life should be spared, adding that he was a man who might be made use of later. Some have thought that Pescara was prompted to his present course of action by the increasing weakness of the Duke of Milan, expecting that on Sforza's decease the duchy would be conferred on him, and that it would be a more desirable possession than the kingdom of Naples. The most favourable construction that can be put upon his conduct is that he was all along loyal to the Emperor, and was only playing with the opposite party in order to learn their secrets ; but, if we accept this interpretation (which hardly seems a likely one), it does not suffice to wipe the stain from his memory, as in any case he broke faith with Morone, and acted throughout with so much fraud and duplicity as even to overstep the limits allowed by a politically unscrupulous age.

However it may have been, what he plotted for he never obtained. The hardships of the last five years had severely tried a constitution which never seems to have been robust, and he never really recovered from the serious wounds received at Pavia. Illness, disappointment, and anxiety broke him down, and, recognising that he was gravely ill, he sent for Vittoria and for his cousin, del Vasto, whom he made his heir, and to whom he confided the care of his wife. The Marchesa set out in all haste, but had only reached Viterbo when the news of her husband's death was brought to her.

Ferrante d'Avalos, Marchese di Pescara, died on November 25, 1525, at the age of thirty-six ; he was

buried with great pomp in Milan, but his remains
were subsequently removed to Naples and placed
before the high altar in the Church of S. Domenico.
Ariosto is said to have written a Latin epitaph for him,
but the authenticity of it is very doubtful.[1] It was
intended that a suitable monument should be erected,
but, for what reason we do not know, this was never
done, and the coffin is now to be seen in the sacristy of
the said Church, bearing simply the name of the
Marchese.

Pescara's best claim to remembrance is undoubtedly
as a great general and a brave soldier ; he was passionately regretted by the army whom he had so often led
to victory : in this, at any rate, he certainly had " the
genius to be loved."

It is a common error to expect the incompatible.
Looking back on the early days of the Marchese, his
literary tastes, his poetic gifts, his romantic marriage,
we allowed ourselves to hope for a fitting sequel ; and
yet what could be more natural, almost inevitable, than
that things should develop as they did. Perhaps leisure
is one of the first requisites of any great and lasting
attachment, the time to occupy ourselves with our
heart's object: it is not sorrow or poverty that can
interfere—or, necessarily, distance ; but it is hurry and
turmoil, and constant change and excitement which
alter our life's centre, which indeed prevent its having
a centre at all, and this dissipation both of the heart
and mind tell fatally on the character, and weaken our
capacity for any strong affection.

[1] *Carm.* iii. 8. The question is discussed by Carducci, *Su Ludovico
Ariosto e Torquato Tasso* (Bologna, 1905), pp. 231–233.

And so Pescara appears before us with the limitations of the life that was thrust upon him, and yet adorned with the virtues proper to his career. Vittoria, wearing out the years of her married life in loneliness and disappointment, is the more to be envied of the two ; no doubt she knew what she had missed, but she stood aside and watched the bearings of things and saw what they entailed, and, in the light of her sane judgment, she gauged the situation, honouring in her husband the gifts that were really his, and making no vain demands and no lamentations. The love of country, the thirst for glory, the talent for leadership, these are great objective facts, and, when we come to study Vittoria's poems, it is these that will stand out to the exclusion of hopes and regrets alike futile.

CHAPTER II

CHOICE AND CIRCUMSTANCE

A white rose thornless that grows in the garden of time.
A. C. SWINBURNE.

IT is a picture of dismay, that of Vittoria hastening
from Ischia on receiving the news of her husband's
alarming state, travelling no doubt as fast as the
circumstances of the time permitted, and haunted by
the agonising fear of being too late—which indeed
proved to be the case, for the tidings of his death
reached her when she was near Viterbo, and she was so
overcome with grief that she fell from her horse and
remained for two hours in a half-dead condition.
When the Marchesa was brought to Viterbo, she begged
to be taken to a convent and to be given a nun's habit.
She would not lie anywhere but on the ground, and
could scarcely be persuaded to touch food. Her
brother Ascanio hastened to her side and returned
with her to Rome, and there she took up her abode in
the Convent of San Silvestro, with which her family
had been connected since the thirteenth century.

This convent was in the hands of nuns of the order
of Santa Chiara, to whom it had first been given by
Pope Honorius IV. An ancestress of Vittoria's, the
Blessed Margherita Colonna, born about the middle of
the thirteenth century, and left an orphan at an early

age, was brought up by her brothers, who destined her to make a brilliant marriage. But the girl had higher views for herself, and was encouraged in them by one brother, who subsequently became a priest and afterwards a cardinal. Living at home she found herself in the midst of dissipation and festivities, which were so foreign to the mode of life she courted that one day she secretly left the house and retired to Palestrina.

Dowered with no common degree of beauty, talent, and riches, Margherita renounced everything, procured the habit of Santa Chiara in which she dressed herself, and cut off her beautiful hair with her own hands. After this she gave herself up to the care of the poor and sick, specially devoting herself to those whose diseases were most repulsive. She kept the rule of St. Francis in all its rigour, but, not being yet of age, she did not attach herself to any convent. When, however, she reached the age of one and twenty and came into possession of her fortune, she distributed the whole of it among the poor and went to the Convent of Santa Chiara at Assisi, into which she begged to be admitted. The Superior accepted her eagerly, but Margherita was never able to realise her darling project, being seized with a violent illness, which was only the beginning of continuous bad health. In consequence of this, she returned to Palestrina and collected round her a number of holy companions, leading with them a life of extreme mortification. Having given away all her wealth, she had no longer the means of relieving the poor, and so the Colonna princess, "ogni vergogna deposta," was seen daily begging alms from door to door.

D

For the last seven years of her life she suffered from a dreadful ulcer, but displayed heroic patience throughout. She died still young in 1284, and was beatified by Pius IX. It was on her death that Pope Honorius IV bestowed the Convent of San Silvestro in Capite on the order of Santa Chiara, and the body of Blessed Margherita was buried there. Hence the Colonna family were closely connected with San Silvestro, which seemed therefore a natural retreat for the Marchesa in her great sorrow.

From this time forward we are face to face with the real Vittoria, and the originality of the woman cannot but strike us. In the eyes of the world, there must have seemed to be three possible futures open to her. First, she might have returned to her own estates and lived there *en grande dame;* secondly, she might have contracted a second marriage (and suitors were never wanting); thirdly, she might have taken the veil. This last course she certainly contemplated, and it is almost surprising that she did not persevere in it. There is no doubt that, in the first desolation of her widowhood, this was her one idea, and the Pope, in giving leave for her to reside in the Convent of San Silvestro, expressly forbade that she should be allowed to take the veil without his consent.

It is abundantly evident, both from her writings and her subsequent career, that Vittoria was not only deeply religious, but that religion was to her the key-note of existence, the meaning and explanation of all life. And surely to have grasped this is the initial vocation to the cloister; only it is this and much more. Perhaps, the true definition of a vocation would be that religion looms large enough in the soul not only to over-shadow, but literally to obliterate everything else. It is an utter detachment and selflessness such as we do not find in Vittoria, with her versatile mind, her varied interests, her affections flowing in so many channels. Keen, alert, many-sided, placed by her position in the foreground, and hopelessly entangled in the troubles of a most troublous time, leaving us in her letters and poems a legacy of talent, though not of genius, Vittoria might have looked down on us through the ages as a noble, intellectual woman, true to the traditions of her race and name; but she elected to be all this, and something very different as well. Henceforth we are not to seek her for the most part in courts and palaces, but moving from convent to convent, leading a life of almost monastic simplicity, her food, her dress, her expenditure, reduced to the very smallest and simplest; so that, though by birth connected with all that was highest, and by intellect with all that was noblest in her country, she yet threw in her lot with the poor, became their friend by living for them and like them, and, from her choice of a retreat in the early days of her widow-hood, down to her interment in the common burial-ground of the nuns, without a stone to mark her resting-place, she stands forth pre-eminently as one of those who *de mundo non sunt.*

It is this which gives her that distinction which is hers, which separates her so markedly from many of her noted contemporaries, which gives her a hold over our hearts as well as our minds.

It may truly be said of her that her " soul was like a star and dwelt apart," yet she was never able all through her life to isolate herself from the fierce discussions of the age. The wars in which Pescara had won his wounds still continued, the bitter quarrels which had hastened his end still raged, and the years 1526 and 1527 are some of the most terrifying in the annals of Christian Rome ; doubly so to Vittoria, who was intimately connected with their horrors.

Clement VII, frightened, as we have seen, at the prospect of Spanish ascendancy in Lombardy, entered into a League in May, 1526, with France, Venice, and the Duke of Milan, for the promotion of the peace of Christendom : the Emperor was invited to join, on condition that he released the sons of Francis I, left the Duke of Milan in possession, and restored to the other Italian powers what had been theirs before the last war. On the proclamation of the League, Ascanio Colonna, the brother of Vittoria, and Vespasiano, her cousin, the son of Prospero Colonna, withdrew from Rome, as being subjects and supporters of the Emperor, Ascanio removing his sister to Marino. Cardinal Pompeo Colonna, a cousin of Vittoria's, had already departed to the Abbey of Subiaco, where he was organising his forces.

Ineffectual as the League proved to be, and possessed of no power of carrying out its professions, it yet embarrassed Charles for the moment, and he sent first the Duke of Sessa, and subsequently Don Ugo de Moncada to try and detach the Pope from his new allies ; but Clement, advised by his datary, Giberti, who is specially interesting to us as the warm friend of the Marchesa, for once stood firm, to his own detriment, and the

Spanish ambassador repaired to Genazzano, a stronghold of the Colonna.

Meanwhile the Pope, alarmed at the hostility of the Colonna, came to an agreement with them in August by which he pardoned them if they would consent to restore the places they had seized, to withdraw their troops into Neapolitan country, and to undertake not to wage war from the lands they held from the Church ; these conditions observed, they were free to help the Emperor. There is an undated letter from Giberti to Vittoria which appears to have been written before the end of August, and from which it may be gathered that the Marchesa had written to her friend on her brother's behalf. The letter runs :—

" In that affair of the most illustrious signor Ascanio I have done what I could, but, as your Excellence knows just cause for the anger of his Holiness, you will not wonder that the result does not follow as quickly as you would like. His Beatitude loves his Excellence, and would take pleasure in every advantage and satisfaction of his, if he sought them by such means as are proper, and not by attempting to compel his Holiness, and assuming too much security on account of his easiness and patience. The desire I have to serve this signor, as your Excellence knows, makes me grieve all the more that the methods of his Excellence preclude me from serving him : however, where I can, I will not fail. And I commend myself as much as possible to your Excellence's favour." [1]

It is difficult to see what Giberti could have done for such a refractory vassal.

---

[1] *Carteggio*, Letter xxx.

It is abundantly evident that Moncada saw his way to striking a blow for the Emperor by trading on the discontent of the Colonna, who, in the event of success, were to be merely the cat's paw of the enterprise. In September, Moncada, having with help from Naples collected a force of some four thousand men, joined the troops of the Colonna and marched on Rome. Meeting with no opposition, they seized the Lateran Gate and drew up at the SS. Apostoli ; in the morning they pursued their way across to the Ponte Sisto and pressed on to the Vatican. If it seems strange that no resistance was made, we must remember that the Colonna was a Roman house ; it had been thought that Cardinal Colonna might have been Pope instead of Clement, and he was still said to be aspiring to that dignity : it was but one house against another, and Roman citizens looked on unmoved while the lords settled their private difficulties. Clement shut himself up in the Castle of S. Angelo, and for three days the Colonna party and the Spanish soldiers pillaged the Vatican with the savage ferocity of pagans, sacking as much of the Borgo as was out of range of artillery.

On September 21, the Pope listened to terms of peace, which were thus dictated by Moncada: a truce for four months was concluded, and Clement was to withdraw his troops and fleet from the service of the League, and pardon the Colonna ; Moncada then withdrew, having achieved his purpose. Cardinal Pompeo is said to have been bitterly disappointed, having dreamed of more far-reaching consequences, and probably foreseeing that Clement would lose no time in wreaking vengeance on his House.

We do not know exactly when Vittoria saw fit to abandon Marino for safer quarters, but she certainly went south to Aquino, to Ischia, and finally to Naples before the end of the year. It was in November that the Papal troops entered the territories of the Colonna, storming Marino, Zagarolo, Gallicano, and other castles of theirs, while at the same time the Cardinal was deprived of his dignity. On December 9, Giberti thus writes to Vittoria: " Your Excellence may rest assured that it was most bitter to me to see our Lord constrained, on account of the great injuries done to him, to set himself to pull down that House which I have always desired to see most great. But, since the hatred of others, which has been the reward of my services, has not taken from me the favour of your Excellence, every other loss appears small to me. Nor can you do me a more singular favour than to command me, for you will find me always most ready to obey you, as I would willingly do in interposing to arrange some kind of peace, as you request, if I saw that any could be arrived at consonant with the dignity and honour of our Lord, to whom after God my service is principally due. And it may be that the divine Goodness will open a way for us, if that goodness and desire for peace be found in the other party which his Holiness has always shown ; and to your Excellence's good favour I commend myself as much as possible." [1]

But the terrible events of 1526 were only a shadow of those which were to follow. In May, 1527, the Imperial army, mad and mutinous, rushed on Rome and took it by assault. The mixed soldiery of Italy,

---

[1] Letter dated Rome, December 9, 1526. *Carteggio*, Letter xxxii.

Spain, and Germany, clamouring for pay of which long arrears were due, half starved, and rendered brutal by every sort of suffering and hardship, found the spoils of the wealthiest and most cultivated city in the world at their mercy, and the scenes enacted present such a story of unparalleled horror as no other page of history can unfold.

The Pope remained shut up in the Castle of S. Angelo, trembling for his life, and, according to his wont, treating with each party in turn.

This must have been one of the bitterest moments of Vittoria's life. Overwhelmed with grief and horror, as only a Catholic and a Roman could be, for the devastation of the Eternal City, the fiercest pang of all must have been that her nearest relations were implicated in it. To this agony came some mitigation in the conduct of Cardinal Colonna, who, entering Rome to exult over the downfall of his enemy, felt his heart wrung for the destruction of so much greatness, and who, possessed of more power than any other Cardinal, opened his palace to the distressed, and was the means of delivering many of his fellow-citizens. Through him and through her cousin, del Vasto, Vittoria did all she could to alleviate the lot of the sufferers, aiding them with money and advice, and interceding in their behalf. It is probable that with her name and wealth she was able to effect much, and her good work brought her a reward in the near future, as we shall have occasion to see very shortly.

Among the hostages whom Clement was obliged to deliver up to his enemies was his favourite, Giberti, and it was while occupying this unenviable position that the

Datary wrote the following letter to Vittoria: "I could wish not to have been already as certain as I was of your Excellence's love and kindness towards me, because these proofs of them that you have given me, and give me every day more efficaciously, if they were new to me and unexpected, would fill me with so much pleasure that they would make every hardship that I suffer delightful; but, even as it is, I feel a wonderful comfort from them; and it seems to me that these chains procure me honour in the sight of everybody who sees the account your Excellence makes of my liberation. I have seen what you wrote to the most reverend and most illustrious Monsignor Colonna, and his Lordship has up to now behaved in such wise towards us all that we are under an obligation to him for it, and he makes us also have a firm hope of bringing our affairs to a prosperous issue, as it will indeed be good, if in this tempest, we be put into a place where we can remain in some quietness. But my desire goes beyond this in seeking to be soon given into the hands of the imperial lords, as I shall go in three months as a hostage for the observance of those things which his Holiness promises. Because, if I obtain this, the liberty and the occupation that I have had in the past will not be so grateful to me as will be the imprisonment with ease, and the delectation of soul which I propose to myself to have there. I have besought the most illustrious Lord Marquis on this account, and his Excellence is desirous to comply with my request, as is clearly shown by himself, and by the work that your Excellence has done for us by letter; but either the difficulty there is in obtaining it, or some misfortune

that is going to take away from me the sweetness of this
tranquillity, is the cause that up till now I see no fruit
therefrom, and little hope of any.   I should thank your
Excellence for the pledges you offer of your State for
me ; but how can I thank you, or what is there in me
that I can still promise you, having already given
myself to you entirely, and being more obliged to you
now than ever ?   To your good favour I commend
myself with all my power."[1]

These hostages, seven in number, were bound and
taken as prisoners to the Palazzo della Cancelleria, where
Cardinal Colonna was living; they were brutally treated
by the soldiers, and even led to the foot of the gallows
many times, and threatened with death, so that Pompeo,
fearing for their lives, connived at their escape, which
was aided by the Spaniards who were encamped near
S. Maria del Popolo.

Giovio, in his interesting little life of the Cardinal,
here remarks that nothing better could have happened
to Rome than the coming of Pompeo : rather a merciful
sentence, considering the ravage he had himself wrought
there the preceding year.   His is a career that would
hardly have been possible at any other period.   The
age bred warlike ecclesiastics, and Pompeo was certainly
more warrior than priest; if he had been only the
former, we might have admired him more, though, even
so, he would not have been free from the accusations of
implacability and overwhelming ambition.   But, along
with these faults, there was certainly an element of
greatness in the man's nature, which, no doubt, appealed

---

[1] Letter dated Rome, November 26, 1527. *Carteggio*, xxxv.

to his illustrious cousin who both loved and was beloved by him.

Character is shown by life's choices, and, perhaps,
no less by life's acceptances. In our intercourse with
people in general, we are free to form our own opinions
of their actions and line of conduct, free to be disappointed in them, to be disillusioned concerning them,
to alter our mind a hundred times as to their moral
and intellectual worth ; but when once we have pledged
ourselves to a friendship, this freedom is no longer ours.
We cannot say: I am disappointed in such an one, I
thought he would have done better or otherwise ; for we
have altered our position, and taken upon ourselves a
new responsibility.

The consecration of a great friendship, while by no
means warping our judgment, requires from us something other than judgment. It takes away our sense of
aloofness and independence, and demands from us a
heart-whole loyalty, an immense self-sacrifice, an un-
limited belief; while, too humble alike for mercy or
generosity, it goes one step farther, and, basing that
belief on the unseen springs of character, will not let
itself be affected by any outward thing, by contradicting
word or action, rightly regarding these as mere human
accidents, and nowise concerned but with the aim and
the ideal.

But if this is the point to which noble friendships
bring us, it would seem to be the starting-point of noble
relationships.

These cannot begin with any freedom of choice ;
they are among the iron circumstances of life, and it
often happens that the natures with whom we have most

to do are those with whom we have least in common, and whose aims (a difference which divides so much more sharply than character) are widely severed from ours. Yet, if we elect to bring to these the same fidelity which friendship pre-supposes, we come to the acceptances of life which are hardly less excellent, though far less responsible, than its choices.

Vittoria lived in her friendships, and it will be interesting later to trace their growth, influence, and variety; for she was never a woman of one friend. But if we consider her attitude towards all the members of her numerous and divided family in the above light, we shall find in it something admirable and at the same time comprehensible, and it is evident that it enabled her to keep alive the flower of family affection which must else have perished in such stormy times.

The Cardinal, Pompeo Colonna, had, as we have seen, a great admiration for his gifted cousin; his book, *Apologia Mulierum*, is dedicated to her in the following letter :—

" Most writers, magnanimous Vittoria, are wont to dedicate their writings and compositions specially to those divinities from whom they hope most grace and protection. Some therefore invoked Jove, others the Muses, many the Cæsars, to guide and favour their work. But I, who am taking up the cause of women (a task not only beyond my powers, but arduous and difficult to any genius), verily have need of a greater deity and a greater defender. To whom then to fly, whose protection to implore, which of the gods to invoke, I know not. But since it is handed down by tradition that when the giants waged war upon Jove, and, having captured him, strove to break into heaven itself by heaping up mountains, a certain maiden, the daughter of Styx, not less adorned with beauty than with virtues, brought succour to Jove, by whose work, counsel, and authority, the war was soon finished, and the Titans annihilated. Jupiter, not unmindful of this so great benefit, decreed that none of the gods swearing by the Stygian swamp should be forsworn, and willed that this oath should be inviolable with them, and he named the maiden, by whose valour he had preserved his empire, Vittoria, for an eternal memory of her name. Oh what a magnanimous maiden, oh what a truly famous and divine name! When I reflect within myself, considering what is said and with what powerful opponents I have to deal, I think it in vain to implore the aid of Jove in so glorious and arduous a struggle, since he was unable to end a much lighter contest without the activity, the authority, the imperturbable fortitude of Vittoria. We need therefore a stronger leader, warrior, guide, and director of this our work, and we see not, if one were to be chosen out of all, whom we can compare to Vittoria herself. To thee, therefore, I fly and invoke thy divinity, thy holy and invincible name, especially since, induced by thy counsel and authority, I have undertaken this great and laborious task; for, albeit I give and devote to it all my studies, all my work, care, industry, yea all my mind, nevertheless, unless thou stretch forth thy hand, all these things will be in vain, and we shall be forced to give the place to the calumniators of the feminine sex. But, although all these things have been naturally considered by me, and I have seen the gravity of the business, nevertheless, because thy love is of such weight with me, thy authority is so great that all things that please thee, and which thou dost order and wish, seem to me right and beautiful. I have, therefore, preferred to be oppressed by the weight of the labour enjoined upon me, rather than give up, owing to the infirmity and helplessness of my soul, that which was once laid upon me by thee. It will be thine, therefore, divine Vittoria, to receive the parts of this our work ; and I doubt not that, especially with such a champion, the assault of their most bitter accusers having been broken and the darts of their detractors blunted, our women, whose cause we have undertaken, will recover their pristine dignity and glory.

" Farewell." [1]

In the first book, Pompeo demonstrates, both by philosophical and theological reasoning, that woman is not an imperfect creature, and cites examples of women great in eloquence, and learning, and poetry among the ancients, such as Hortensia, Aspasia, and Corinna ; and notable examples of constancy, as Portia and Læna, adding : " I omit those most holy virgins of Christ, Catherine, Lucy, Agatha, Cecilia, and innumerable others, who on account of singular fortitude, piety, and constancy, having despised the threats and tortures of tyrants, possess the crown and palm in the heavenly

---

[1] Pompeii Cardinalis Columnæ, S.R.E. Vicecancellarii, ad illustrem ac magnanimam Victoriam Columnam Marchionissam Piscariæ, Apologiæ Mulierum Liber Primus, ff. 320–321. This, and the following quotations, are from the manuscript of this (unpublished) treatise in the Biblioteca Vaticana, Cod. Lat. 3370.

kingdom, in the presence of their Spouse who is Christ."

Then follow more classical examples of woman's piety, charity, and other virtues, such as were found in the Spartan women, in Rutilia, Servia, Lucretia, and Claudia, whence he argues that women, being most capable of acquiring all virtues, ought not to be kept out of public offices and magistracies.[1]

In the second book, *De fortitudine, magnanimitate atque constantia Mulierum,* the author cites Vittoria herself as a shining proof of womanly virtue, first describing the great deeds of her husband—his victory at Pavia, and his refusal to be tempted from his fidelity to the Emperor by the promise of the crown of Naples (this being apparently Colonna's version of the Morone affair). "Oh divine faith, oh singular wisdom and prudence of a leader! And when these things came to thy ears, Vittoria, not the royal sceptre, not any desire of ruling, not any lust for domination, nor the common opinion that right may be violated for the sake of a kingdom, ever turned thee aside from the right and virtuous course. Nay, they declare that thou thyself, considering the claims of thy noble nature, didst say thou preferredst to die the wife of a most brave marquis and a most upright general, than to live the consort of a king dishonoured with any stain of infamy."[2]

Pompeo then goes through all the Aristotelian virtues, defining them as he goes, and giving pagan and Christian examples of each, and ends thus: "Receive then, magnanimous Vittoria, this little work,

---

[1] MS. *cit.,* ff. 321 *v*–333.   [2] MS. *cit.,* ff. 338 *v*–340.

begun and composed in these days recently passed by, as the first-fruits of my vigils and studies for thee, who art going to receive afterwards much richer fruits, if perchance they ripen. Nevertheless, by the greatness of thy lofty and invincible soul, and by our supreme devotion towards thee, I pray thee again and again not to let it see the light unless mingled with thy eloquence and illustrated by thy divine songs. Farewell."[1]

The *Apologia Mulierum* is pre-eminently the work of a humanist, and exhibits stores of learning, especially pagan ; it is the only one of Pompeo's writings that remains to us, with the possible exception of one poem, though he is known to have written many which were highly esteemed by Minturno and others of his contemporaries. The Cardinal is interesting as an example of that many-sidedness which characterised the men of the Renaissance. We would very willingly divorce the priest from the soldier, but there still remain the administrator, the student, the collector, the lover of books and of gardens.

Made Viceroy of Naples in 1530, we have rather con-flicting accounts of his career there. Some praise his astuteness and his wonderful cleverness in restoring order and holding that mixed population in check, curbing the insolence of the nobles and showing such favour and leniency to the army that he was worshipped by the soldiers ; but others lay stress on his extreme severity, on which account, they say, his life even was in danger.

---

[1] For the whole of this I am indebted to the kindness of Mr. Edmund Gardner, who transcribed it for me from the manuscript in the Biblioteca Vaticana.

At the same time that Pompeo was elevated to the viceregal dignity, he was made Bishop of Monreale in Sicily, and he built for himself a beautiful palace on the shore at Chiaja.   Here he planted his trees and "noble shrubs and strange flowers," lecturing the while on the science of gardening.   Here he studied, wrote his fugitive poems, and composed his book.   Here his friends visited him, rejoicing in his wonderful courtesy and his unfailing readiness to grant favours; and here in June, 1532, he died, surrounded by learned and charming companions, regretting only that he was forced prematurely to forego that intercourse from which he had derived such incomparable pleasure.   His end, as related by Giovio, has a grace and dignity which seems to touch the very summit of pagan perfection.

To return to the hostages on whose behalf the Cardinal had interfered so successfully.   In Giberti, the one who interests us most as the friend and frequent correspondent of Vittoria, we have an entirely different type.   He had suffered so much during his fifty-two days of imprisonment, that he had no thought but to retire from public life and settle at Verona, of which he had been made bishop in 1524.   Indeed, he had long since desired to take this step, but Clement would not part with an adviser in whom he trusted so much ; though to us Giberti appears as but another instance of a supremely wise priest whose political judgment was beneath contempt.   Giberti's real leaning was to that reform within the Church to which all great souls were yearning, which might be fitly described in the words of St. James as "primum quidem pudica est, deinde pacifica, modesta, suadibilis," and which was so different

E

from the noisy revolt going on outside. As early as
1519, there was established in Rome a small society
called the Oratory of Divine Love, whose members
numbered only fifty or sixty men, among whom we note
the names of Caraffa, Contarini, Sadoleto, Pole, Priuli,
and Giberti. They used to assemble first in the
rectory of Giuliano Dati, a Florentine, and afterwards
in the Church of San Silvestro and Santa Dorotea in
Trastevere, adjoining the rectory. The members of
the Oratory pledged themselves to visit the churches
more diligently, to celebrate Mass more regularly, and
to pray more frequently at sacred spots ; they had as
their aim a reform, not so much individual as collective,
which from these humble beginnings might permeate
through the whole hierarchy.

Giberti, once free, resigned his dataryship and gave
up all his offices, asking leave to be allowed to retire to
Verona ; further, he renounced the many benefices with
which he was invested, and only retained the bishopric
of Verona and the Abbey of Rosazzo.

From this time dates the interest of his life and personality. He is indeed a dignified and attractive figure,
this Bishop chiefly concerned with the reform of his
clergy (wherein many difficulties awaited him), living
in the strictest simplicity, so that his house resembled
a monastery in the keeping of the canonical hours and
the severe regulations regarding food and sleep. On
the other hand, magnificence was not wanting. He had
a noble love of books and collected a splendid library,
rich in rare codices ; he also set up a private printing-
press with a special view to the accurate printing of the
Greek character, and he issued many valuable works,

notably the commentaries of St. John Chrysostom on St. Paul's Epistles. He welcomed the best minds of the age, and thither thronged literary and scientific men, artists and nobles. For all these he kept open house, calling them "the dearest of his family," and entertaining them with a kind of splendour which he said befitted this mode of life. Liberality and courtesy seem to have been the key-notes of his character. He remained Vittoria's life-long friend, and his death was one of the keenest griefs of her closing years.

The Marchesa, in repairing to Ischia, had not passed out of reach of hostility, and the great naval battle of Salerno must have been fought under her very eyes. This fight, which took place on April 28, 1528, and only lasted four hours, consisted chiefly in a desperate hand-to-hand struggle in which the Imperial party, trusting more to the valour of their leaders than to the strength of their ships, were completely beaten by the superior skill of the enemy. France was then strong in her Genoese allies (though the situation was already becoming strained) and her fleet was commanded by Filippino Doria, cousin of the great Andrea. Filippino with his galleys was occupying the Gulf of Salerno and there the Viceroy, Don Ugo de Moncada, determined to attack him, and having only six galleys, four light boats, and six brigantines, he augmented the appearance, though certainly not the strength, of his fleet by adding to it a large number of fishing boats to present a formidable front to the enemy. Though Ugo was nominal admiral, the command of the expedition was really entrusted to Fabricio Giustiniani, who pointed out the rashness of opposing the famous naval

power of Genoa with such an undisciplined and inex-
perienced force. Ugo, however, was not to be dissuaded from his purpose, and further wasted precious
time by taking his ships to Capri to be harangued by
a Spanish monk whose ardour, it was supposed, would
inspire them with the like feeling. Putting forth from
Capri, two galleys were ordered to approach the enemy
and then feign flight so as to draw their adversaries
into the open sea. In the meantime, Filippino Doria
had got wind of the enterprise, when the only possible
chance of success lay in its secrecy.

Having obtained reinforcements from Lautrec, Doria
prepared to meet the Imperial fleet whose numbers,
formidable in the distance, filled him with dismay; but
when they came near, and he saw the long line of fishing
boats, he felt more than equal to the encounter, and
detached three galleys, ordering them to gain the open
sea and to return at a given signal and join in the
combat. The fight was an obstinate one; Doria,
surrounded by the hostile fleet and blinded by their
smoke, yet directed his cannon so well that he killed
the commander of Ugo's vessel and several officers;
at the same time the captain of his own ship fell.
Coming to close quarters, the Imperialists fared worse
than the Genoese, who were more used to this kind of
warfare and more accustomed to defend themselves.
But two of the Genoese galleys found themselves so
hard pressed by three of the Imperial ships that they
were on the point of surrendering, when, at the sign
agreed on, Doria's three reserve galleys came up and
turned the fortune of the day. The Spanish flagship
was riddled with bullets and her mainmast shot down.

Moncada, wounded in the arm, continued to exhort his men until killed by an arquebus.

Perhaps the decisive stroke was given by Doria liberating his slaves, and these threw themselves on the Spaniards with the special ferocity of private hatred. The number of prisoners taken was enormous and included the Marchese del Vasto, Ascanio Colonna, Fabricio Giustiniani, and the Prince of Salerno, who were all immediately sent to Andrea Doria. This must have been a cruel reverse for Vittoria, not only on account of the defeat of the Imperial party, but because of the capture of her brother and her adopted son.

It would seem that the Pope interceded in their behalf, communicating with Andrea by means of Giovan Battista Sanga, one of the papal secretaries, and also a great friend of Giberti whose secretary he had been ; and Sanga wrote the following comforting letter to the Marchesa :—

"My most illustrious and excellent Lady. The ardent desire of my Monsignor of Verona to serve your Excellence has obscured that of your more humble, but not less affectionate servants. Therefore I bewail my sad fate which has kept for me the occasion I desired until such troublous times ; still, even in these I should be well content if, in my good offices towards the most illustrious Signor Marchese and Signor Ascanio, I could make your Excellence understand that there is imprinted on the minds of those that serve him the same observance and service towards your Excellence. Our Lord commissioned me some days ago to write on his behalf to Signor Andrea Doria, recommending the said signors to him. This I did,

and, because I knew how much M. Andrea loved my
Monsignor, I added thereto an account of the works
done last year by your Excellence and by the most
illustrious Signor Marchese for the benefit of his Lordship. He replied to me that, though by reason of war
they are his prisoners, he does not regard them as such,
and that he endeavours to treat them with all possible
consideration and affection. This I believe your
Excellence has heard by letter from the Signor
Marchese himself. I have written of it to my Monsignor, and I know that his Lordship will also write
efficaciously. Nor, even without this, can one believe
that, in the hands of so valiant a man, these signors
should have to endure any treatment unbefitting their
station." [1]

What we have to notice is that the capture of two
such generals and strategists was to have a notable
effect on the fortunes of Spain. History shows us
that, before this engagement, the relations were much
strained between Francis I and his haughty ally, Andrea
Doria. The aim of this man, and how far he was
swayed by patriotism, and how far by vulgar self-
interest will always remain a problem: in a world
where motives are so mixed, it is probable that he was
never able to answer that question to his own satisfaction. But at this crisis two facts are patent. Francis
owed him large arrears of salary, which he seems to
have had no intention of paying, and further offended
him after the battle by laying claim to Doria's two
illustrious prisoners. Colonna and del Vasto had made
it their first entreaty not to be given up to the French,

---

[1] Letter dated Viterbo, June 3, 1528. *Carteggio*, XXXVI.

and Doria was determined to abide by his word, main-
taining at the same time that he had an absolute right
to the captives.

Del Vasto, who must have been fully aware of all
the friction that was going on, now boldly proposed to
Doria to go over to the Emperor, promising that
Charles would guarantee him an immense salary and
would reinstate Genoa in her rights over Savona.   It
would appear that Doria gave in very rapidly to this
suggestion, signed an agreement with the Emperor,
revictualled Naples, took the command of the Imperial
fleet and went in pursuit of the French galleys, of which
he captured four to indemnify himself for the money
owed to him by Francis.   We are hardly concerned
here with the ethical side of Doria's conduct: it is
manifest that his proceedings set Ascanio Colonna and
del Vasto at liberty, and Vittoria had no longer to
concern herself with intercessions on their account.

But we have one other instance of her activity on
behalf of a soldier, Fabricio Maramaldo (or Maramaus),
of Spanish origin, who had served both under the
Marchese di Pescara and del Vasto.   This man had an
unenviable reputation for cruelty even in that age, but
perhaps this did not render him unacceptable to Pescara,
whose memory is blackened by the sack of Como and
Genoa.   In the present juncture, Maramaldo seems to
have been the victim of mere party-jealousy.   The
following is the letter Vittoria addressed to Filiberto,
Prince of Orange, on the subject :—

"If by my writing about a thing of this kind it
may, perhaps, appear that the authority is less than the
subject and my audacity greater than it ought to be,

your Lordship must attribute the fault to the chance
that so many and such of my relations as would have
helped Fabricio Maramaldo, both by obligation and
goodwill, are either absent or dead. Therefore of
necessity I, with the sole light of their living memory,
am constrained to esteem my darkness clearer than it
sometimes is, but I would far rather be considered bold
than ungrateful. The sincerity of Fabricio and the
virtue of your Lordship make me feel certain that it
does not befit me either to implore for the one, or
to excuse the other for a fault. But because the sinister
information, which is made use of to-day, might make
your Excellence suspect that to be possible which is a
thing remote from all possibility, I have wished to
write to you and to assure you that in affairs of a
similar kind the Marchese, my lord of blessed memory,
made trial an infinite number of times of the virtue,
sincerity, and faith of Fabricio, and at a time when he
was in a lower position than he is to-day. On that
account, it would seem to me a strange thing that the
malice of a wretch could injure or stain the pure faith
of such a knight, made fine by such a hand. I therefore beg your most illustrious Lordship that, considering the prudence of the Marchese, my lord, which
approved Fabricio as trustworthy, that of the lord
Marchese del Vasto which confirmed this, your own
which confided to him in the past a part of your army,
you will remove every doubt from your mind; and
that, with that clearness, and generous will, and excellent judgment which befit such a Prince, you will
decide conformably to justice and reason, and restore
him to the honourable position and authority which

his services demand. For the Spanish nation, as specially jealous for the honour of knighthood, will praise you for it, and the Italian nation will believe that your Lordship holds her in more estimation than has sometimes been thought, and we shall all of us consider it a singular favour. And Our Lord God preserve you always.

"The Marchesa di Pescara."[1]

This letter is undated, but seems to have been written in July, 1528. Vittoria's intercession obtained for Fabricio what was only his due, namely, his re-instatement in his command. An intrepid soldier, we find him the following year at the siege of Volterra, which the Florentines under their patriotic general, Francesco Ferruccio, were defending.

There is a story that Ferruccio had live cats nailed to the walls of Volterra that the horrible noise they made might deride the name of his adversary, " Maramaus." If this be so, it forms a small excuse for the latter's savagery after the battle of Gavignana when, Ferruccio being dangerously wounded and a prisoner, Maramaldo is said to have killed him with his own hands : this outburst of tiger-passion may be considered an over-payment of revenge for the cats of Volterra.[2]

Once again we come across Maramaldo in connexion with the Marchesa, when in 1531 she appears to have commissioned him, he being then in Mantua, to apply

---

[1] *Carteggio*, Letter xxxviii.

[2] The manner of Ferruccio's death is variously reported ; some say that Maramaldo dispatched him with a dagger ; others that he ran him through with a sword or a javelin, calling to his men to finish the work, while Ferruccio exclaimed : " You are killing a dead man ! "

to Federigo (who had been made Duke by the Emperor in the preceding year) for a picture of the Magdalen, for whom she evidently had a special devotion. On this subject several interesting letters were exchanged. First the Duke wrote :—

" Most illustrious Lady and honoured Sister,

"The fraternal love that there was between the most illustrious Signor di Pescara of blessed memory and myself, and the close friendship and intimacy which I have with the most illustrious Signor Marchese del Vasto, cause me to feel a singular love for your Ladyship, joined by matrimony to the sweet memory of the one, and by the closest relationship to the other; and this love of mine towards you is made greater by your singular virtues. . . . And not knowing just now in what else I can please you, excepting what I have heard from Signor Fabricio Maramaldo, who has told me that you desire to have a fine picture of St. Mary Magdalen from the hand of an excellent painter, I have sent immediately to Venice and have written to Titian, who is certainly the most excellent artist of our time, and who is entirely at my service, earnestly begging him to paint a Magdalen, more beautiful and tearful than can be imagined, and to let me have it quickly. And because of the excellence of the artist, and the importunity with which I have assailed him, I feel sure that the work will be most perfect. I hope to have it here perhaps by Easter, and when it comes I will send it to your Ladyship, to whom I continually commend myself.

"From Mantua, March 11, 1531."[1]

---

[1] *Carteggio*, Letter XLII.

It would appear that Titian executed this commission very rapidly, and that the picture was sent to Mantua on April 14. Its subsequent history is shrouded in mystery. It was certainly sent to the Marchesa, for, in May, Vittoria wrote to Federigo, thanking him for the Magdalen "infinite volte," and sending him some costly perfume of roses. On July 28, the Duke wrote: "I have received two letters from your Ladyship just lately, which were most acceptable to me ; one which accompanied the most magnificent and precious gift which you sent me of most sweet perfumes and cosmetic of roses, in a beautifully-wrought casket; the other in which you informed me that you had been pleased with the Magdalen that I had sent you. I thank you most warmly for everything, and not less for having been so pleased with my little gift than for having made me such a beautiful present, which indeed could not have been more acceptable to me, both for being precious in itself, and on account of the place from whence it came. That your Ladyship should have been gratified by me as regards the Magdalen, and that I should have forestalled all the others who might have gratified you in this, pleases me, since, as you have seen some little alacrity on my part to content you, I hope that you will have recourse to me all the more confidently to do you a pleasure whenever you see that you can make use of me in this part of the world, as I beg you with all my heart to do, because this is one of the greatest desires that I have. I have had much pleasure in letting the artist who painted the Magdalen know what your Ladyship wrote to me about it, because I know how much encouragement it will give him to hear your judgment on his work, to which he will have to be grateful, if, under the stimulating effects of your praises, he adds something to the perfection of his art. Our Lord God grant your Ladyship all that content which you desire, and I commend myself always to you."[1]

Nevertheless, for what reason we know not, the picture found its way back to Mantua; that it did not remain long in the Marchesa's possession is attested by the fact that only two years later, in 1533, del Vasto was again trying to procure a Magdalen for her, which occasioned Isabella Gonzaga, the Duke's mother, to write the following gracious epistle to Messer Giovanni Tommaso Tucca, del Vasto's secretary:—

"I saw a few days ago, in a letter which you wrote to my Count Nicola di Maphei, a passage about the wish of the Marchese del Vasto to have my picture of St. Mary Magdalen to make a present of it to the Signora di Pescara. And because I have nothing in the world that I should not wish to belong equally to his Excellence, it gave me the greatest satisfaction to see that he had this desire, and I should have sent him the picture immediately, but, because I wished first to have a replica made of it, it was necessary to keep it until the artist had done copying it. Now that he has finished it, I send the picture by the same bearer as this letter of mine, and I address it to you, begging you to present it in my name to the aforesaid Signor Marchese, giving his Excellence to understand that I

---

[1] Letter dated Mantua, July 28, 1531. *Carteggio*, Letter XLVI.

Giovanna d'Aragona.
by Raphael.
(The Louvre.)

am sorry it is not much more beautiful, although, if it pleases him, it cannot but be most beautiful."[1]

This letter is rather an evidence of the great desire of the house of Gonzaga to stand well with del Vasto, who was a powerful imperial favourite, than of anything else, but it is disappointing that we do not know by what artist the picture was painted, nor have we any account of its reaching Vittoria, who would have been in Ischia at that date. But this is anticipating events by some years. In 1528, the pestilence which had devastated Naples spread to Ischia, and the Marchesa was obliged to leave the island and go to Arpino, from whence she proceeded to Rome, where she remained during the greater part of 1530.

Ascanio Colonna, with his beautiful wife, Giovanna d'Aragona, and del Vasto, who was married to Giovanna's sister, Maria, were all in Rome at this time. Vittoria was singularly blessed in the women with whom she was most closely connected. Each name that comes to our notice as that of one of her near relations, whether it be that of her aunt, Costanza d'Avalos, Principessa di Francavilla, or of the ladies of the court of Urbino, or of the two just mentioned above, gives forth a fragrance of its own, and is marked with its own distinction. This is, perhaps, especially the case with the Lady Giovanna, whom poets and painters have delighted to honour. Raphael and Titian painted her, Ariosto celebrated her, and in the curious anthology, called *Il Tempio alla divina Signora Donna Giovanna d'Aragona*, collected by that rather ineffectual

---

[1] Letter of March, 1533, published by Luzio, *Vittoria Colonna*, p. 19.

person Ruscelli,[1] if there be not much of marked
interest, it yet testifies to " the great merits and supreme
worth, and the infinite beauty of body and soul " of
this most illustrious lady ; and the charms of her sister,
the Marchesa del Vasto, are linked with hers in a
graceful manner.   Luca Contile was one of Giovanna's
ardent admirers, and wrote about fifty sonnets in her
honour, while Maria was sung by the poet Tansillo.
Giulia Gonzaga, herself a far-famed beauty, used to
say that of these sisters Giovanna was undoubtedly the
most beautiful and Maria the proudest.   Life in Rome
with these paragons must have had many agreeable
features; it is also pleasant to know that among the
children of Ascanio and Giovanna there was one
daughter, named after her aunt, Vittoria, who was a
special favourite of hers, and was said to resemble her
greatly in mind and person.

Vittoria Colonna is, perhaps, nowhere more charming
than viewed in regard to these family ties which nothing
could ever weaken, and she seems to have been adored
by her relations.   She was indeed a woman to be proud
of : untouched by scandal, unspoiled by praise, incapable
of any ungenerous action, unconvicted of one un-
charitable word.   Living in the midst of such religious
and political dissensions as divided and uprooted
families, she yet preserved in all relations of life that
jewel of perfect loyalty which does not ask to be
justified.

---

[1] *Il Tempio alla divina Signora Donna Giovanna d' Aragona, fabricato
da tutti i più gentili Spiriti, et in tutte le lingue principali del mondo.*   In
Venetia, per Plinio Pietrasanta, MDLV.

CHAPTER III

EARLY POEMS

When God helps all the workers for His world,
The singers shall have help of Him, not last.
                                        E. B. Browning.

We have to ponder carefully the feelings with which Vittoria probably regarded her husband before we can quite understand either her conduct after his death, or the long, and, to say the truth, somewhat dreary set of sonnets which he inspired. Bold, high-spirited, fantastic, eager for fame (who is after all but a vulgar mistress), we cannot feel that Pescara's character would have been the complement to that somewhat severe beauty of face and mind that we associate with Vittoria. Her deep tranquil affection may have been half a mystery to him, for if, as chroniclers hint, he had various loves, the only one of which we possess any record redeems him from being found the plaything of mere passing fancies, and shows him to have been capable of such a lasting passion as the cruelty of which he was certainly guilty, and the shadow of treachery which darkens his name, would hardly have led us to expect.

The record is slight enough and dates are everywhere wanting, but it is certain that Pescara's affections were given to one of the ladies-in-waiting of Isabella d'Este, Marchesa of Mantua, whose name was Delia, and who seems to have been a relation of the Marchesa's secretary, Mario Equicola, who was always a go-between in the affair. Isabella's ladies were all noted for their personal charms. We cannot precisely say when Pescara first made Delia's acquaintance, but we know that, after the defeat at Ravenna, he went to Mantua, and was so cordially received by Isabella, that his aunt, Beatrice d'Avalos, wrote to thank the Marchesa for her extreme kindness to her nephew. This would have been in 1512. Two years later Isabella went to Ischia, certainly accompanied by the fair Delia, and had a magnificent reception from Fabrizio Colonna, which was not only in acknowledgment of the treatment he had received from her father during his imprisonment in Ferrara, but still more on account of the Duke's courtesy in not letting him pass into the hands of the French.

There are only four letters extant from Pescara to Equicola, one of which mentions an enclosure to Delia; they obviously cover a long period of time, and contain the history of a passion which had survived the chill and torment of continuous absence. The letters have few dates; to the first, written from Naples, October 1, the date 1519 has been assigned, but Professor Luzio thinks it should rather be 1517: the time of Pescara's return from his diplomatic mission to Brussels, and his journey to and from Flanders, are here mentioned. The second letter was from Rocca Secca on December 14; the others were probably written in 1522. In the second, he writes of "Delya da chi penso me nasce omne bene, omne alto pensiero et omne gratia"; in the last, he prays that he may see her once more before he

dies: one wonders if he did.[1]   It is difficult to know
exactly what importance to attach to this episode,
though some expressions in the letters make it impossible to consider it otherwise than as a serious
affair; and this would, in some sort, explain the total
lack of confidence and intimacy in the relations of
Pescara and his wife.

Equicola died four months before the Marchese, who
wrote to condole with Isabella on the loss of such a
faithful servant, while he promised to watch over the
interests of Mario's nephews and heirs, and wrote to
Vittoria begging her to do the same, a request which
she faithfully obeyed. We cannot tell whether she
knew that Equicola had been her husband's confidant
in his love-affair; but, in any case, hers was not a mind
to harbour mean jealousies.

We shall never know how much Vittoria guessed of
the real situation, but the facts as they stand throw
some light on the scope and the tone of her poems. If
it is difficult to imagine that the extravagant grief she
displayed on receiving the news of her husband's death
was lavished on the man who was unfaithful to her, we
can well imagine her weeping over a lost ideal, and can
realise that it was not only her widowhood that she
bewailed, but that " marriage of true minds " which
had never been hers. The grief for what we never had
is so much sorer than the grief for a lost possession;
nor is it only happiness that we mourn in this world;
perhaps, as many tears are shed over the mere apprehension of the unreturning past. Our joys leave us so
much even when they are gone from us, but the

---

[1] These letters are given by Luzio, *Vittoria Colonna*, pp. 4–8.

F

mutability of mortal things—the sense that we can
retain nothing—this makes half the tragedy of life: so
was it with Vittoria, looking back over sixteen chequered
years of married life. We can see her outlook so
clearly; her life has been shaken to its depths, storm-
swept and broken, but from all these wrecks and strays
something must be gathered up, and, if she is to be
ennobled by the past, she realises that nothing remains
to her in the present but a great fidelity.

And so, with a fine pride that would not betray itself,
she closed up the door through which inspiration and
feeling might have come forth, and, disdaining to make
a show of the supreme sorrow of her life, she no doubt
sought relief in song, but elected to keep to the outside
of things, and only to present to the world the image of
the soldier's widow, exulting in her husband's honour,
and deploring, not her own, but her country's loss.

Two causes contribute to the monotony of the
hundred and odd elegiac sonnets ; one is, as we have
noted, the repression exercised in them ; the other, the
total lack of any personal touches. All that is said of
Pescara might have been said of any general; there is
no trace of any individuality, and, though the measure-
less grief expressed deceives us a little at first, the
repetition of the same words and images becomes wearisome beyond bearing, and we feel that one genuine
heart-cry would be preferable to all the glory with
which the singer would fain surround her "bel sole."
No doubt something must be allowed for the taste of
the age which tolerated, rather expected, the recurrence
of accepted symbols, and which demanded that poetry
should be Petrarchan or nothing.

Vittoria does not live by her poems, least of all by those inspired by Pescara, but no presentment of her would be complete that did not give some idea of the work on which she was engaged for seven years, and to which she must have owed in part that rich record of literary friendships which will form the subject of the next chapter.

We will turn then to the *Rime* which form the first part of her literary output. Only one of these poems, the *Epistola a Ferrante Francesco d'Avalos, suo Consorte, nella Rotta di Ravenna,* was certainly written during her husband's lifetime, and it is curious that this is not contained in any of the early editions; it was first published in 1536, by Fabricio da Luna, in his *Vocabulario di cinque mila Vocabuli Toschi,* but P. E. Visconti (1840) was the first to include it among her poems. This long epistle, which seems to us a rather heavy composition, with conventional, classical imagery, has this one great interest attaching to it, that it has a far more personal note than any of the sonnets. The few lines at the end are, perhaps, reproachful, and would seem to imply that the soldier was more willing to be gone than the wife to suffer his absence, but this may be called the fortune of war and will be eternally the case as long as wars last. There are really touching lines of personal attachment to the man Pescara, not to his wounds, or his exploits, or his glory, which is all we shall get hereafter. She writes:—

> " But now in this most perilous assault,
> In this so cruel and relentless battle
> By which my heart and mind are turned to stone,

Your mighty valour has proclaimed you kin
  To Hector and Achilles.   But for me,
  Forlorn and weeping, what can this avail?
My mind was evermore a prey to dread;
  Whoever saw me melancholy, judged
  That jealousy and absence wounded me.
But I, alas! had ever in my thoughts
  Your daring courage, your audacious soul,
  With which injurious fortune ill accords.
Others cried out for war, but I for peace.
  My speech was ever: it suffices me
  If my dear lord rest ever at my side.
You are not hurt by hazardous emprises,
  But rather we who, mournful and afflicted,
  Wait on, sore wounded by our doubts and fears.
But you, spurred on by rage, and heeding naught
  Save honour, 'tis your custom to go forth
  Against all perils with fierce fury armed;
While we for you hold fear within our hearts
  And grief within our eyes; while sister yearns
  For brother, wife for spouse, for son the mother."[1]

---

[1] " Ma or in questo periglioso assalto,
      In questa pugna orrenda e dispietata
      Che m' ha fatto la mente e il cor di smalto,
  La vostra gran virtù s' è dimostrata
      D' un Ettor, d' un Achille.   Ma che fia
      Questo per me, dolente, abbandonata!
  Sempre dubbiosa fu la mente mia:
      Chi me vedeva mesta, giudicava
      Che m' offendesse assenza e gelosia.
  Ma io, misera me! sempre pensava
      L'ardito tuo valor, l'anima audace,
      Con che s' accorda mal fortuna prava.
  Altri chiedeva guerra, io sempre pace,
      Dicendo: assai mi fia se il mio marchese
      Meco quieto nel suo stato giace.

This was, of course, written in the early years of Vittoria's marriage, when her disillusion had not taken place, and when probably she had no cause to be disillusioned. We learn from Giovio that, in the *Dialogo d'Amore* which Pescara sent to his wife from Ravenna, he urged her to choose for her device a cupid embracing a serpent, the symbol of prudence, with the legend: *Quem peperit virtus prudentia servet amorem.* We do not know whether she ever adopted the suggestion, and Giovio subsequently designed another one for her, representing rocks lashed by the waves, with the motto: *Conantia frangere frangunt;* but the device actually used by her was a juniper, and she writes of it and its signification in the following sonnet, which was perhaps addressed to Costanza d'Avalos:—

" By angry winds is this fair juniper
    Encompassed, and with all her leaves unspread
    And close-shut branches, she defends her head,
    Kept thus within herself a prisoner.
Such shall my soul be, lady; tempests stir
    Around, yet to no freedom she aspires
    From honourable cares and high desires,
    But beats back all who seek to conquer her.
She loves, adores her sun, so is she bound
    Beneath great thoughts of him, and safe is she,
    And victor in all combats proudly found.

Non nuoce a voi tentar le dubbie imprese ;
    Ma a noi, dogliose afflitte, che aspettando
    Semo da dubbio e da timore offese !
Voi, spinti dal furor, non ripensando
    Ad altro che ad onor, contro al periglio
    Solete con gran furia andar gridando ;
Noi timide nel cor, meste nel ciglio,
    Semo per voi : e la sorella il fratre,
    La sposa il sposo vuol, la madre il figlio."

Nature has taught this tree of her fierce foe
Resistance meet; and reason wills in me
That in my grief my faithfulness should grow."[1]

There is no doubt that Vittoria had written poetry
from her youth ; the works of Britonio testify to this;
they are dedicated to her and pay her the most extravagant compliments. The little life of her by
Filonico is also full of small quotations from her early
verses which have now been lost.[2] In fact, the Marchesa
would never formally consent to the publication of her
poems. In 1537, Varchi, writing to Molza, states that
he had been to see her and had begged her to have her
sonnets printed, but that she would by no means
consent. Nevertheless, five editions appeared during
her lifetime, the first in 1538, which is extremely rare.
We get the fullest details of these from P. E. Visconti,

---

[1] " Quel bel ginepro, cui d' intorno cinge
　　Irato vento, che nè le sue foglie
　　Sparge, nè i suoi rami apre, anzi raccoglie
　　La cima, e tutto in se stesso si stringe ;
Qual sia l'animo mio, donna, dipinge,
　　Che fortuna combatte e non si scioglie
　　Dall' alte cure ed onorate voglie,
　　E chi vincerlo pensa addietro spinge ;
Perchè sicuro, sotto i gran pensieri
　　Ristretto di quel sol ch' ama ed adora,
　　Vincitor d' ogni guerra altero riede.
A quell' arbor natura insegna i fieri
　　Nemici contrastar ; ed in me ancora
　　Ragion vuol che nel mal cresca la fede."

[2] This practically contemporary life by Filonico Alicarnasseo (who
is probably to be identified with Costantino d'Atripalta, a member of
the household of the Marchese del Vasto) is reprinted as an Appendix
to the *Carteggio* by Ferrero and Müller.

to whom we owe the standard edition of Vittoria's
poems brought out by him in 1840, corrected from
the original manuscripts which he discovered in the
Corsini and Casanatense libraries.   These manuscripts
appear to have her very latest and most careful
emendations ; some are in her own handwriting, some
in that of Innocenza, the daughter of her agent, Carlo
Gualteruzzi, a beautiful and intelligent girl, whom the
Marchesa brought up and educated.

These early editions contain one hundred and forty-
three sonnets, as against the one hundred and seventeen
given by Visconti, but he includes several of these in
the second part, *Rime sacre e morali*, and it is probable
that the remaining ones are of uncertain authorship.
In the sixteenth century six more editions appeared,
two more in the next century, and in 1760 a *corrected*
edition was published by Lancellotti.   That these
corrections did not show much critical insight is proved
by the fact that they contain some famous stanzas by
Veronica Gambara, and also still include the canzone,

" Spirto gentil che sei nel terzo giro,"

which, though given in all the early editions, is now
generally attributed to Ariosto.   One sonnet is repeated
ten times, and seven are given which are the work of
other authors—three of them by Molza.

It is not wonderful that the text should vary immensely, owing to Vittoria's habit of sending stray
copies of sonnets to innumerable friends, some of
whom she invited to offer improvements.   Giovanni
Guidiccioni was one of these, and two of his letters,
one to the Marchesa, the other to her secretary,

Giuseppe Jova, are full of interest: both are undated.
To Vittoria he writes: " Your Excellence would make
me think far more of myself than I do, and than I
ought to do, if I did not know the poverty of my
expression and your habit of exalting the humble:
seeing that you make excuses to me for having delayed
writing to me, and are prodigal of such praises to my
sonnets as would be due, though insufficient, to yours.
But I know for certain that I know nothing, and I do
not seek any other glory from my writings than to
know that they have been read by you.   Because I
shall feel that I receive a great reward for any labour
of mine, whether small or great, in being certain of
this, and in being able to assure you that they come
from someone who is never tired of talking about
you, and of thinking of the high powers of your mind.
And I would it might please God that I might approach
so near to your learned and graceful style as to be able
to compose a poem, I do not say with the hope of
praise, but without fear of blame.   But, since you
have such a good opinion of me, I will endeavour
with all diligence to act so that you shall not be
greatly ashamed of having hoped for fruit from so
sterile a plant. . . . I thank you also for your last
most beautiful sonnets, which have so filled my mind
and my ears as those things do which delight one's taste
and please one immensely; and it seems to me that
there are some of them that Bembo would have been
glad to have written.   But I have no doubt at all that
you will acquire more every day, and surpass yourself
by more admirable things; which, up till now, my mind
would not have been able to conceive, as it seemed to

me that you had arrived at the truest finish and perfection of style and of thought that one could imagine. And I understand that the ancient glory of Tuscany will be renewed, nay, it will pass entirely into Latium."[1]

The emendations were sent in the following letter to the secretary: "I have examined the three wonderful sonnets that her Excellence has sent me, which have made me believe that the spirit, I will not say only of Petrarca, but of Plato, has passed into that holy breast. I have read them over several times, and always with more commendation, and, in order not to depart from her Excellence's commands, I will rashly tell you what I should like altered. . . . I should express the first three lines of the sestet otherwise, if it could be done conveniently, where it says:—

> 'The instant it arrives, happy and eager,
> There where I send it, such brief joy surpasses
> By a great measure every mortal rapture.'

There I should add a verb—the brief joy that *it feels* surpasses every mortal rapture: or, perhaps, in this sense: 'There where I send it, it becomes such that it surpasses'—— See now, in order to be obedient, I have ventured greatly. Now let it be your business either not to reveal or to excuse my arrogance, and so I beg you to do."[2]

---

[1] Letter xxx (undated), in *Opere di Monsignor G. Guidiccioni*, ed. C. Minutoli.

[2] Letter xxxi (also undated). *Loc. cit.* In the letter these three lines stand :—

Two other sonnets are corrected in this letter, but neither are to be found in the printed editions of Vittoria's poems. In the one quoted, though the Marchesa made two slight alterations, she did not apparently avail herself of Guidiccioni's suggestions, acting after the usual fashion of those who ask for advice. She, however, altered and corrected most extensively herself, and worked on her sonnets till the very end of her life.

Besides fugitive gifts, Vittoria seems to have had some special collections of her poems made, one of which was sent to Giberti's relative and secretary, Francesco della Torre, but this was only a loan, as we see from the following letters. In January, 1540, della Torre wrote thus to the Marchesa's agent, Carlo Gualteruzzi :—

"I have heard through letters of Messer Lattantio of the production of many most beautiful sonnets, and I have a great desire to have them, if that may be without importunity. I wanted you to know my wish; the rest will be for you to decide, but I know how much reason I have to confide in this lady's kindness and in your good offices."

That the sonnets were sent appears from another letter from della Torre to Gualteruzzi :—

> " E 'n quel punto che giunge lieto e ardente
> Là 'v'io l' invio, sì breve gioia avanza
> Qui di gran lunga ogni mortal diletto."

The sonnet is the sixth of those printed for the first time by Visconti, beginning: *Vivo su questo scoglio orrido e solo*. The only alterations that she seems to have made are *'ve* for *'v'io* in the second line quoted, and *mondan* for *mortal* in the third.

" The longer your letters are, the dearer they always
are to me ; but this short one of yours of the 11th is
full of so many favours that it is a long time since I have
had such an agreeable one.   I have read the sonnets of
our most illustrious Lady many times, but since I shall
not be satisfied without reading them a great deal
oftener, you must please to obtain forgiveness for me
if I do not send them back this time.   For I will send
them very soon, when I have first made a copy of
them, with the promise not to let them go out of my
hand ; which promise you may safely make for me,
since, as I make a profession of some talent in other
things, I confess that in this I am envious.   For,
indeed, I should not like such rare compositions to be
in any other hands than mine in this neighbourhood.
For how much honour and favour and grace will they
not be the occasion of to me, if, in order to see such
beautiful gems, people come to my treasure-house ;
as you and whoever else has a taste for such beautiful
things will see ; for the more one reads them, the more
one discovers new beauties.   I pray you kiss the hands
of her Excellence for me for the favour she has deigned
to grant me, which I esteem as much as I admire her
divine intellect and the grace of God therein."[1]

Another copy was sent by Vittoria to that remarkable
woman, Marguerite d'Angoulême, Queen of Navarre,

---

[1] Letters dated Verona, January 30, 1540, and February 16, 1541.
Pino, *Nuova Scelta di Lettere*. Lib. III. p. 132, and Lib. IV. p. 26.
The "Messer Lattantio" mentioned in the first letter was Lattantio
Tolomei, a cousin of Claudio Tolomei, and Sienese ambassador at the
court of Clement VII.   He was a great lover of literature and art, and
a friend of Michelangelo.

with whom she had so many things in common. The meeting of these famous ladies, if it had ever taken place, would have been a matter of historical interest. Marguerite is one of history's picturesque figures—*la Marguerite des Marguerites*, as her brother loved to call her. Her crest a daisy, her motto *Non inferiora secutus*, her character so blended of sweetness and strength, simplicity and courage, that she almost seems the embodiment of Chaucer's ideal flower:—

> " She that is of alle floures flour,
>   Fulfilled of al vertu and honour,
>   And ever y-lyke fair, and fresh of hewe."

She had strong points of resemblance to Vittoria in her love of letters, her great literary gifts, and the interest she manifested in reform. Indeed, the protection she extended to the reformers laid her open to the accusation of heresy, but it is difficult to ascertain her position accurately, as it was to the interest of her political enemies to make her out disaffected to the Church. It is certain that her brother, Francis I, never entertained any suspicions of her, and it is equally certain that she died a Catholic.

It was probably after Vittoria's long visit to Ferrara, where she would have heard so much of Marguerite from the latter's cousin, the Duchessa Renata, that the two authoresses felt a great desire to arrange a meeting, for which Milan appeared the most eligible place. But many circumstances arose to prevent the carrying out of this plan, and Marguerite therefore deputed the French ambassador, Georges d'Armagnac, Bishop of Rhodes, to beg for a copy of the Marchesa's sonnets,

which he did through Gualteruzzi. The precious
manuscript was sent through Alberto Sacrati, the
Ferrarese ambassador, but it fell into the hands of the
Constable, Montmorency, who informed the king that
he had retained it, judging many things in it to be
contrary to the Christian faith. The king, however,
to whom the name of the Marchesa di Pescara was
well-known, ordered the book to be delivered immediately to his sister. This manuscript is nearly
certainly that which is now to be found in the Biblioteca
Mediceo-Laurenziana of Florence; for, on the last page
of it, is written in another hand a sonnet in French
which is thought to be by Marguerite. The collection
comprises one hundred and two sonnets, but three of
them are variations of the same, which reduces the
number to ninety-nine, and of these only thirty-seven
are to be found in the printed editions of 1538 and
1539.[1]

Yet another copy was made for Michelangelo, " più
che carissimo," as we learn from the following letter
from him to his nephew, Lionardo Buonarroti, in
March, 1551 : "Messer Gianfrancesco begged me
earnestly about a month ago for something of the
Marchesa di Pescara's, if I had anything. I have
a little book in parchment which she gave me about
ten years back, in which there are one hundred and
three sonnets, not counting those she sent me from
Viterbo on paper, of which there are forty, and which
I had bound in the same volume with the others, and
I lent them to a great many people, and now they are

---

[1] See Domenico Tordi, *Il codice delle rime di Vittoria Colonna
appartenuto a Margherita d'Angoulême, Regina di Navarra.*

all in print. I have also several letters that she wrote me from Orvieto and Viterbo ; this is what I have of the Marchesa's. So show this letter to the said priest and let me hear what he says."[1]

Fattucci was evidently desirous of having the book of sonnets lent to him, but the artist, writing to his nephew two months later, says : "As for the Marchesa's book of sonnets, I do not send it, because I shall first have it copied, and then I shall send it."[2]   From this it would seem that Michelangelo had become aware that, though Vittoria's sonnets had all been published, they yet differed very greatly from the manuscript copies, which would enhance the value of those he possessed. Among the hundred and forty-three sonnets given to him, there must have been many of those subsequently printed as *Rime sacre e morali ;* with these we shall not concern ourselves at present ; they belong to a later, calmer period, the greater part of them probably to the time of Vittoria's sojourn at Viterbo, and it is nearly certain that her vision, *Del Trionfo di Cristo,* which seems to be the dividing line between her early and her later style, was written then.

For full seven years Vittoria poured out her laments for her husband. In Sonnet cxv she writes :—

> "I hoped that time would somewhat modify
> My fervent longings, that this seventh year
> From such long distance none should overhear
> Sighs from a heart o'ercome by misery.

---

[1] Letter ccxliii in Milanesi, *Lettere di Michelangelo.* The Messer Gianfrancesco mentioned is Gianfrancesco Fattucci, prete di Santa Maria del Fiore.

[2] Letter ccxliv, *loc. cit.*

But since the pain augments, and since on high
  The sun still runs his course, these cannot make
  My loss less heavy nor my heart more weak ;
  My grief despises time, and sufferings I.
Burning yet weeping, still I do not grieve ;
  Faithful perhaps shall be my title meet,
  Dearer than any deathless honours lend.
I will not change my faith, nor will I leave
  This rock which pleased my sun, where I would end
  These bitter hours as those which erst were sweet."[1]

This was obviously written from Ischia, where the Marchesa did pass a good deal of her time, but family circumstances were perpetually causing her to move from one place to another, and she always seems to have preferred convent-residences.

It would be impossible, without being wearisome, to give more than a few specimens of Vittoria's style. There is a fine sonnet here and there, and many fine lines throughout, but the poems on the whole are artificial and monotonous beyond words. Sonnets v and vi are among the happiest.

---

[1] " Sperai che 'l tempo i caldi alti desiri
        Temprasse alquanto, o da mortale affanno
        Fosse il cor vinto sì che 'l settim' anno
        Non s' udisser sì lunge i miei sospiri.
    Ma perchè 'l mal s' avanzi o perchè giri
        Senza intervallo il sole, ancor non fanno
        Più vile il core o men gravoso 'l danno ;
        Che 'l mio duol spregia tempo, ed io martiri.
    D'arder sempre piangendo non mi doglio ;
        Forse avrò di fedele il titol vero,
        Caro a me sopra ogn' altro eterno onore.
    Non cambierò la fè, nè questo scoglio
        Ch' al mio sol piacque, ove fornire spero,
        Come le dolci già, quest' amare ore."

" My light eternal, in thy victories
    Nor time nor season took a favouring part ;
    Thy sword, thy strength, and thy undaunted heart,
    Summer and winter were thy sole allies.
In so short time didst thou, prudent and wise,
    Disperse the foe, the manner did no less
    Than did the deed thine inward worth confess,
    And lent more honour to the high emprise.
Never did haughty minds arrest thy course,
    Nor streams nor mountains ; cities that were great
    Were conquered by thy favour or thy force.
The world's great prizes unto thee were given ;
    Other and true thy triumphs now in heaven,
    With other leaves thy brows incoronate."[1]

" O upon what smooth waves and tranquil seas
    My bark erewhile sailed onward with her prize,
    A load of rich and noble merchandise,
    Through the pure air and with propitious breeze.
Heaven, that now hides her lovely brightnesses,
    Lent me a light serene and free from shade.
    Ah ! let who blithely travels feel afraid :
    The first stage with the last not oft agrees.

---

[1] " Alle vittorie tue, mio lume eterno,
    Non diede il tempo o la stagion favore :
    La spada, la virtù, l' invitto core
    Fur li ministri tuoi la state e 'l verno.
Col prudente occhio e col saggio governo
    L' altrui forze spezzasti in sì brev' ore,
    Che 'l modo all' alte imprese accrebbe onore
    Non men che l' opre al tuo valore interno.
Non tardaro il tuo corso animi alteri
    O fiumi o monti, e le maggior cittadi,
    Per cortesia od ardir, rimaser vinte.
Salisti al mondo i più pregiati gradi ;
    Or godi in ciel d' altri trionfi e veri,
    D' altre frondi le tempie ornate e cinte."

Behold where fell and fickle fortune shows
    Her angry, evil face, the hurricane
    Bred of her fury doth around me close,
And savage beasts are ravening at my side ;
    Against me fight the winds and storms and rain,
    But still the faithful star my soul doth guide."[1]

Sonnet LXXIII is, perhaps, the most truly auto-
biographical of the series :—

" Even my serenest days were clouded all
    With mists, and so it was that hopes and fears
    Held me alternately 'twixt smiles and tears,
    And now of sweet, now bitter thoughts the thrall.
Heaven was not then of gifts so prodigal
    As sparing of them now, yet the soul would
    Endure sheer ill for that imperfect good,
    Which in the dear past years did her befall.
This is the law of that so cruel lord,
    Prompt to our hurt and slow to profit us ;
    Dark days and sunny hours he doth accord.

---

1 " Oh che tranquillo mar, oh che chiare onde
        Solcava già la mia spalmata barca,
        Di ricca e nobil merce adorna e carca,
        Con l' aer puro e con l' aure seconde !
    Il ciel ch' ora i bei vaghi lumi asconde,
        Porgea serena luce e d' ombra scarca ;
        Ahi quanto ha da temer chi lieto varca !
        Chè non sempre al principio il fin risponde.
    Ecco l' empia e volubile fortuna
        Scoperse poi l' irata iniqua fronte,
        Dal cui furor sì gran procella insorge.
    Venti, pioggia, saette insieme aduna,
        E fiere intorno a divorarmi pronte ;
        Ma l' alma ancor la fida stella scorge."

G

Devoid of faith and full of falsity,
　　Trust not the outward show to judge him by,
　　You who have reached the passage perilous."[1]

We have noble expressions of faithfulness in
Sonnets XLVI and LXXX, and the series ends with a
madrigal, which seems to be the only one Vittoria
ever wrote.

" This honourable tie that binds my soul,
　　Since the high cause immortal hath become,
　　Drives from my heart that evil which in some
　　Changes to violence the lover's dole.
No longer love false pictures doth unroll
　　Before my mind, nor fear doth now assail ;
　　Nor gold nor leaden dart doth now prevail
　　By curb or spear my motion to control.
With steadfast faith, in this unshaken mood,
　　By one fair, faithful thought he is exprest :
　　Above the stars, beyond all change and fate,

---

[1] " Erano in parte i miei giorni più chiari
　　Di nebbia impressi, che in timore e spene
　　Mi tenner sempre fra diletti e pene
　　Or con dolci pensier or con amari.
Non fur sì larghi allor, ch' or tant' avari
　　Mi sieno i cieli : e pur l' alma sostiene
　　Intiero mal per l' imperfetto bene,
　　Che si godeva già negli anni cari.
Questa è la legge di quel rio signore,
　　All' altrui danno pronto, all' util parco,
　　Che i dì ne fa infelici e liete l' ore.
Egli è vôto di fè, d'inganni carco ;
　　Non vi fidate a quel ch' appar di fuore,
　　Voi che giungete al periglioso varco."

Whose noble scorn nor grows nor doth abate,
  He stands for ever firm, for ever blest.
  This love fast-founded is the true, the good."[1]

" That flower of every virtue planted well
  With breath of my glad hope, in a fair field,
  In bygone days such perfume sweet did yield
  As makes the bitter fruit desirable.
Shall fate be kind to us, we cannot tell,
  Or adverse, none can know until the end;
  Loosed from one load, 'neath some new weight we bend:
  Such is our wretched lot with change to dwell.
But neither change of time nor destiny
  Can alter in my mind the high intent
  To praise the subject and the loss lament.
From the old passion one fidelity
  Springs in my bosom, that no less sincere
  Than the first day shall be the latest year."[2]

---

[1] " Questo nodo gentil che l' alma stringe,
      Poichè l' alta cagion fatta è immortale,
      Discaccia dal mio cor tutto quel male
      Che gli amanti a furor spesso costringe.
    Tanto l' immagin false or non dipinge
      Amor nella mia mente, nè m' assale
      Timor, nè l' aureo nè 'l piombato strale
      Tra freni e sproni or mi ritiene, or spinge.
    Con salda fede in quell' immobil stato
      Me l' appresenta un fido e bel pensiero,
      Sopra le stelle, la fortuna e 'l fato,
    Nè men sdegnoso un giorno nè più altero
      L' altro; ma sempre stabile e beato.
      Questo amor, ch' ora è fermo, è il buono, e 'l vero."

[2] " Quel fior d' ogni virtute in un bel prato
      Con l' aura della mia gioiosa speme
      Tal odor mi diè già, che 'l dolce seme
      Fa il frutto amaro ancor soave e grato.

MADRIGAL

" From sovereign desire are born the fears
  Which to the soul bring mingled smiles and tears.
  The wretched heart in its infirmity
  Is hurt by that fierce heat
  Whose supreme worth it faileth to descry.
  But when the mind becomes irradiate,
  Evil and woe are gone,
  And joy remains alone;
  The height of my fair fancy makes me view
  False things as false, and true things doubly true."[1]

These, then, are specimens of the poems which won
their author such great fame in her generation, a time,

Se n'è benigno o pur contrario il fato,
  Non si discerne infin all' ore estreme :
  Chè se l' un mal s' allevia, l' altro preme :
  Sempre è dubbioso il nostro miser stato.
Ma per cangiar di tempo o di fortuna
  Non fia cangiato in me l' alto pensiero
  Di lodar la cagion, piangere il danno.
Dall' antica passion nacque sol' una
  Fede al mio petto ; che non men sincero
  Del primo giorno sarà l' ultim' anno."

[1] " Dal soverchio desio nasce la tema
    E fa che l' alma in un gioisca e gema :
    Sente l' ardor che 'l miser core offende,
    Quando dal suo imperfetto
    Il sublime valor non si comprende.
    Ma poi che 'l lume irradia l' intelletto,
    Il mal fugge e la noia,
    E sol m' apporta gioia,
    E fa l' altezza del mio bel pensiero
    Il falso falso, e 'l ver più che mai vero."

we must remember, when other poetesses were not wanting, and women of culture and taste abounded. Yet among all Vittoria reigned supreme, and, to realise this, we cannot be content to devote ourselves solely or chiefly to the works she has left behind : we feel that the real worth must have been in the woman herself, and we cannot hope better to arrive at a more intimate knowledge of her than by studying her in her manifold friendships.

CHAPTER IV

A CHRONICLE OF FRIENDSHIPS

Truly the losse should be much more than the gain if that high degree of friendshippe should be taken from the fellowshippe of man, which in mine opinion ministreth unto us all the goodness conteined in our life.—CASTIGLIONE, *Il Cortegiano* (Hoby).

SOME people choose their friends on the rough and ready principle that "it takes all sorts to make a world," and thence results a possibly pleasing, but bewildering, mixture, of which the chief disadvantage is that it will not mix. But, with the greater number of us, allowing always for those friendships of circumstance which are, as it were, thrust upon us, and for which we are scarcely responsible, there is a certain similarity. of aims and tastes running through any group of friends which explains them to each other.

This is notably the case with Vittoria Colonna : from her early days two things distinguish her—love of family and friends, and love of literature ; and, in her later life, Friendship and Poetry were her guiding-stars. And, fixing our eyes on her large circle of friends, it is their likeness to each other that will most strike us: the same sense of proportion, of the relative value of things, the same ideal, and the same notion of how to attain it. For in this, at any rate, Vittoria was essentially unlike many of her sparkling sisters of

the Renaissance : brilliancy was not her chief feature,
and she was not conspicuous, as so many of them
were, for a restless and insatiable curiosity. Rather do
we find in her the patience and reserve which mark
the mind of the scholar, and that quality of aloofness
which also characterises those who are not even
scholars, but only the humblest students. These are
not attracted by the world ; they feel a need of being
alone, a sense of finding themselves in solitude, and of
losing the best part of themselves in society, as though
light, and talk, and a crowd, far from giving them
anything, appeared, on the contrary, to rob them of
what they had that was most precious. And, as this is
a world of compensations, natures of this kind, if not
reclusive, seem to have a special gift for friendship and
to find their best expression in it.

If there is one thing that the present age has lost
completely, it is the solid love of letters, though
education was never more talked about. The times
may compare favourably with the last century, or
century and a half, in that intellectual pursuits are, at
worst, indulgently permitted, and, at best, regarded
as the legitimate development of a certain order of
mind ; but that does not falsify the statement that the
humanistic point of view has been wholly lost. It was
the noblest idea that the Renaissance had to give, and
very nobly did the men and women of that epoch rise
to realise it.

It is probable that the wave of scientific discovery
which rolled over the last century diverted men's
minds to the positive and the practical ; for the charm
of certainty, the possibility of proof, is attractive to

some characters ; but while we cannot but respect the patience and devotion which science demands of her votaries, there is no doubt that the general effect has been to induce a preference for such knowledge as can be measured, and to make men attach an undue importance to tangible results.

On the other hand, it may be said that in education we tend more to be individualists : we consider each one's taste and capacity, and perceive that all cannot have the same talent or reach the same level. And this is good from one point of view : our error is not in expectation, but in aim. *Mensura hominis;* this is what we have lost sight of : for the humanists, the man did not exist apart from his highest capabilities, while we can be bribed for the neglect of these by some lesser gift. One little talent, which would have a definite value as a graceful superstructure, built on when the main edifice was strong enough to bear it, and imparting thereto the stamp of individuality, is regarded at present as the only thing worth reckoning with. All education is to be specialised with a view to utility, and so we have lost the loftier standpoint of former times, and men grow up half developed, one-sided, and needlessly limited.

If we would have the clue which shall admit us into Vittoria's charmed circle, it is this very " measure of a man": they all measured with the same golden reed.

It will help us to visualise the Marchesa's manner of life, if we understand clearly her different places of residence. For the ten years succeeding her husband's death, she may be said to have resided at Ischia, though her sojourn there was diversified by moving to Naples,

and Arpino, and Aquino, and by at least two visits of
some duration to Rome and Marino. In 1537, she
made a long stay at Ferrara, which is important for
her relations with Ochino and the Cappuccini, and
will require a separate chapter. In the summer of
1538, she went to the Bolognese, then to Florence and
to Lucca, after which she stayed in Rome until the
Salt War broke out in 1541, when she went for some
months to Orvieto, returning to Rome for a short time,
and then settling at Viterbo for three years in the
Convent of Santa Caterina, making, however, frequent
visits to Rome to see Michelangelo. From 1544 until
her death, in 1547, she lived in Rome at the Convent
of Sant' Anna de' Funari. In all these places Vittoria's
mode of life was the simplest and most retired, but in
all of them her friends sought her out, and if, for any
reason, intercourse was interrupted, it was made up
for by frequent correspondence, and the exchange of
verses and other literary productions.

We have already mentioned Sannazzaro as one of
the early friends as well of the Marchesa as of her
husband, and in this connection we must also consider
the poet, Girolamo Britonio, who, while following Pescara's fortunes for many years, was also a devoted
admirer of Vittoria, for whom he had a chivalrous
affection, appreciating her intellect as much as her
beauty. A sonnet of his praising her style was published in 1519, which shows that Vittoria must have
done a good deal of literary work before that date,
though none except the *Epistola* has come down to us.
Britonio's sonnet, somewhat high-flown and flattering,
is contained in the *Gelosia del Sole*, which has other

honourable mention of her, and is dedicated to her. If the work is conventional and the compliments exaggerated, it was at least accompanied by a rather charming letter, which ends thus :—

"I pray then that you will deign to accept it, because I send you with it the perpetual pledge of a mind devoted to you. I do not deny that I should have delayed sending it to you, but a great part of it having appeared against my will, and a great many verses being incorrectly given therein, I judged better to send it you in the same guise, as under the shadow of your so famous name I am persuaded that it will not be so unjustly blamed by malevolent judgment. Therefore, do not be contemptuous when you find it bare of great thoughts ; read some part, if not for the merit of this most unpolished work, at least in remembrance of the long-standing devotion which I have borne to you, and which I will bear you as long as I live."[1]

Another poet—lover rather than friend—was Galeazzo di Tarsia. This man was evidently a recluse; he was a native of Cosenza, who lived a retired life in his Castle of Belmonte and cultivated poetry. He was a devoted adherent of the House of Aragon, and his castle afforded shelter to all the refugees of that party. How intimately he was acquainted with the Marchesa we have no means of knowing, but his poems in her honour have the ring of true feeling and convey a vivid impression of her beauty. We are indebted to him for descriptions of her speaking eyes and her

---

[1] *Opera volgare di Girolamo Britonio di Sicignano intitolata Gelosia del Sole.* Dedication.

golden hair—"bright shining tresses, nets of curling gold," he writes—and one sonnet begins thus :—

> "I bless the day when tender hands and white
>   Opened my heart, when one curled golden head
>   So swift and soon me into bondage led;
>   And most those eyes which with a burning light
> Fulfilled these eyes of mine."[1]

A man of fastidious taste and secluded life, he was content that both his love and his genius should remain hidden. His contemporaries seem to have had scarcely any knowledge of him, and his poems were never published until 1617—more than half a century after his death. Where all attain to a high level of excellence, selection is difficult, but the subjoined sonnet is at any rate particularly appropriate.

> "Fair marble, honour is thine ornament,
>   Showing the image high of Love divine,
>   Even as a gem's translucent colours shine
>   On the blest bosom of the Orient.
> Who can one small bright ray make evident
>   Of the great splendour which encircles thee?
>   Or can the power that other light to see
>   That fires thy heart to pen or mind be lent?
> Heaven should have granted such a style or thought
>   As subject so sublime aright portrays;
>   Or should not in such wondrous wise have wrought.

---

[1] "Io benedico il dì, che il cor m' apriste,
    Man bianche e molli, e te, veloce e presta
    A legarmelo poi, cresp' aurea testa,
    Occhi, e più voi, che di bel foco empiste
    Quest' occhi miei."

But since the truth exceeds what either tells,
Angels must stoop to speak of thee, or else
The longing must suffice without the praise."[1]

During the Marchesa's brief appearance at the court of Leo X, she made at least three lifelong friendships, namely with Giberti, Sadoleto, and Bembo. These men, together with Cardinals Pole, Contarini, and Morone, will be seen to have been most intimately connected with her, and to have had the greatest influence over her life—an influence which was, in all cases, mutual. We have already sketched out the life of Giberti, and given some of the letters that passed between the friends. All their correspondence shows a very real respect and affection.

There is a picturesque element in what we know of Sadoleto. He, too, was a poet, and wrote both in Italian and Latin; his *Curtius* and *Laocoon* were much praised by his contemporaries, and there is a charming incident connected with the latter poem. Sadoleto first went

---

[1] " Chiaro, e di vero onor marmor lucente,
Che l' alta imago del divino Amore
Serbi, qual gemma lucido colore
Nel più felice sen dell' Oriente ;
Chi può segnare un picciol raggio ardente
Dell' immenso splendor che t' orna fuore ?
O l' altro in parte che ti alluma il core,
Ombreggiar con la penna e con la mente ?
Doveva stile il Ciel darne, o pensiero
Conforme a sì sublime e raro oggetto,
O non fuor del mortale uso intagliarti.
Ma poichè questo, o quel non giunge al vero,
Scenda a parlar di te puro Intelletto,
O almen basti il desio senza lodarti."

to Rome under the protection of Cardinal Oliviero
Caraffa ; it was just at the time when, by order of
Pope Julius II, excavations were being made and art-
treasures were being constantly recovered. Sadoleto
was keenly interested in the work, and frequently
assisted at it. One day, the workmen sent to him to
report that they had unearthed a colossal marble group,
which seemed to be a Grecian masterpiece. Sadoleto,
hastening to the spot, recognised the Laocoon as described by Pliny. He immediately apprised Bembo of
the fact, and the Laocoon, crowned with flowers, was
borne in procession through the city and into the
Vatican. In a few hours Sadoleto improvised his
Latin ode, which he recited in the presence of the Pope
and an assemblage of courtiers, standing before the
laurel-wreathed statue. The Pope was so struck with
the poem that, the next day, he sent the author a beautiful manuscript of Plato. This anecdote indicates that
the hero might be a fitting friend for Vittoria, which
fact further details of his life and character fully carry
out, for his charm does not reside solely in his poetry.
He became secretary to Leo X, and his life at the
papal court was exemplary ; in an age of bargaining
and self-seeking, he was distinguished by never asking
anything for himself and firmly refusing all presents.
He was made Bishop of Carpentras, and remained
there during the pontificate of Adrian VI. Clement
VII recalled him to Rome, and, not deeming it right
to refuse, he obeyed, sorely against his will, only stipu-
lating that he should be permitted to return in three
years. At the end of that time, like an ecclesiastical
Cincinnatus, he went back to his own see, and re-

sumed his quiet, studious life. He was adored by his
flock ; he was the arbiter in all quarrels, the settler of
all difficulties, and did justice under the trees in his
garden. Amongst his writings was a commentary on
St. Paul's Epistle to the Romans, which was greatly
approved by Erasmus, but incurred ecclesiastical cen-
sure, which, however, was removed, the book being
warmly defended by Cardinal Contarini.

Paul III recalled Sadoleto to Rome and made him a
cardinal in 1536, and, five years later, he was sent on a
diplomatic mission to Francis I. His intercourse with
Vittoria must have ceased during his residence at
Carpentras, but was no doubt renewed when he returned to Rome. Their friendship, however, never
languished, and he was one of her executors. It is
curious that no letters remain as a memorial, since it
is obvious that many must have been exchanged.

Intellectually, it is probable that Vittoria owed more
to Bembo than to anyone else. By age and standing,
he was eminently fitted to be her master and adviser,
while his infallible taste made him the universal censor
at that time. No story of this date would be complete
without some sketch, however slight, of the man who
seemed so curiously to dominate it ; but he was so
entirely the creation of his own age that it is difficult
to find a niche for him in ours—not because our age is
better, but because it is different. We wonder what
kind of a personality was his, to achieve the position
which he did, for it was not his age or rank, and assuredly not his literary output, which seems to raise
him so prominently above his contemporaries. Men
of more real genius—riper scholars, as Jacopo Sannaz-

zaro; greater poets, as Ariosto—deferred to his opinion,
and measured the worth of their work by his judgment of it. His ideal of a national language was
indeed a high one; he besought his countrymen, when
leaving Latin, to use, not the common tongue of the
people, but only the very purest Italian. But he was
not original : a close copyist of Virgil and Cicero in
Latin, servilely Petrarchan in Italian, he made his mark
not so much by his matter as by his manner, inculcat-
ing the doctrine of doing little and perfectly, with an
immense expenditure of thought. Bembo was the
high-priest of form, that most vital requisite of all
good literature, and he was never tired of dwelling on
the distinction that should characterise true poetry :
and men who have recognised these things have won
their immortality.

A Venetian citizen, Pietro Bembo had yet lived
some time in Florence, and had thus acquired that
pure Tuscan which played so conspicuous a part in
his literary career, while his Greek he learned in Mes-
sina from the celebrated Costantino Lascaris. About
the year 1498, his father having been appointed *vis-
domino* for Venice at the court of Ferrara, Pietro proceeded thither, and remained there for several years.
There was indeed every inducement to him to do so.
Always more occupied with literature than with anything else, he found himself in a most congenial en-
vironment in Ferrara, which was then one of the effec-
tive literary centres of Italy, and had attracted to itself
a great circle of *literati* and notably of poets. He was
still residing there when, in 1502, the golden-haired
Lucrezia Borgia wedded Alfonso, son of Duke Ercole,

and it is certain that Bembo desired to add yet another
experience to the very varied ones of which that lady's
life was made up.

In 1505, he published the *Asolani*, which was dedicated to Lucrezia.   These celebrated discourses, inter-
spersed with poems, some extraordinarily graceful and
some singularly monotonous, were supposed to take
place at Asolo, a castle in the Trevigiano, where lived
Caterina Cornaro, the ex-Queen of Cyprus, and where,
amidst a brilliant court-circle, she was celebrating the
marriage of one of her ladies.   On three successive
days, three noble youths and maidens meet together in
the court-garden to discuss the nature of Love, the
aspects of which are thus presented.

The speaker of the first day, Perottino, demonstrates
that love is synonymous with desire, and is wholly evil.
He is refuted on the second day by Gismondo, who
defines love as the ordered desire for the beautiful,
and, as such, bringing only blessing.   The speaker of
the third day takes a yet loftier flight, and represents
love as the desire for the intrinsic, immutable beauty,
aspiring so high and so far as to find its only fulfilment
in the Eternal Beauty, which is God.

The outcome of his Ferrarese sojourn, but deeply
tinctured with Florentine Platonism, the *Asolani* quickly
became the model of all contemporary treatment of
love, just as the *Prose della Volgar Lingua*, published in
1525, became the standard of language.

In 1506 Bembo proceeded to Urbino, and was for
six years an ornament of the famous court where
Guidobaldo had ruled, and the Duchessa Elisabetta and
Emilia Pia reigned.   Made papal secretary in 1513,

Bembo immediately took rank as one of the most
notable men in Rome, on account of his varied attainments, his magnificent library—the best private one
in Rome—and, probably, no less, for his captivating
manners. Possessed of these, it seems strange that his
diplomatic missions, both to Venice and Ravenna, were
failures. Bembo evidently was no politician, but in all
other relations of life he seems to have been largely
endowed with that quality which is at once a gift and a
grace, the indefinable attribute of tact, which is, as della
Casa says, " either a virtue, or the thing that comes
very near to virtue." All the accounts of him that are
preserved to us give an unfailing impression of
appreciative courtesy and sympathy, constantly given
forth by a man who was the leader and the admiration
of his contemporaries.

To us this ecclesiastic (though only in minor orders ;
he never became a priest till he was on the point of
being made a cardinal), who had buried one passion in
Ferrara and another in Venice, and was living in Rome
with his mistress, Morosina, is rather a repulsive
spectacle, though his own age seems to have seen
nothing startling in the situation. At any rate, he
tenderly loved Morosina and the children she bore
him, and she had no rival during her life, and after
her death no successor.

The most fascinating portion of Bembo's life was
certainly the twenty years that he spent, more or less
continuously, at his favourite villa, Noniano, near
Padua. Here we find in him the double charm of the
highly cultivated, many-sided connoisseur, and the
greater attraction of the mind of the student ; here

H

he seems to deepen and to expand. We can picture to ourselves his beautiful garden, full of rare plants and herbs, for he was a great botanist; his collection of medals, coins, and antiquities, for he was a noted judge of such things; and here we can see him in his extensive library, leading studious days, holding ever before him the ideal of the scholar, making patient researches, polishing his every work laboriously. At the same time he was no recluse, for he was consulted from far and near; no literature of any kind was considered safe that had not received his *imprimatur*, and he was surrounded by a band of friends and worshippers, who hung upon his every word and relied upon his lightest judgment, so that his small villa became the centre of the humanistic world, and he the idol of the whole literary community. The man's nature must have been rich and sweet to be unspoiled by all this adulation, and to give out, unfailingly, wise advice, courteous encouragement, and generous approbation.

We are at no loss to account for the friendship which grew up between Bembo and Vittoria, for, besides the tastes they had in common, there was a fund of sanity and generosity in the character of each which could not fail to render them attractive to each other. That he greatly admired her writings we learn from one of his letters to her, dated January 20, 1530, in which he says, having just seen several of her sonnets written upon the death of her husband, " how much I exult over our age—an age which has both had him, who among men was equal in arms to the valour of the most praised and most illustrious of the ancients, and also you, who among women have attained to more excellence in this art than seems possible for nature to concede to your sex."[1]   All their letters show on what pleasant terms they stood with each other; they exchanged portraits and addressed sonnets to one another. One of the Marchesa's commends the *Asolani;* the following, which is, perhaps, the most interesting, reminds us that she was instrumental in procuring Bembo's elevation to the purple, and also indicates that she would not have been averse to seeing him invested with that further dignity of which he is said to have stood a chance.

> "O happy spirit, whose noble gaze and bright
>   Pierces the distance; and whate'er surrounds
>   The elements, or day within its bounds
>   Unveils, falls far below your thought's high flight:
> If, live and pure, you raise to the true light,
>   Whose splendour decks you, the immortal eye,
>   In that abode your lofty destiny
>   Of sacred rule you will behold aright.
> Wherefore do thou in us that sacred seed
>   With neither tired nor sparing hand renew,
>   Which to immortal fruit the soul doth lead.
> Then, when the royal wills are unified,
>   The scattered flock they shall assign to you
>   To rule, O father, shepherd, master and guide."[2]

---

[1] *Carteggio,* Letter XL.
[2] " Spirto felice, il cui chiaro ed altero
    Sguardo lunge discerne, e quanto intorno
    Circonda gli elementi, e quanto il giorno
    Discopre, è basso al vostro alto pensiero:
  S' alzate puro e vivo al lume vero,
    Che v' ha del suo splendor fatto sì adorno,
    L' occhio immortal, vedrete in quel soggiorno
    L' alto destin del vostro sacro impero.

From Bembo it is natural to turn to the man who delighted to honour him, and from whom it is likely that most of us derive our most vivid conception of the literary Cardinal. Baldassare Castiglione was the ornament in turn of nearly every famous court in Italy, but was the special darling of the court of Urbino, where he was cherished as a son or brother. He seems to have been one of those *âmes d'élite* who are endowed with all the gifts in the world and out of it; the accidents of noble birth and personal beauty are lost sight of in the lustre of his mind and character. Through all his eventful life, his faith, his loyalty, and his devotion shine forth, and no less excellent is the sense of values which placed the good soldier and the most finished gentleman of the age in the forefront of scholarship and literature. The name of Castiglione, of course, suggests the *Cortegiano*—the portrait of the ideal courtier, whose character was so happily realised in that of the author. The book was written to keep alive the glory of the court of Urbino in the days of Guidobaldo and his Duchessa Elisabetta, and no rulers could wish for a more enduring monument. It would be idle to give an account of a work so well-known and so often described, yet it is tempting to linger over anything so perfect. The charm, and wit, and wisdom of all those men and women are made alive for us for

---

> Onde poi non sarete o stanco o scarso
>> Di rinnovar fra noi l' antico seme,
>> Ch' a frutto eterno alfin l' alma conduce.
> Allor le regal voglie unite insieme
>> Daran la verga in man del gregge sparso
>> A voi padre, pastor, maestro e duce."

ever, and so enlightened are their sayings that we
wonder how succeeding generations should dream of
adding anything to the ethics of manners, of letters,
and of love.   Jest and earnest alternate swiftly; we are
sometimes kept on the surface and sometimes taken
down into the deeps of thought; until we are led up
to those farthest heights for which neither moon nor
stars would suffice, and so the author created the sunrise of a new day.

The *Cortegiano* seems to have been begun in 1514,
when Castiglione was residing in Rome as the ambassador of Francesco della Rovere, Guidobaldo's
nephew and adopted successor.   He had there a noble
circle of associates—poets, men of letters, and artists;
among the former Bembo, Sadoleto, and Federigo
Fregoso; among the latter, Raphael and Michelangelo,
the former of whom was his most intimate friend and
constantly asked his advice.   The book was completed
about 1518, and submitted to Bembo, but countless
alterations were made in it during the next few years,
and, in 1524, it was sent to Vittoria Colonna, doubtless
for two reasons—that her opinion in such matters was
continually sought for, and that the book in question
would be particularly interesting and acceptable to her
as extolling her famous aunt, the Duchessa of Urbino.

It is at this juncture that we have to relate the only
unpleasant episode that ever occurred between the
Marchesa and any of her literary friends.   Castiglione,
being about to set out for Spain, wrote to request that
his manuscript might be returned to him, and the
following is a part of Vittoria's answer: "I had not
forgotten my promise to you ; on the contrary, I am

sorry that I have remembered it so well, because it has
continually taken from me the pleasure of such a beautiful book, thinking that I should have to send it back
without reading it as often as I should have liked,
which, at least, would have helped me by keeping it
well impressed on my memory. Since you have been
disobliging enough to press me for it, and since I am
already in the middle of my second reading of it, I
pray your Lordship to allow me to finish it, and then
I promise to return it to you, as soon as I hear from
you by letter that you are going to leave Rome. You
will not need to send anyone for it, for I will return
it carefully and safely. It would not be fitting that I
should tell you what I think of it, for the same reason
that your Lordship says you cannot speak of the beauty
of the Signora Duchessa,[1] but for the promise I made
you ; and I shall not trouble to write you an elaborate
letter telling you what you know better than I do. I
will simply tell you the plain truth, affirming it with
an oath which will demonstrate its efficacy, when I say
por vida del Marchès, my Señor, that I have never seen,
nor expect to see, another work in prose superior to
this, or to be compared to it ; nor, perhaps, one that
deserves to be ranked second to it. Because, besides
the new and beautiful subject, the excellence of the
style is such that, with a sweetness never felt before, it
leads you to a charming and fruitful hill, ascending
always, without ever letting you perceive that you are

---

[1] "I confess not only that I have not expressed, but that I have not
even indicated, the excellence of the Signora Duchessa, because not only
is my style insufficient to express it, but also my mind to imagine it."—
Dedication of *Il Cortegiano*.

no longer on the plain where you entered ; and the
way is so well cultivated and adorned, that it is difficult to discern whether art or nature has most embellished it. Let us pass over the wonderful wit, the
wise sayings, that shine upon us no less than gems set
in just enough gold to hold them together without
taking away the smallest part of their light ; nor do I
think that other such jewels can be found, nor any
artificer to improve on their setting."[1]

Whether Vittoria's flattering remarks so softened
the heart of Castiglione that he permitted her to con-
tinue to be the custodian of the *Cortegiano,* we do not
know ; but it is certain that she retained possession of
it, at the same time remaining a fast friend of the
author, as we have a cordial letter of his to her from
Madrid, congratulating her on the "glorious suc-
cesses" of her husband at the battle of Pavia. But in
September, 1527, he writes complaining that she has
not kept his manuscript safely ; that he hears that
many fragments of it are in Naples, in divers hands,
and that, on that account, he is having it printed. And
in the dedication of the *Cortegiano* to Don Michele de
Silva, Bishop of Visco, there stands this passage, which
must surely have been a painful one for the Marchesa,
although the rights of authorship were very differently
regarded in those days to what they are now :—

"Finding myself in Spain, and hearing news from
Italy that the Signora Vittoria della Colonna, Marchesa
di Pescara, to whom I had already lent the book, contrary to her promise had had a great part of it transcribed, I could not but feel some annoyance about it,

---

[1] Letter dated Marino, September 20, 1524. *Carteggio,* XVIII.

fearing those many inconveniences which may happen
in such cases. Nevertheless, I trusted that the talent
and prudence of that lady (whose virtue I have always
held in veneration as something divine) would be sufficient to prevent any prejudice coming to me from
having obeyed her commands. But at length I learned
that part of the book was in Naples in the hands of
many; and, as men are always covetous of novelty, it
seemed likely that these persons might try to have it
printed. Wherefore, terrified at this danger, I determined to revise the book quickly, in the little time at
my disposal, with the intention of publishing it; thinking it less bad to see it a little defaced by my hands,
than much lacerated by the hands of others."[1]

So the *Cortegiano* saw the light in Venice, in 1528;
and there would not appear to have been any undue
hurry in this, as the book had been practically finished
ten years earlier.

It is fortunate that Castiglione's expostulatory letter
ends in a forgiving strain : "If your Ladyship should
think that this might have had the power to weaken in
any way the desire I have to serve you, you would err
in judgment, a thing which you have never done in all
your life. On the contrary, I am really indebted to
you, because the necessity of having the book printed
immediately has relieved me from the trouble of adding
many things to it, as I had already made up my mind
to do, and these would only have been of slight importance, like the rest; and thus fatigue will be less-
ened to the reader, and blame to the author; so that
there is no occasion for your Ladyship, or for me, to

---

[1] Dedication of *Il Cortegiano*.

repent or amend. It now only remains for me to kiss your hands and to commend myself to your favour."[1]

We do not know whether any other letters passed between them before death overtook Castiglione in 1529, when all Spain and Italy mourned the man who had so adorned both.

Several literary men of note are associated with the Marchesa's life at Ischia. Hither came Marcantonio Flaminio, as early as 1514, to make the acquaintance of Sannazzaro. This remarkable youth, who began his literary career at the age of sixteen, when he went to Rome to present his own poems and those of his father to Leo X, seems in no wise to have disappointed his early promise. Leo is said to have been so struck with his extraordinary ability that he said to him : *Macte nova virtute, puer: sic itur ad astra.* Patronised and admired by every man of note, he went for a time to Urbino, at the invitation of Castiglione, who, charmed with his intelligence, kept him at his side and gave him all manner of advice and instruction, for which Flaminio expressed his gratitude in an ode which is said to have been a marvellous production for a lad of seventeen. It is probable that he knew the Marchesa from the time of his first visit to Naples ; at any rate, he played a large part in her later life, particularly during her sojourn at Viterbo, and we shall have to speak of him later, when we come to deal with Ochino and his followers.

We are not sure when Vittoria first came to know the historian, Paolo Giovio, but he certainly visited her

---

[1] Letter dated from Burgos, September 21, 1527. *Carteggio,* XXXIV.

at Ischia in 1528 ; his life of Pescara is dedicated to her, and is specially interesting from the fact that she probably supplied many of the details ; and she was greatly pleased with the historian's life of her cousin, Pompeo Colonna, whose force of character and elements of greatness are so happily set forth therein. It was Giovio who presented to her notice the scholar, Antonio Minturno, a man who seems to have been in some sort a protégé of the Colonna family, as he resided sometimes in Rome, sometimes in the Colonna castle of Genazzano, and among his works was a Latin poem on the origin of that illustrious house, which he desired to dedicate to Cardinal Pompeo, and so brought it with him to Ischia and begged the Marchesa to recommend it to his attention. The poem was published under the title *Geneazanos*. Minturno also brought out a well-known treatise on the Art of Poetry, which was written both in Latin and Italian, and some poems in both languages, among which was a canzone on the death of the Marchese di Pescara.[1]

Another friend and poet connected with the South was Bernardo Tasso, and, though his name is overshadowed for us by that of his more celebrated son, he was accounted great in his own time, and the fame of his *Rime* made him known to Ferrante Sansovino, Prince of Salerno, who invited him to his court. He followed the prince on various expeditions, but, when not so engaged, he was allowed to live at Sorrento and devote himself to poetry. Tasso wrote the following sonnet to Vittoria after her husband's death :—

---

[1] *Rime et prose del Sig. Antonio Minturno*, Venice, 1559, p. 158.

" Blest Lady, unto whom it may be said,
 Thou in this stormy, evil world hast showed
 That, with the soul's eyes ever fixed on God,
 Thou liv'st a life joyous and honourèd ;
And there, where all desire is perfected,
 Borne upward on the wings of thy fair thought,
 As though to thy dear native country brought,
 Each day in happiness is finishèd ;
And gazing gladly on each angel-band,
 And on the noble people, verily,
 Thy heart contains a joy that nothing mars.
O perfect life, O true felicity !
 To watch the wandering Sun and Moon, and stand
 Above the elements, above the stars."[1]

It is probably to this that the Marchesa refers in a letter to Bembo, when she writes of " that most beautiful and, perhaps, unique sonnet that he (Messer Bernardo) has made, for which I think that he is more indebted to me than I am to him. For it has been with him as with those perfect painters who, seeing a person who has been very badly finished by nature,

---

[1] " Hor vi si può ben dir, Donna beata,
     Che in questo mondo tempestoso e rio,
     Volta cogli occhi de la mente a Dio,
     Lieta vita vivete ed honorata ;
  E con le penne del pensiero alzata
     Là, dove si finisce ogni desio,
     Sì come in un terreno almo e natio,
     Felice trapassate ogni giornata :
  E l' angeliche squadre ad una ad una
     Mirando allegra, e le ben nate genti,
     Sentite a mezo 'l cor gioia infinita.
  O perfetto piacere, O vera vita :
     Scorger gli error del Sole e de la Luna,
     E star sovra le stelle e gli elementi."

seek to copy that imperfect work, it being sufficient to them that one should see the excellence of the art, not the perfection of the thing ; wherefore, whosoever looks upon it is compelled to the consideration of the skilful hand, without thinking at all of the unworthiness of the effigy."[1]

Bernardo wrote a good many sonnets and canzoni to the Marchesa, and they have a distinct charm as conveying a real impression of the woman, not a mere conventional image. His letters are elaborate pieces of flattery, but his poems seem to be much nearer his heart. The following lines occur in one of the canzoni :—

> " Rest quiet and secure
> Into this harbour cast.
> Let reason with her twisted rope make fast
> Unto this happy shore
> Thy laden bark, which tires
> Beneath the burden of thy high desires.
> Of thy great virtue let me now behold
> The sunshine luminous,
> Pouring its thousand lovely rays on us ;
> Dispelling fold by fold,
> As dawn makes mists of morning fly,
> Each dreadful cloud of cruel destiny."[2]

---

[1] *Carteggio*, Letter CLX.
[2] "State secura e queta
> In questo porto sorta ;
> E con la fune da ragione attorta
> A questa riva lieta
> Legate pur la barca
> De' vostri alti desii gravosa e carca :
> Ch' io veggio il chiaro sole
> De la gran virtù vostra,

And these lines come in the second of the *Libri de gli Amori* :—

> " Then driving from her heart all other wills,
> Inflamed with high desire celestial,
> To sign more excellent she lifts her thought :
> God doth the clear eyes of her mind enthral,
> Nor do they ever close, for this fulfils
> With joy, compared to which all else is naught.
> Can surer pledge be sought
> To be of that fair country citizen
> Where life lives ever? Mid the angel-band,
> Dear to the supreme Father, aye to stand,
> Not fearing any dawning morrow, when
> Thought's piercing cry shall all thy grief awake,
> Or mortal misery thy slumber break."[1]

No doubt Vittoria responded liberally with praises, of which the following letter is an acknowledgment :—

> Che con mille be' raggi a noi si mostra,
> Disgombrar, come suole
> L' alba l' ombre al mattino,
> Ogn' atra nebbia di fiero destino."

[1] " Poi sgombrando dal cor tutt' altre voglie,
Accesa d' un celeste e bel desio,
Alza la mente a più lodato segno :
E gli occhi del pensier fermando in Dio
Senza chiuderli mai, piacer ne coglie
Tanto ch' ogn' altro a lato a quello è un sdegno.
O che securo pegno
D' esser di quella patria cittadina,
Ove sempre si vive ; e fra le squadre
De gli Angeli più cari al sommo Padre
Di star ; senza temer ch' a la mattina
Acuta squilla di pensier molesti,
O mortal noia dal sonno ti desti."

"Many have been found in past ages who have given states, money, goods, and other benefits of fortune; but glory none that I know of except you, who, by dispensing your own praises on my compositions, contrive to make me immortal with your glories. The beauty, the variety, the loveliness, the sincerity that you tell me you find in my Canzoni are fruits born of the seed of your merits, sown by you in the arid field of my intellect, notwithstanding which, they are not in any way equal to the seed. I do not know what reason moves you to despoil yourself of your own praises in order to honour my productions, which of themselves, and without the ornament of your name, haply would not deserve either to be seen or read; unless that, in order to surpass everybody in liberality, as you do in virtue and in judgment, you have wished to employ this new method. I confess to having little judgment about anything, but in this I have, at least, so much as makes me acknowledge these praises as being due to your goodness and not to my merits. Farewell, and keep me in some part of your good favour."[1]

It may also be interesting to give the dedication of the Eclogues and Elegies, and there is certainly truth in the assertion that their connection with Vittoria's illustrious name has served to keep them in some sort of remembrance.

"Most illustrious and virtuous Lady, it being a common instinct of Nature that man should desire to live eternally in this world, those especially who are of a higher and nobler intellect, not being able, by the ordinance of Him who governs us in this which we

---

[1] *Carteggio,* Letter CLXXIX.

call life, to overpass the prescribed limits of age, strive
to procure this immortality for themselves in one way
or another, as they best can. So that if death, who
spares none, takes them away from this light, their
name at least shall remain alive in men's memory. For
which reason I, having fallen a victim to this same
desire, and knowing that these my writings cannot of
themselves resist the injurious force of time, but that
a few years will take from me the second life, have
decided, by availing myself of your favour, to procure
for them that with the white wings of your name,
without which they would not dare to raise themselves
from the ground, they may mount so far that the
rapacious hand of the years may not hide them under
the ruins of the world. Hoping that, as you alone
are found to have attained to that highest degree of
perfection in every art and science, far surpassing
Sappho and all others who are most famous in good
literature, and, soaring above the stars on your own
wings, have illuminated this our age with the rays of
your virtue, you will even be content that these my
eclogues and elegies should live in the bosom of your
glory. With the light of your honour clearing away
the darkness of their imperfections, they will be read
all the more willingly by the world the more the adorn-
ment of your virtues shall render them beautiful.
Nor, on this account, shall I be bound to you by a
lesser obligation than for many other benefits of which
(thanks to your generous mind) you have made me
worthy; nay, by a greater ; seeing that the former will
have helped to defend me from the troubles of this
life, but these will deliver me from eternal death and

the perpetual darkness of oblivion."[1] Tasso had a troublous and melancholy life, and his unbroken friendship with the Marchesa must have been one of his happiest records.

One of Vittoria's most fascinating friends was Giovanni Guidiccioni, of whom Caro said that, while still a boy, he had arrived at that perfection of sense, and judgment, and cultivation of mind to which few attain in later life. He took major orders and entered the service of Cardinal Farnese, with whom he went to Rome in 1528, and subsequently to Lucca and Bologna. But the life of courts and cities was completely distasteful to him, and he obtained leave at one time to retire to Gradoli, a castle of the Farnese near Viterbo. From there he sent to a friend some sonnets " nati tra quei boschi," and said that he was devoting himself to the study of Plato. He had such an ardent admiration for Vittoria that he said (in a letter already quoted) that by her means the ancient glory of Tuscany had entirely passed into Latium, and the Marchesa was accustomed to consult him. Their philosophy of life would have been much the same, for Guidiccioni says of himself: " I wish to live to God, to myself, to my friends, and to enjoy an honourable leisure for the pursuit of literature "—an ambition hard to realise in any time, and impossible then, when every able man was called to fill some onerous post and undertake some difficult mission : both fell to Guidiccioni's share, and he would certainly have been made a cardinal but for his early death at the age of forty-one. He was a writer as well as a good judge of literature. Three of his sonnets

---

[1] Letter inserted among the *Rime* of Bernardo Tasso, pp. 160–162.

are addressed to Vittoria, but his poetry is chiefly interesting from its patriotic note, a note seldom struck by the men of his age, and it is on that account that we have selected the following sonnet for quotation.

" From that dead slumber which has been thy grave
    These many years, now breathe and rise again,
    And gaze upon thy wounds with deep disdain,
    My Italy, no less a fool than slave.
The lovely liberty that others have
    Deprived thee of, for thine insanity,
    Now seek and sigh for; let thy footsteps try
    The straight road that to crookèd pathways clave.
For if thou ponder ancient memories,
    Then those who graced thy triumphs thou shalt see
    Are those who chain and bind the yoke on thee.
Others have reaped, whilst thou abid'st undone;
    Thine impious wills, thine own worst enemies,
    Have brought thee to this end, most wretched one!"[1]

Francesco Maria Molza was probably a friend of the Marchesa's later Roman days, though he has been said by some to have been her master in the art of

---

[1] " Dal pigro e grave sonno, ove sepolta
    Sei già tanti anni, omai sorgi e respira,
    E disdegnosa le tue piaghe mira,
    Italia mia, non men serva che stolta.
La bella libertà, ch' altri t' ha tolta
    Per tuo non sano oprar, cerca e sospira ;
    E i passi erranti al cammin dritto gira
    Da quel torto sentier, dove sei volta.
Chè, se risguardi le memorie antiche,
    Vedrai che quei, che i tuoi trionfi ornaro,
    T' han posto il giogo e di catene avvinta.
L' empie tue voglie, a te stessa nemiche,
    Con gloria d' altri e con tuo duolo amaro,
    Misera ! t' hanno a sì vil fine spinta."

I

poetry—a very unlikely thing, as he was but one year her senior, and also having regard to the character he bore. Three sonnets of hers, however, are addressed to him, two on the death of his parents, one, strangely enough, on the death of his mistress.[1] Molza was certainly in Rome during Vittoria's sojourn there in 1530, and accompanied her in her various visits to the antiquities ; on one of these occasions, she exclaimed : "*O loro beati che furono a tempi sì belli !*" to which he replied : "*Essere eglino stati meno felici per non averla veduta,*" an incident which he has preserved in a sonnet.

It is rather surprising to find how many letters the Marchesa exchanged with the notorious Pietro Aretino ; we can only suppose that he imposed upon her as he did on so many learned men of the time. Certainly he had the wit to try all lines, and plied the Marchesa with his Lives of the Saints and paraphrases of the Penitential Psalms.

Claudio Tolomei is another interesting figure connected wholly with Rome. He founded the Accademia della Virtù, to which Molza and Flaminio belonged, and, when that came to an end, he was instrumental in starting the Accademia Romana, which flourished in the days of Julius II and Leo X ; Sadoleto belonged to this, and has given an alluring description of it, telling how the meetings were held in beautiful houses, or in gardens on the banks of the Tiber, or in shady groves. We have two letters from Tolomei to Vittoria, one in which he says he is trying to recover for her a part of a small work of his on the Tuscan language which he

---

[1] *Rime,* Sonnets XXXVII, XXXVIII, CXIV.

fears has perished in the sack of Rome ; another in
which he offers her a copy of his *Orazione della Pace*,
and gracefully says that it will be much better off re-
posing with her at Ischia than if it remained with him.
Luca Contile was another literary light who was at the
opening of the Accademia della Virtù ; he was later in
the service of the Marchese del Vasto, and was devoted
to Vittoria.   There is a letter from him to a friend in
1541, saying how he had been to visit the Marchesa
and had stayed with her four hours as he was wholly
unable to tear himself away.[1]   The Florentine poet
and patriot, Luigi Alamanni, wrote that he never expected to have left Rome with such regret as he felt
when leaving her.

No list of the friends of this gifted woman would
be complete that did not make mention of her two
secretaries, Carlo Gualteruzzi and Giuseppe Jova, who,
besides being devoted to her interests, were themselves
men of gifts and distinction, and were held in esteem
by the most eminent literary men, as is abundantly
shown in the letters they received and the mention
made of them in Vittoria's correspondence.   Jova numbered Caro and Varchi among his special admirers.
A further interest attaches to Gualteruzzi in that he
had a daughter Innocenza, who was brought up and
educated by the Marchesa, who loved her as much for
her sweetness of disposition as for her talent ; the girl,
as we have noted, often acted as her amanuensis and
made copies of numbers of her sonnets.   Innocenza
eventually took the veil in the Convent of San Silvestro.

---

[1] See below, pp. 237, 238.

Vittoria seems to have found her women-friends chiefly among her large circle of relations. First of all we may place her illustrious aunt, the Duchessa Elisabetta of the *Cortegiano*, and scarcely less remarkable was her husband's aunt, Costanza d'Avalos, Duchessa (afterwards Principessa) of Francavilla, who brought up Ferrante d'Avalos and is thought by some to have educated Vittoria with him : there is no clear proof of this, but it is certain that Vittoria passed a great part of her married life with her. There was another Costanza, sister of the Marchese del Vasto, also brought up by this aunt, who married Alfonso Piccolomini, and became a firm adherent of Valdès ; she greatly resembled the Marchesa in her love of retirement and her intellectual gifts. The three lengthy letters that Vittoria addressed to her are, in reality, religious treatises. Costanza ultimately entered the Convent of Santa Chiara in Naples. The same ties of religious interest formed a bond between Vittoria and two ladies of the House of Gonzaga, Giulia who married the Marchesa's cousin, Vespasiano Colonna, and Eleonora, the beautiful Duchessa of Urbino ; the latter was the daughter of Isabella d'Este. We cannot picture Vittoria and Isabella as friends, their outlook on life must have been too different : the one lived too much in her affections to sympathise with the cold and brilliant nature of the other. Burne-Jones, in summing up the qualities of gems, said : " Diamond is strength, but it fidgets and sparkles and is all of this world. Amethyst is devotion." So we might sum up the characteristics of these notable women. With the Duchessa Renata and Caterina Cibo we shall be concerned later, when Ochino and Carnesecchi come into our story, and the poetess, Veronica Gambara, must have a chapter to herself.

Of Vittoria's three special friends among the Cardinals, we shall also hear more when dealing with the Ochino episode, but we may here remark that they were all men who had the inner reform of the Church at heart, and never ceased to work for it with the most intelligent zeal and charity. Cardinal Contarini was probably the most learned of the three, and addressed his letter *Del libero arbitrio* to the Marchesa.[1] Morone, who was the son of the man Pescara had betrayed, became, nevertheless, a close friend of his widow, particularly after Contarini's death. But the man who influenced her most was Cardinal Pole, with whom her intercourse has a charm and poetry of its own, speaking the language of maternal affection and devotion. When he was made legate of Viterbo, "a government of ease and leisure which he enjoyed for many years," as Beccadelli tells us, Vittoria also took up her abode there, and they were constantly together. Sadoleto and Giberti were Pole's particular friends, which must have made an additional tie with the Marchesa.

We feel instinctively that Vittoria can have been no less attractive in the dignity of her widowhood than in her younger years. Hers was probably more the beauty of woman than of girl ; her golden hair, of which Galeazzo sang so much, may have faded a little,

---

[1] It is dated Rome, November 13, 1536, and published in *Quattro Lettere ai Monsignor Gasparo Contarino Cardinale* (edited by A. M. Faroso), Florence, 1558.

but her starry eyes would have been no less luminous ; and the years, that write so many things upon our faces, must have left on hers the impress of a great purity and an ever-soaring ideal. No friend ever dropped away from her, but, on the contrary, their number was always increasing. Nor was it only her talent that drew her large circle around her, though no doubt men came, full of admiration for her intellectual powers, to get the benefit of her criticism. Bembo said of her that she had better judgment in poetry than he had found in the greatest and most learned masters ; and Annibale Caro and countless others echoed his opinion. But it is evident that that was only a small part of her charm, for learning in itself does not make anyone lastingly interesting. The people with whom it is good to talk, whose possibilities we do not exhaust, are not those who know most, but those who have thought much and felt deeply ; for these are they who have got the keys. The impression that Vittoria left upon all was not only, or chiefly, that of the gifted poetess and the intellectual woman, it was the spell of her unworldliness, her religion, her spirituality, and her humility : she had the supreme gift of making goodness attractive. Nor were hers an ordinary set of friends : each has some corner, and nearly all a well-assured place, in literature, while with scarcely an exception they are distinguished by a high cast of character and a true appreciation of the things worth striving for. Yet all this wealth of friendship dwindles to nothing before the unique friendship which was, indeed, the crown and glory of Vittoria's life, and would itself have sufficed to keep her name in undying remembrance.

CHAPTER V

THE LOVE OF FRIENDSHIP

Id quod amatur amore amicitiæ, simpliciter et per se amatur.
                                        St. Thomas Aquinas.

IF there is one thing that is certainly known to everyone about the subject of the present volume, it is her
friendship with Michelangelo, which is so full of pathos
and sentiment, so sublimated by the characters and
enriched by the high gifts of each, that there is
nothing quite like it in all the history of friendships.
Yet, as the world has invariably failed to grasp the
fact that real romance does not belong to the ephemeral
passions which grow up from vague connections and
last some few years and die, but attaches in reality
to that wedded love which has survived the severest
of all strains—the commonplaces and the monotony
of daily life ; so neither is it capable of apprehending
the beauty of a friendship between a man and a woman,
but always drags in some other element, as though
something were wanting : not realising that divine
thing, the Love of Friendship, which has its own distinct individuality, which is unlike the love of brothers
and sisters, and of all relationships where natural ties
and interests supervene, and which—setting apart the
love of husband and wife, the highest and most perfect
union of which human nature is capable (*Sacramentum*

hoc magnum est)—rightly considered is the most ethereal and the most spiritual of all loves. Truly it may exist between man and man, woman and woman, but the reason why a friendship between man and woman is, perhaps, the more complete thing is that each is more surely the complement of the other. A friendship to be ideal must be equal ; each must give in like measure, but need not give the same ; and, as the gifts of men and women are essentially different, each is able, in a more certain and definite manner, to contribute what is wanted by the other.

Michelangelo is one of the many instances of the penalties that wait on the artistic nature. Great geniuses, whether artists, poets, or musicians, have rarely been those to whom any great degree of earthly happiness has seemed possible. The poet, Wordsworth, is the most notable exception to this. But, for the most part, our greatest have been heavily weighted by temperament ; their lives have been in some sort overshadowed ; friendship has not come easily to them ; toleration is no part of their character ; and it would seem as if those who had so clear a vision of the Divine could not brook the human. Of none is this more true than of Michelangelo, the greatest artist the world has ever seen; enamoured of Beauty, he could not be satisfied with the loveliness of any created woman ; in love with Perfection, each individual fell short of his demand. Even so in youth, it may have happened to some of us that we have had vouchsafed to us such transcendent visions of Beauty that nothing in nature, whether " of sea or sky or woman," can fulfil our expectations ; but we are not strong enough to cling to

our inward convictions, and, as the years go by, we
accept our surroundings, and open our eyes wide to
admit and enjoy all lovely things, feeling all the while
a wound in our hearts because we cannot but know
that our loss is greater than our gain. But Michelangelo, straining after the unfulfilled, went on into old
age a solitary man. The best of sons and brothers, a
generous master to the few pupils whom he could
endure to keep about him, there is yet something
terrible in his loneliness and aloofness. Fate, indeed,
made him the sport of circumstance; after his first
happy working-time in Florence, he became the servant of capricious masters and was never able to take
his life into his own hands, while the "Tragedy of the
Tomb," as he aptly termed it, wasted his best years.

It was with this burden upon him that he entered
upon that friendship which was henceforth the glory of
two lives. Most writers agree in thinking that he
probably made Vittoria's acquaintance in 1538, when
she was forty-seven and he sixty-three. At the same
time, it is possible that they had met as far back as the
days of Leo X; and, again, as it is certain that they
were both in Rome in 1533, it seems hardly likely
that they should have remained strangers to each other,
at a time when all great ladies interested themselves so
particularly in painters and their work. The Marchesa's
circle always included all that was best in art and
literature, and it seems inconceivable that some friend
should not have introduced the illustrious artist to her
notice. The argument against this is that there are
no records and no correspondence, but the latter may
very easily have existed and been destroyed, because,

though we know from Vasari and from Michelangelo himself that they often exchanged letters, very few have come down to us ; there are only two letters of his and five of hers. Milanesi heads Michelangelo's letters *da Roma*, 1545, but in the collection of Vittoria's letters, published by Ferrero and Müller, these, together with three of the Marchesa's, are assigned to the years 1539–40 ; a later letter of Vittoria's is obviously from Viterbo, and there is one other to which no date can be given.

Gotti, in his life of the artist, inclines to place the meeting between 1532 and 1533, but he gives for this a very unconvincing reason, which is entirely rejected by J. A. Symonds as unworthy and improbable. There are five letters from Michelangelo to his great friend, Tommaso Cavalieri, a young Roman nobleman, which are dated 1533. These letters are so extravagant in tone, both as regards affection and adulation, that it has been suggested that the phrases really apply to the Marchesa, and were sent to Tommaso, he being a mutual friend, that he might pass them on to her. It is certainly difficult to see in what sense Michelangelo could have addressed a very young man of no particular attainments as *Luce del secol nostro unica al mondo*, and profess to regard him as his superior in all talent ; but love is nothing if not humble, and for many minds youth has such a glamour and fascination that it seems to outweigh all other gifts. That Michelangelo should have desired to employ an intermediary is apparently contradicted by one of his two letters to be given below. In any case, it would have been a strange expedient, and, considering the age and

position of the two persons in question, it appears singularly unfitting.

We must, therefore, be content to leave the date of
their first meeting an uncertainty, and we can but
rejoice that we have a full record of their intercourse
from the Portuguese miniature-painter, Francisco
d'Ollanda, who was visiting Rome in 1538, and who,
through Lattantio Tolomei, was introduced to the
artist and to the Marchesa.[1] Yet, from his description,
it must surely strike us that the terms on which these
two stood with each other were those of a friendship
of long standing, and not the ways of people who have
just come across each other for the first time.
Vittoria's informal summons to " come and lose a little
of the day with us " seems to show how ordinary and
frequent the invitation must have been, while her
gentle familiarity with him, and her way of managing
him, argue an intimate acquaintance with his character.

It is from d'Ollanda that we derive one of our
clearest impressions of Vittoria, for though there is
abundant testimony to her attraction in the letters
from her friends, these are often formal and always
flattering, while her own letters are, for the most part,
too purely conventional to be anything of a self-reve-
lation ; but the conversations reported by d'Ollanda
give us a sensation of being brought face to face with
the real woman.   We get first a glimpse of her way of
life ; she was then living, as in the first days of her
widowhood, at San Silvestro in Capite, leading that

---

[1] Three Dialogues on Painting, composed by Francisco d'Ollanda, a
Portuguese miniature-painter who was in Rome in the year 1538 ; in
an Appendix to Sir Charles Holroyd's *Michael Angelo Buonarroti*.

life of humbleness and charity which she had long since chosen. She was attending a set of lectures given by Fra Ambrogio of Siena,[1] on St. Paul's Epistles, in the Church of San Silvestro di Monte Cavallo, then in the hands of the Dominicans, and there, or in the convent garden which adjoined that of the Colonna palace, Vittoria would remain after the lectures, to discourse on art and poetry with her friends, till the evening closed in on them. D'Ollanda gives at great length the discussions that took place between himself, Tolomei, Michelangelo, and Vittoria on two successive Sundays, but the Marchesa is the leading figure of the group; it is she who arranges and directs the conversation with infinite tact, and there is a sweetness and playfulness in this representation that we find nowhere else : conventionality has fallen off, and we see her dominating by her individuality, and essentially winning and attractive.

These discourses are so well known, or at any rate so accessible, that it would be waste of time to give a detailed account of them, interesting as they are ; there are, however, two points that we may note specially connected with the Marchesa. She mentions to Michelangelo a project for building a nunnery at the foot of Monte Cavallo, on the spot where Nero is said to have stood to watch Rome burning, and he replies that it would be a good thing to go and look at the site, as he could give her some design for it : but the idea

---

[1] Fra Ambrogio Politi, a famous Dominican preacher and controversialist, called Catarino from his devotion to St. Catherine of Siena. He was the author of an abridged version of Fra Raimondo's great life of the Saint.

was never carried out. On the same occasion, Vittoria makes the rather surprising statement that Flemish painting appears to her more devout than the Italian style, and Michelangelo seems in a manner to assent to her proposition, saying that it " will generally satisfy any devout person more than the painting of Italy, which will never cause him to drop a single tear, but that of Flanders will cause him to shed many." Though we may wonder what induced him to be of this opinion (for, surely, succeeding ages have awarded the palm of devotional painting to Italy), it is certain that his was the prevalent view at the time. We have evidence of the great respect with which Flemish painters were regarded in the fact that Duke Federigo of Urbino sent for a Fleming, Justus of Ghent, to paint the portrait of his duchess, and to adorn his library with figures of poets, doctors, and philosophers. Leonello d'Este also invited Roger van der Weyden to stay some months in Ferrara, where he painted for him a picture representing the Descent from the Cross and the expulsion of Adam and Eve from Paradise, which was one of Leonello's most prized treasures ; and when the artist proceeded to Rome, Florence, and all the principal cities of Italy, his journey was somewhat in the nature of a triumphal progress, with such honour was he welcomed in all parts. In Naples and in Spain, Flemish art was no less regarded ; the travelling altar-piece of Charles V was by Memling, and represented the Adoration of the Kings, the Nativity, and the Presentation in the Temple ; and at Naples the poet, Sannazzaro, had a painting of Christ enthroned, by Petrus Christus, which must have been well-known to

Vittoria. The Flemings in their religious art would seem to have been imbued with the spirit of earnestness, gravity, and sorrow, while the Italian school set itself to follow nature in a broader, more comprehensive, and yet simpler manner. It is, in fact, a difference of aim, as Michelangelo points out when he goes on to state his own ideal of devout painting in these words : "As for the good painting of this country, there is nothing more noble or devout, for with wise persons nothing causes devotion to be remembered, or to arise, more than the difficulty of the perfection which unites with and joins God ; because good painting is nothing else but a copy of the perfection of God and a reminder of His painting." This satisfies us as coming from the master-mind, and is thoroughly in accordance with his character, and it also recalls Dante's saying that—

> " Filosofia . . .
>   Nota non pure in una sola parte
>   Come natura lo suo corso prende
> Dal divino intelletto e da sua arte ;
>   E se tu ben la tua Fisica note,
>   Tu troverai non dopo molte carte
> Che l' arte vostra quella, quanto puote,
>   Segue, come il maestro fa il discente,
>   Sì che vostr' arte a Dio quasi è nipote." [1]

---

[1] "Philosophy . . .
>   Noteth, not only in one place alone,
>   After what manner Nature takes her course
> From Intellect Divine, and from its art ;
>   And if thy Physics carefully thou notest,
>   After not many pages shalt thou find
> That this your art as far as possible
>   Follows, as the disciple doth the master ;
>   So that your art is, as it were, God's grandchild."

Longfellow (*Inferno*, xi. 97).

It is impossible to friendship not to consecrate its gifts, so we find Michelangelo offering drawings and poems to Vittoria, and she, on her side, addresses sonnets to him and has all her verses transcribed for him. Condivi mentions at length two designs made for the Marchesa, one a Deposition from the Cross, in which the dead body of Our Lord is supported by two angels, while His most holy Mother, seated at the foot of the Cross, stretches out her arms to heaven ; and underneath the legend :

Non vi si pensa quanto sangue costa.

The other was a Crucifixion, the original of which is said to be in the Taylorian Museum at Oxford. The Pietà was engraved by Giulio Bonasoni and Tudius Bononiensis about 1546. Vasari makes mention of a third drawing, Christ talking to the woman of Samaria, and Vittoria refers to it in one of her letters, but all trace of it is lost.

The first of these letters of Michelangelo's refers to the drawing of the Crucifixion. Having no knowledge of the circumstances under which it was written, we are at a loss to account for the tone of vexation which it certainly betrays.

"Signora Marchesa,

"As I am in Rome, there seemed no need to leave the Crucifix to Messer Tommaso, and to make him an intermediary between your Ladyship and me your servant, for me to serve you, and especially as I have desired to do more for you than for anyone I have ever known in all the world. But the great work, about which I have been and am occupied, has prevented your Ladyship from knowing this. And because I know that you know that love needs no master, and that he who loves sleeps not, still less were any intermediaries needed. And if it seems as if I had forgotten, I was doing what I had not mentioned because I had planned a surprise. But my purpose has been frustrated :

"*Mal fa chi tanta fè sì tosto oblia.*

"Your Ladyship's obedient servant,

"Michelagniolo Buonarroti in Rome."[1]

The answer was a note of a few lines which ends charmingly : "If you are not at work to-day, you might come at your leisure and talk with me" ; this is a side-light worth many letters. Referring to the design for the Crucifixion, Vittoria writes thus, and her meaning is difficult to seize :—

"Unique Messer Michelangelo
AND MY MOST SINGULAR FRIEND,

"I have received your letter and examined the Crucifixion which has certainly crucified in my mind all other pictures that I have ever seen, nor could one find another figure more beautifully designed, more living, and more perfectly finished. Truly, I cannot express how subtly and how marvellously it is done. For this reason, I have made up my mind that it is from no hand but yours, therefore enlighten me ; if it belongs to another, I must have patience. If it is yours, I

---

[1] Letter cdlv, Milanesi, *Lettere di Michelangelo.*

Alinari.

Michelangelo Buonarroti.
(Portrait in the Gallery of the Capitol, Rome.)

must have it at all costs ; but in case it is not yours and you wish to have it copied by your assistant, we will talk it over first. Because, knowing how difficult it would be to imitate it, I could more easily resolve to have some new thing rather than have this copied. But if this is really yours, be patient, for I shall never send it back to you. I have examined it carefully in the light, and with a lens and a mirror, and I never saw a more perfect thing.

"Yours to command,
"The Marchesa di Pescara."[1]

The next letter relates to the Pietà.

"Your works forcibly awaken the judgment of whoever looks at them, and I spoke of adding goodness to things already perfect because I have seen actual instances of this in your works. And I have seen that *omnia possibilia sunt credenti.* I had the greatest faith in God that He would grant you a supernatural grace to make this Christ, and, when I saw it, it was so wonderful that it surpassed all my expectations in every way. Then, emboldened by your miracles, I desired that which I now see marvellously fulfilled, which is that the design should reach the highest perfection in every part, and one could not desire more, nor attain to desiring so much. And I tell you that it rejoices me greatly that the angel on the right hand should be so much the most beautiful, because Michael will place you, Michelangelo, at the right hand of the Lord in the last day. And, mean-

---

[1] *Carteggio*, Letter cxxiii.

K

while, I do not know how else to serve you than by praying for you to this sweet Christ, Whom you have drawn so well and perfectly, and I beg you to command me as altogether yours in all things.

" Yours to command,

"THE MARCHESA DI PESCARA."[1]

The following is the only other letter we possess from Michelangelo to Vittoria, and it is specially interesting because to it was appended a sonnet which embodies the same idea as is here expressed.

"Before I took possession of the things your Ladyship has many times wished to give me, in order to receive them as little unworthily as I could, I desired, Lady, to make something for you with my own hand. Now, however, seeing and recognising that the grace of God cannot be bought and that to keep it waiting is a grievous sin, I acknowledge my fault, and willingly accept your said gifts. And when I possess them, not because I shall have them in my house, but because I shall be in their house, I shall seem to be in Paradise. On which account I shall remain more obliged, if I can be more so than I already am, to your Ladyship. The bearer of this will be Urbino who is with me ; your Ladyship can inform him when you would like me to come and see the head you promised to show me.

" And to you I commend myself,

"MICHELAGNIOLO BUONARROTI."[2]

---

[1] *Carteggio*, Letter CXXIV.
[2] Letter CDLIV, Milanesi, *Lettere di Michelangelo.*

" Seeking at least to be not all unfit
    For thy sublime and boundless courtesy,
    My lowly thoughts at first were fain to try
    What they could yield for grace so infinite.
But now I know my unassisted wit
    Is all too weak to make me soar so high,
    For pardon, lady, for this fault I cry,
    And wiser still I grow remembering it.
Yea, well I see what folly 'twere to think
    That largess, dropped from thee like dews from heaven,
    Could e'er be paid by work so frail as mine.
To nothingness my art and talent sink ;
    He fails who from his mortal stores hath given
    A thousand fold to match one gift divine."[1]

What the gifts referred to in the letter were we have
no certain means of knowing, but it seems likely, from
the way in which they are mentioned, that they were
pictures, and the idea is borne out by two sonnets
which the Marchesa addressed to Michelangelo, which

---

[1] Translation by J. A. Symonds.   The original runs :—

" Per esser manco almen, signiora, indegnio
    Dell' immensa vostr' alta cortesia,
    Prima, all' incontro a quella, usar la mia
    Con tutto il cor volse 'l mio basso ingegnio.
Ma visto poi c' ascendere a quel segnio
    Propio valor non è c' apra la via,
    Perdon domanda la mie colpa ria,
    E del fallir più saggio ognior divegnio.
E veggio ben com' erra, s' alcun crede
    La grazia, che da voi divina piove,
    Pareggi l' opra mia caduca e frale.
L' ingegnio e l' arte e la memoria cede :
    C' un don celeste mai con mille pruove
    Pagar può sol del suo chi è mortale "

must have been sent with pictures, though the usual
interpretation is that they refer to the master's own
designs.

" Because your mind, girt and adornèd well
 With the eternal light, preserves of God
 The likeness in that innermost abode
 Where never may unfaithful image dwell,
Haply, since ardent longing doth impel,
 Which never knows fulfilment but increase,
 As is true lovers' wont, even this may please,
 And prove in painted form acceptable.
And thinking thus, my lord, your humble, new
 Mother and handmaid sends the work to you
 A better Master fashioned in your heart.
Nor be it troublesome to tell, she prays,
 If this resemble that in any part
 On which your high desires for ever gaze." [1]

" As much as human mind can apprehend
 By long-time study with the guidance dear
 Of heaven, whose lovely light the truth makes clear,
 So much I think your noble soul has gleaned.

---

[1] " Perchè la mente vostra, ornata e cinta
 D' eterno lume, serbi la sembianza
 Del gran motor nella più interna stanza,
 Ove albergar non puote immagin finta ;
Forse da quella ardente voglia spinta
 Che mai non s'empie, anzi ad ognor s' avanza,
 Com' esser suol de' veri amanti usanza,
 Aggradir la potrebbe anco dipinta.
Ciò pensando, signor, la vostra umíle
 Nova madre ed ancella ora v' invia
 L' opra, ch' in voi miglior mastro scolpío ;
Pregandovi ch' a dir grave non sia,
 Se questa in parte a quell' altra è simíle
 Cui sempre mira il vostro alto desio."

Wherefore, in no wise, light or strength to lend
  Unto the ray of your rare steadfast faith,
  That by its works to the world witnesseth
And of the other is sure pledge, I send
To you His image Who unto the spear
  Upon the cross His breast did offer, so
  That upon you the sacred blood may pour;
But only, lord, because to you below
  A book more learnèd never opened here
  To make you live above for evermore."[1]

The next letter from Vittoria has an allusion to the third and last design made for her; it is also intrinsically interesting.

"MAGNIFICENT MESSER MICHELANGELO,

"I have not answered your letter sooner because it was, so to speak, an answer to mine; for I thought that if you and I were to go on continuously, according to my obligation and your courtesy, I should have to neglect the Chapel of St. Catherine here and be

---

[1] "Quanto intender qui puote umano ingegno
  Per lungo studio con la scorta cara
  Del ciel, da cui bel lume il ver s' impara,
  Credo ch' intenda il vostro spirto degno.
Sicch' io non già per dar luce e sostegno
  Al raggio della vostra e salda e rara
  Fede, per l' opre al mondo mai sì chiara
  Ch' a noi dell' altro è ben securo pegno,
L' immagin di Colui v' invio ch' offerse
  Al ferro in croce il petto, onde in voi piove
  Dell' acqua sacra sua sì largo rivo;
Ma sol perchè, signor, qua giuso altrove
  Più dotto libro mai non vi s' aperse,
  Per là su farvi in sempiterno vivo."

absent from the company of these sisters at the appointed hours, while you would have to leave the Chapel of St. Paul, and no longer find yourself passing the whole day from before sunrise in sweet intercourse with your paintings, which with their natural accents speak to you no less clearly than to me the living people with whom I am surrounded. So that I should fail the brides, and you the Vicar of Christ. Wherefore, knowing our steadfast friendship and most sure affection bound in a Christian knot, I do not think it necessary to procure by my letters the testimony of yours ; but I would rather wait with a well-prepared mind for some substantial occasion of serving you, praying that Lord of Whom you spoke to me with such a fervent and humble heart, on my departure from Rome, that I may find you on my return with His image so renewed and alive by true faith in your soul as you have so well painted it in my woman of Samaria. And I commend myself always to you and also to your Urbino.

"Yours to command,

"THE MARCHESA DI PESCARA.

"To my more than magnificent and more than dearest M. Michelangelo Buonarroti."[1]

Michelangelo wrote eight sonnets and three madrigals to Vittoria ; the former are so well known in the admirable translations of J. A. Symonds that they will not be given here. The following is a rendering of one of the madrigals :—

---

[1] *Carteggio.* Letter CLVII.

" A man within a woman, rather say
   A god, speaks through her mouth ;
   And having heard, in sooth,
I am no longer mine in any way.
   Outside myself, my place
   I take, and verily
Have pity on myself, since saved by her.
   Above vain longings, I,
   Urged on by her fair face,
See naught but death in beauty otherwhere.
   O Lady, who doth bear
The soul through flood and fire to a bright shore,
Unto myself let me return no more."[1]

We should like to apprehend, if it were possible,
the spiritual colour of this unique friendship, which
found so much on both sides to foster it.

There was everything in the great artist to appeal to
a noble woman ; his integrity, his high sense of
honour, his many-sided genius, and, above all, his firm
religious faith would have pre-eminently attracted her
whose religion was her life, and her beauty and talent

---

1 " Un uomo in una donna, anzi uno dio,
        Per la sua bocca parla :
        Ond' io per ascoltarla
   Son fatto tal, che ma' più sarò mio.
        I' credo ben, po' ch' io
        A me da lei fui tolto,
   Fuor di me stesso aver di me pietate :
        Sì sopra 'l van desio
        Mi sprona il suo bel volto,
   Ch' io veggio morte in ogn' altra beltate.
        O donna, che passate
   Per acqua e foco l' alme a' lieti giorni,
   Deh fate ch' a me stesso più non torni ! "

mere accessories; while there must have been something peculiarly attractive to Michelangelo in the
quietness, the austerity, and charity of Vittoria's self-
chosen life, and there is always a great repose in the
society of those who give themselves time to think.
There was never anything small about Vittoria; her
life was full of broad spaces, of silences, of worthy
occupations and interests, and sorrow, that brings sweet
and bitter things, had but laid a consecrating hand on
her, and enriched her with a wide sympathy. In such
wise was she fitted to be the friend of Michelangelo;
her proficiency in poetry, her knowledge of art and
literature, her cultivated mind, must have made her
companionship delightful, but we must look far deeper
and higher than this if we wish to arrive at any right
understanding of what this friendship really was. To
both these minds, religion was of the first importance;
they had devoted to it the best of their thoughts; it
was supremely interesting. Vittoria may have had the
ineffable happiness of making it more paramount in
the life of Michelangelo than it had been : at any rate,
it is manifest from his writings that that is what he
attributes to her influence. But, comparing their
religious poems, the spirit is essentially the same—a
spirit of contrition, humility, and unwavering faith;
tending ever more and more in each to the realisation
that there is only one thing that really matters.

Mr. Swinburne has written finely on this subject:—

> " As light that blesses, hallowing with a look,
>   He saw the godhead in Vittoria's face
> Shine soft on Buonarroti's, till he took,
>   Albeit himself God, a more godlike grace,

A strength more heavenly to confront and brook
    All ill things coiled about his earthly race,
From the bright scripture of that present book
    Wherein his tired grand eyes got power to trace
      Comfort more sweet than youth,
      And hope whose child was truth,
And love that brought forth sorrow for a space,
      Only that she might bear
      Joy: these things written there,
Made even his soul's high heaven a heavenlier place."[1]

The history of a great friendship is, before all things, complex; it has as many notes as the birds' songs, as many colours as the sky can show from dawn to sunset. Nothing is alien to it; it could not be so great if it were not so comprehensive; for the touchstone of ideal companionship is this, that it is not only the great things of life that are affected by it, but the least and lowest are invested with a new meaning and are transfigured thereby.

It is sacrilegious to attempt to inquire which of these two friends gave the most: rather for all time do they stand

    "As happy equals in the flowering land
     Of love that knows not a dividing sea."

This chapter cannot close more fitly than with the words of Condivi, taken, as they were, out of the master's mouth: "In particular he greatly loved the Marchesa di Pescara, of whose divine spirit he was enamoured, being in turn tenderly loved by her, and he had received from her several letters full of pure

---

[1] A. C. Swinburne, *Studies in Song*.

and most sweet love, such as would have issued from such a heart. She returned to Rome from Viterbo and other places, whither she had gone for pleasure or to spend the summer, for no other reason than to see Michelangelo, and he on his part bore her so much love that I remember to have heard him say that nothing grieved him so much as that, when he went to see her when she was passing from this life, he did not kiss her on the brow or face, but only kissed her hand. On account of her death, he remained for a long time overcome with grief and as one bereft of his senses."

CHAPTER VI

A SISTER POET, VERONICA GAMBARA

The world is too much with us: late and soon,
Getting and spending, we lay waste our powers.
WORDSWORTH.

VITTORIA COLONNA was not the only poetical light of her time; at least two other ladies take rank with her as writers of some distinction, Veronica Gambara and Gaspara Stampa; and of these the former was possibly personally acquainted with the Marchesa. At any rate, they were known to each other through the medium of literature, for they exchanged sonnets testifying to their mutual regard and admiration.

In turning from the contemplation of Vittoria to review the life of Veronica, the first thing of which we are conscious is difference of atmosphere; yet their positions have many points of resemblance. Veronica was the daughter of Count Gianfrancesco Gambara of Brescia, and of Alda Pia, sister of Emilia Pia of *Cortegiano*-fame. She was born on November 30, 1485, at Pratalboino, a fief of her family, whence she seems to have imbibed her most interesting characteristic—an abiding love of the country. Her education was evidently the widest and best that could be had, and she must have responded to it very remarkably, for she won fame for herself from her early youth by her letters and poems, her knowledge of Greek and Latin, and the deep study she had made of philosophy.

It is probable that she was instructed in Greek by Britannico Giovanni who was teaching in Brescia until 1518, while her poems give evidence of the very close acquaintance she had with Virgil and Petrarca; indeed, there was a literary coterie in Brescia which met every week to study Petrarca and, in due time, the *Asolani*. Veronica is said to have had a quick mind and a wonderful memory; in later years she was certainly an excellent letter-writer and a brilliant conversationalist; the one gift nature withheld was that of beauty; her features were frankly ugly; coarse, and masculine; but her face must have been redeemed by her eyes and by her vivacious expression. Nearly all her poems and letters belong to her married or widowed life, and we have to construct the story of her girlhood as best we can, out of very scanty materials. A great love of study seems to have characterised her then and always, and her range was wide, including theology and the works of the Fathers, to which several of her sonnets bear witness.

Many eminent literary men must certainly have visited Brescia; Trissino was there in 1505 and also Bembo, but different opinions are held as to the date of Veronica's intercourse with the latter. To Bembo has been assigned the part of literary godfather to every budding genius of his time, and there is no doubt that his opinion was anxiously sought by writers of every degree. Hence we find Veronica's earliest biographer, Rinaldo Corso, referring to him as her master, and saying that her first poetical efforts were made under his auspices, but facts contradict this statement. The earliest record that we have of any intercourse between them is in a letter of Bembo's dated September 11, 1504, from which it would appear that Veronica had first written to him two years before, she being then seventeen, and no doubt desirous of numbering such a famous man among her friends.[1] The correspondence, however, seems to have languished, and in 1504 the lady sent Bembo a sonnet, which he acknowledged in the letter just referred to, and of which the first line (given thus in a later letter of his, *S' a voi da me non pur veduto mai*) shows that they had never met. Bembo's reply-sonnet states the same thing, *ancor mai non veduta*, and in a second one, sent either with this letter or almost immediately afterwards, he asks : *Vedrò mai raggio, udirò mai parola ?*[2]

In the following year, however, he was certainly at Brescia, and from that time there began a steady friendship between them, he evincing a warm admiration for her talents, and she constantly seeking his judgment and deferring to his opinion. In 1530 we find them still exchanging sonnets, and in 1531 she writes : " I have just made two sonnets on the death of Sannazzaro, and send them to you as to my light and guide"; to which Bembo replies : "As for the sonnets, both seem to me most beautiful. They are simple, they are lovely, and infinitely affectionate and graceful : I congratulate you upon them. . . . I cannot say for certain which is the most charming, but the

---

[1] Bembo, *Opere*, Vol. VIII, pp. 55–58.
[2] Bembo, Sonnets 52 and 53 (*ed. cit.*, Vol. II).

one which begins *Se a quella* takes my fancy most."[1]
Both these sonnets are unfortunately lost. In 1532
Bembo, wishing to reprint his poems and to include
with them the first sonnet sent to him by Veronica, to
which one of his was an answer, wrote to her in the
following terms :—

"I am going to have my poems reprinted, and I
have collected two sonnets which I once wrote to you,
and I want to put them with the others. One of mine,
already printed, was an answer, rhyme for rhyme, to
that sonnet which you wrote to me when you were a
child, which begins thus: *S' a voi da me non pur veduto
mai.* But it happens that I have lost that sonnet
of yours, and have nothing of it except the first line
which I quote, nor can I find it anywhere. So I beg
you to be kind enough to look for it among your
papers and to send it me, so that I may put it together
with my own in this volume which will be reprinted,
and I hope to make amends for the fault committed in
the first edition, and that you will no more have cause to
complain of me as you have had in the past. I confess
this, that you may punish me the less. I will not say
anything more, except that I live with the memory of
your worth always in my soul. Farewell.

"From Padua, May 27, 1532."[2]

We have not got Veronica's answer to this, but the
sonnet was not included in Bembo's new edition ;
whether she could not find it, or objected to anything
so immature being reprinted, we cannot tell. For a

---

[1] *Opere,* Vol. VIII, p. 61.
[2] *Ibid.,* pp. 61, 62.

long time it was believed that the sonnet was lost, but in 1845 it was reprinted from a manuscript of the Seminario of Padua, though the first line differs slightly from that which Bembo quoted, evidently from memory. It certainly appears to be a very bad piece of work, even for a girl of nineteen, and it is likely that the author elected to suppress it.

We have in all twenty-one letters from Bembo to Veronica, and ten of hers to him ; an enormous number must be missing, as also many of the sonnets mentioned therein, but it is abundantly evident that Bembo still continued to be her "lume e scorta." Two sonnets of hers on Our Lady are still extant, the second of which is particularly interesting, as we have both their letters concerning it.

> " Virgin most pure, to-day by means of thee
>   On earth is shown so wonderful a thing
>   That nature fails, and gazes wondering
>   Upon the work, and all amazed is she.
> God is made man, 'neath human tendance, He
>   With weary mortal flesh is clothed upon,
>   Remaining what He was, He putteth on
>   An infant form, veiling divinity.
> Confused He was not, nor divided e'er,
>   But very God and very man alway,
>   As powerful on earth as even in heaven.
> Turn then thy rays of grace, O Virgin fair,
>   On me, that so the comprehension may
>   Of this deep mystery to me be given."[1]

---

[1] " Oggi per mezzo tuo, Vergine pura,
    Si mostra in terra sì mirabil cosa,
    Che piena di stupor resta pensosa,
    Mirando l' opra, e cede la natura.

Of this sonnet Veronica says :—

"As I am writing, I have resolved to send you a sonnet of mine which has not been seen by anybody, and which originated I know not how, as it is already a long time since I left off writing poetry. You will see what I have meant but have not known how to express, and, when you have seen it, you will treat it as its simplicity deserves. It is enough for me that, as I dedicated my first-fruits to your most reverend Lordship, I also send to you that which I think will be my last." [1]

Replying to this, about five weeks later, Bembo writes :—

"I have not replied sooner to your Ladyship's most sweet letter, which I received through Signor Girolamo, your son, together with the sonnet to Our Lady, because I wanted first to give the sonnet to his Holiness, and then to write to you about it. But now that that has been delayed longer than I wished, on account of his innumerable occupations, I will at least answer you and tell you that the most sweet memory of your

Fatto uomo è Dio, e sotto umana cura,
　Vestito di mortal carne noiosa,
　Restò qual era, e la divina ascosa
　Sua essenzia tenne in pueril figura.
Misto non fu, nè fu diviso mai ;
　Ma sempre Dio e sempre uomo verace,
　Quanto possente in ciel, tanto nel mondo.
Volgi dunque ver me, Vergine, i rai
　De la tua grazia, e 'l senso mio capace
　Fa' di questo misterio alto e profondo."

[1] Letter xiii, Correggio, October 29, 1540.

Ladyship lives very much in my mind. And it also pleases me that you do not forget the affection I have always had for you, and that you keep me so sweetly in your good favour. May Our Lord God grant that I may see you again this year, as it seems there may be an opportunity. As for the sonnet, it seemed to me very beautiful, and graceful, and thoughtful, as I told the reverend Monsignor your brother. And, therefore, I would not have you abandon this art as you say, but rather not refrain from making others of them. I will give the sonnet to his Holiness by all means, at a time when he can read it more than once. If I could be with your Ladyship as often as I am with your reverend Monsignor, my residence in Rome would be much more dear to me than it is. Nevertheless, it is made dear to me on account of the proximity of his Holiness, more than for any other reason. Farewell, my lady, my most admirable and dearest and sweetest sister.

"From Rome, December 7, 1540."[1]

The last of Bembo's letters to her that remains is written when he had fallen into very bad health ; he thanks her for another lost sonnet, one to Cardinal Farnese, and says : "O how far I am from poetry ! "[2] This was in December, 1544, and he died two years later.

We have wandered a long way from Veronica's first poetical essays, and must return to the events of her girlhood. It is probable that she had very intimate

---

[1] *Opere, loc. cit.*, p. 73.
[2] *Ibid.*, p. 82.

L

relations with the House of Este and especially with that remarkable woman, Isabella d'Este, who was eleven years older than herself. Of her early letters only one very formal one to Isabella remains, and two to her brother, the Cardinal Ippolito; but we find that the latter baptised Veronica's eldest boy and Isabella was godmother; the tastes and talents of the two ladies certainly lay in the same direction, and public affairs also tended to bring them together, so that, in later life, a real friendship subsisted between them. Veronica's letter, written when she was about seventeen, is a very stiff and frightened performance, but Isabella could hardly have been otherwise than a formidable correspondent; it runs thus :—

"If it might be granted to me, most illustrious and most excellent Lady, and my most singular patron, to be able to thank your Excellence with a thousandth part of that gratitude which would befit the exceeding kindness of your most friendly letter, I should consider myself happy above every other servant. But knowing myself insufficient for such a high attempt, having regard to the infinite kindness of your Excellence, I know not to what else to apply myself except to the bewailing of my sad fate which has created me of such lowness that I find myself unworthy to accomplish this end. Still, if I deserve to be in the number of the lowest servants of your Excellence (as I hope), by the divinity infused into you, if ever I complained of fortune in the past, I shall strive henceforth with all zeal to thank you for so great kindness by praising you. And thus at the feet of your Excellence I humbly commend myself, as also do the Count my father and my Lady-mother and Isotta, who is not less the servant of your Excellence than I am.

"Brescia, February 1, 1503.

"From your Excellence's unworthy servant
for all time,

"Veronica di Gambara with my own hand."[1]

There is one other early letter of Veronica's of July 20, 1504, which is thought to have been addressed to some nobleman of the court of the Estensi, as it was found in the ducal archives of Modena.

"I am sorry, Messer Barone, that the lot should have fallen to your Lordship to be the first to write the desire you have to know me, because, as my desire is by far the greater, I should like to have been the first to express it. But patience! And you can gather that it is true that mine was the greater, since I have heard from an infinite number of persons what you have heard from one. So that I shall not say anything more, except to commend myself numberless times to your favour.

"Veronica di Gambara."[2]

There is a spice of unconventionality in this note which is refreshing, and we should like to know if the incident had any *suite*. Veronica's marriage at the age

---

[1] Letter published from the Archivio Gonzaga by Rodolfo Renier in the *Giornale Storico della Letteratura Italiana,* Vol. XIV, pp. 442, 443. I regret not to have seen Luigi Amaduzzi's work, *Undici lettere inedite di Veronica Gambara* (Guastalla, 1889).

[2] Letter published by Emilio Costa, *Sonetti amorosi di Veronica Gambara,* p. 9 *n.*

of twenty-four to Giberto X, lord of Correggio, a
widower with growing-up daughters, can hardly have
been other than a *mariage de convenance*, and thence-
forward her writings and her way of life are slavishly
conventional.   It is, therefore, tempting to linger over
her girlhood, to gather up the few letters that are left,
and to study the fugitive sonnets.   The tone of these
is not that of her later poems ; here she would seem
to have known something of passion, something of
regret, and the most pathetic piece, usually included
among her later writings, is supposed to have been
written before her marriage.   This is the Ballata, *Or
passata è la speranza,* of which the following is a translation, and we subjoin an early sonnet and a madrigal.

BALLATA

" Now has hope passed away
  That kept me once aglow ;
  Less mourn I since I know
  That nothing here can stay.
      Now has hope passed away.

  This false one formerly
  My heart on fire did keep ;
  Mocking my misery,
  She leaves me now to weep
  O'er love and longings deep.
  Ever she leads to death
  Whom passion governeth
  With strong persistent sway.
      Now has hope passed away.

  I hoped and hope made burn
  In me a gracious fire ;
  I hope no more but mourn

That longing sweet desire.
I call in sorrow dire
On death to soothe my smart,
For hopeless is the heart
Where hope made once sweet stay.
    Now has hope passed away.

While I had her to lead,
All ills seemed light to me ;
Without her, lost and dead,
Least things most grievous be.
Brief joy, long agony,
The sole reward I have
Since I became her slave :
This feel I since that day.
    Now has hope passed away.

My gentle hope and fair,
Alas ! from me has fled ;
Why took she not with her
Tired life and heart nigh dead ?
Me such dark fears dismay
As of all hope deprive,
Not living, yet alive
Without hope's faintest ray.
    Now has hope passed away." [1]

---

[1] " Or passata è la speranza,
   Che mi tenne un tempo ardendo ;
   Men mi duol, poichè io comprendo
   Nulla cosa aver costanza.
      Or passata è la speranza.

   Questa falsa un tempo in foco
   M' ha tenuta pur sperando ;
   Or prendendo il mal mio a gioco
   M' ha lassata lagrimando,
   Ed amando e desiando
   Mi conduce ogn' ora a morte

SONNET

"Free am I not, nor ever hope to be,
   From that hard bond with which I erst was bound,
   Because the wound was all too mortal found
   Which pierced the pure and truthful heart of me.

Con passion tenace e forte
E con più perseveranza.
    Or passata è la speranza.

Io sperai, e quel sperare
Mi nutriva in dolce fiamma;
Nè più or spero, e lagrimare
Sol quest' alma desia e brama,
E la morte ognora chiama
Per soccorso al suo dolore,
Poichè senza speme è 'l core
Che già fu sua dolce stanza.
    Or passata è la speranza.

Mentre ch' ebbi lui per scorta,
Ogni mal mi parea leve;
Senza lui smarrita e morta,
Ogni poco mi par greve;
Lungo affanno e piacer breve
Da indi 'n qua sempre ho sentito
Per aver con sè servito;
Questo premio sol m' avanza.
    Or passata è la speranza.

Mia soave e dolce speme,
Da me dunque ahimè! è fuggita;
E al partir ne portò insieme
L' arso cor, mia stanca vita;
Tal ch' essendo sbigottita,
E di speme al tutto priva,
Non vivendo, resto viva
Senz' alfin nulla speranza.
    Or passata è la speranza."

Nor from one single thought shall I be free
 Which day and night my mind doth occupy—
 The fear lest my surrendered liberty,
 Proud heart and ruthless, be despised by thee;
Nor free from fear, nor free for evermore
 From torment, cruel one, from bitter pains,
 Which constantly through thee must work me woe.
In fine, I shall not ever from thy chains
 Be free, since divers passions hour by hour,
 Pleasant and sweet through thee, within me grow."[1]

MADRIGAL

" The grief is so extreme,
 It well-nigh matches so extreme a pain,
 And in this fashion I alive remain.
 I had been dead ere this,
 But that the grief, so heavy on my heart,
 With death can have no part;
 My woes can neither grow nor yet decrease.
 Ah, cruel injury!
 And what defence have I,

---

[1] " Libra non son, nè mai libra esser spero
 Dal crudel laccio, ove già fui legata,
 Perchè troppo mortal la piaga è stata,
 Che già ferì mio cor puro e sincero.
Nè libra mai sarò da un sol pensero,
 Nel qual dì e notte isto sempre occupata,
 Che la mia libertà, qual t' ho donata,
 Non sprezzi ohimè, tuo cor superbo e fiero.
Nè libra da timor, nè libra ancora
 Mai sarò da martir, de acerbe pene
 Che me affligon per te, crudele, ogn' ora.
Alfin nè libra mai da tue catene
 Starò, crescendo in me più d' ora in ora
 Varie passion per te suave e amene."

Whose burdened heart is in such woful plight
That the enkindled soul can nowise die,
And lives in my despite?
But of all pangs this is the crown and chief
Not to be able to bewail my grief."[1]

After her marriage, in 1508, Veronica looks forth
upon us as the great lady of Correggio, and we some-
how feel that, whereas in the case of Vittoria the
woman is always paramount, where Veronica is concerned the position overshadows the woman. She
adored her husband, who was a brave soldier and re-
nowned for his justice and generosity, and she wrote
poems to his "*occhi lucenti*," of which the following
madrigal is the prettiest :—

    " Lovely and shining eyes,
      How can it be that there are born in you
      At one same time so many forms and new?
      You are both glad and sad in the same breath,

---

[1] " Così estrema è la doglia,
    Ch' a così estremo mal mal non arriva ;
    E a questo modo i' me ne resto viva.
    Sarei ben morta homai,
    Ma il duol che ho in cuor sì grave e forte
    Non dà luoco a la morte,
    Nè accrescer può, nè sminuir mei guai.
    Ahi dispietat' offesa !
    Come faro diffesa
    Che m' hai sì pien d' angoscia l' alma e 'l petto
    Che fuor non può spirar l' anima accesa,
    E vivo al mio dispetto ?
    Ma fra tutti i martir quest' è 'l maggiore
    Non puotermi doler de 'l mio dolore."

This madrigal and the preceding sonnet are quoted from *Sonetti
amorosi di Veronica Gambara*, edited by Emilio Costa. The others are
all included in the *Rime e Lettere* edited by P. M. Chiappetti.

Humble and haughty; hence it doth befall
That fear and hope fulfil
This heart that burns for you and harboureth
Fierce feelings, bitter, sweet, continual,
Which crowd here at your will.
Now since you are my very life and death,
Oh happy eyes, eyes beautiful and dear,
Be ever joyful, ever bright and clear." [1]

Veronica's literary reputation drew many celebrated
men to Correggio, and no less did the magnificence of
her far-famed pleasure-place, the Casino, of which two
rooms were subsequently decorated by Antonio Allegri.
The description of the garden, the views, the number
and size of the rooms, and the treasures they contained, seem hardly consonant with aught but a fairy
palace.   Ariosto visited it, when he came to Correggio
to see del Vasto, and has immortalised its mistress in
his *Orlando* :—

> " Veronica da Gambara è con loro,
>   Sì grata a Phebo e al santo aonio coro "; [2]

---

[1] " Occhi lucenti e belli,
     Com' esser può che in un medesmo istante
     Nascan da voi sì nove forme e tante ?
     Lieti, mesti, superbi, umili, alteri
     Vi mostrate in un punto ; onde di speme
     E di timor m' empiete,
     E tanti effetti dolci, acerbi e fieri
     Nel core arso per voi vengono insieme
     Ad ognor che volete.
     Or poi che voi mia vita e morte sete,
     Occhi felici, occhi beati e cari,
     Siate sempre sereni, allegri e chiari."

[2] *Orlando Furioso,* XLVI. 3.

and here also congregated Bembo, Mauro, Molza, Cappello, and many others; and hither came Isabella d'Este, ever on the search for rare and artistic things.

It is curious to think that, at the date of which we are writing, the name Correggio would have stood for the Count Giberto of the ruling family, or, perhaps, still more for his wife, whose name was widely known throughout Italy as a lady of great literary attainments: in our time Correggio means one man, the painter, Allegri.

Antonio Allegri was born in 1494, and was therefore only fourteen when Veronica married, but she seems to have been from the first a real friend to him, and he is believed to have accompanied her to Bologna at various times. Her patronage probably had a great effect on his life, as Veronica is known to have brought him to the notice of the Emperor on the occasion of one of his sojourns at Correggio, and, indeed, it was in honour of Charles' second visit that Allegri painted two of the rooms of the Casino. It is also fairly certain that Veronica introduced him to Isabella d'Este, for we notice that, in writing to the Marchesa in 1528, to describe a picture Allegri had just finished for her of the kneeling Magdalen (of which no trace has been found for years), she refers to the painter as " our Antonio." Isabella employed him to execute the Allegories of Vice and Virtue for her Grotto; they were done in tempera and are now to be seen in the Louvre; and in the last years of his life he worked almost exclusively for Isabella's son, Federigo, the first Duke of Mantua, by whom he was commissioned to

paint the Leda and the Danae to be sent as a present
to the Emperor.

Vasari's graphic description of the painter's extreme
poverty and miserliness does not bear the light of
more recent researches; on the contrary, his family
appears to have been one of some standing and importance, holding property which Allegri looked after
and increased; that he had some position is shown by
his having been chosen as one of the witnesses to the
marriage settlement of Veronica's son, Ippolito. Allegri seems to have been singularly modest and un-
ambitious, and no doubt preferred a retired life. That
he stood before great masterpieces murmuring *anch' io
son pittore* is, says one of his biographers, a story now
completely discredited : might we not rather say that
it is a truism? Has not every artist, in whatever line,
felt the same? Nor is it necessary to be an artist;
one gleam of inspiration, or even of insight, prompts
the possessor, at however great a distance, to say
I also.

We wonder if it would be doing an injustice to the
keen-sighted lady of Correggio to hint that she, no
doubt, knew the value of a court-painter, and would
not have liked to be behind the age in lacking one :
however that may be, she always showed herself Allegri's friend as well as his patron.

Veronica had two sons, Ippolito and Girolamo, and
it was immediately after the birth of the second boy
that she lost her father, which caused her to proceed to
Brescia to console her mother, and thus it happened
that she was there in 1512, at the time when the town
was taken and sacked by the French under Gaston de

Foix; no quarter was given either to women or children, but Veronica, after remaining in hiding for some days, was able to escape to Correggio. A more agreeable incident in her married life occurred in 1515, when she went with her husband to Bologna to render homage to Leo X and Francis I ; on this occasion the French monarch declared that he had never met any woman endowed with so many gifts. But Veronica was destined to have but a brief time of happiness, for her husband died in 1518, and her grief for his loss brought on such a severe illness that her life was endangered. This violent affliction, however, had a somewhat theatrical element in it, for we find her registering vows never to go out of mourning, to have her rooms always draped with black, and to drive only coal-black horses, and over the doorway of her apartment she had these two lines from the *Æneid* carved :—

> " Ille meos, primus qui me sibi junxit, amores
>   Abstulit ; ille habeat secum servetque sepulchro."

At the same time, she does not seem to have lost interest in mundane things, for, as early as 1520, we find her writing for some plush, which is to be so beautiful that there shall be nothing more beautiful in the world, and again, a little later, for some Flemish cloth " fra tutti i belli bellissimo " ; also for washes for the complexion and to keep the hair golden : this is not like the abandonment of a very profound sorrow. Yet she had certainly been attached to Giberto, and had given him probably as much love as was possible to a nature of her kind ; for Veronica was not a woman to live in her affections, things did not go deep enough with her for that; it was rather the kaleidoscope of life that attracted her—events not emotions.

She had been left sole guardian of her two sons and administratrix of the estate, and she fulfilled these onerous duties excellently, but it is, perhaps, in this connection that the least agreeable side of her character becomes prominent. She felt the necessity of keeping in touch with and conciliating all great people, and the way was by flattery and adulation; her gift for verse is used almost entirely to this end, and many of her letters have the same aim in view. The career of her sons becomes her ruling passion, and all is done with a keen eye to their advancement; the world dazzles her, though it may be only for their sake, and all its prizes are to be striven after. Dowered with a liberal education, the eldest son, Ippolito, adopted arms as his profession, while Girolamo, the youngest and favourite, was destined for the Church and eventually became a cardinal—but that was ten years after his mother's death. In 1528, when Veronica's brother, Uberto, was appointed governor of Bologna, she seized eagerly on this as a means of advancement for her family, and obtained from him an excellent military command for Ippolito, while sending the younger son to his uncle to study diplomacy and become acquainted with court life. At the same time, she went herself to live at Bologna in the Palazzo Massilia, which became the most brilliant and learned centre in the city. A letter of Veronica's on the occasion of her brother's appointment is worth quoting in full, as it is so very characteristic. It is written to Lodovico Rosso, one of her principal correspondents, a noble Bolognese,

who was a senator of the city and several times Gon-
faloniere di Giustizia ; he has left no printed works,
but was a great scholar and student.

" I understand from your letter, my dear Messer
Lodovico, all the gladness that your mind feels at the
coming of Monsignore my brother to the government
of Bologna. I see that your joy is very great, and
almost like to mine ; only, with mine there is mixed a
little discontent. Nor does that surprise me at all,
knowing that fortune is wont never to give me anything that completely satisfies me. And the discontent
is this, that the said Signor, my brother, warns me that
he shall only remain in this post as long as will suffice
to allay the suspicions of the Germans, which are very
great ; and I am certain that the second miracle will
perhaps be greater than the first, which God forbid.
The fear, then, that the time will be short, does not let
me enjoy my satisfaction in giving effect to the desire
that I have had for many years of staying some months
in that delightful city with an occasion of this kind ;
nor do I quite believe that the heavens, as they have
seemed to favour this my desire by finding the means
most desired by me, will similarly find the other to end
it as I should like. Yet I will not entirely despair
considering the instability of fortune. You, my
Messer Lodovico, will offer devout prayers to God
that He will inspire the mind of the Pope to keep
him at least a year, so that I may enjoy him like a
brother whom I love, I will not say more than any
sister ever loved, but like my own life. Signor
Girolamo, my son, is coming, as happy as it is possible
to say and will reside with Monsignore ; I commend

him to you, not only as my son but as a part of myself; and why do I say a part, since he is the whole? I commend him then to you as myself, for he is Veronica herself. My Ippolito will go in a week to Milan, with a good and honourable salary. I wanted to give you this news, knowing that you would care to hear it. I thank you for your kindness, though it is nothing new. Commend me to Monsignore my brother, and kiss his hand for me. I am expecting all those things without which I could not appear with my wonted magnificence; understand me sensibly, and do not take magnificence for ostentation, which was always far from me and from anything that I do. Always remember me, and farewell."[1]

There were great rejoicings in Bologna in 1530 for the coronation of the Emperor, which took place on February 24, St. Matthias' day and his own birthday, and all that Italy had to offer of splendid, beautiful, and learned congregated there. Isabella d'Este, somewhat embarrassed with her court ladies, was a central figure of the group, but Veronica seems to have been the presiding genius. Her lively letters prepare us to believe that she shone in conversation, and she possessed the additional charm of a very musical voice, so that it was said that, when she began to speak, her audience hoped she might never leave off. All the most famous *literati* of the age were to be found in her palace, and all of them sang her praises. The Emperor himself was at her feet, and his admiration for her decided him to visit her at Correggio. This flattering determination obliged Veronica to leave Bologna and return

---

[1] Letter XL. (undated).

home to prepare for Charles' reception. He was to
stay at the Casino, and a new street was made by way
of approach. According to the fashion of the time, a
magnificent pageant was arranged on this occasion, and
the Emperor's progress through the town must have
been a gorgeous spectacle. Nor was this the only visit
with which Veronica was favoured, for the Emperor
returned two years later, and made another sojourn,
which fact probably testifies to her talent as a hostess
and her brilliant conversational powers. It was for
this second visit that the Casino was further embellished
by Allegri's paintings.

The Marchesa di Pescara was not among the splendid
circle that assembled for the coronation : we feel that it
was not her *milieu*, though she would well have known
how to shine in it. It is more likely than not that she
and her sister-poet never met, and that their intercourse
was confined to the sonnets they exchanged. As those
of Veronica are rather above her average, we will give
both ; the first is distinctly pathetic, the second noble,
though conventional.

> " What time on youthful wayward thoughts I fed,
> 　Now fearing and now hoping, sorrowing
> 　With bitter tears, and now with heart to sing,
> 　By longings false or true still harassèd,
> I told in accents pitiful and dread
> 　The fancies of my heart, which rather would
> 　Seek its own hurt, than follow after good ;
> 　And all my days thus sorrowfully sped.
> On other thoughts and wishes now I feed
> 　My mind, and hence the once dear rhymes and style
> 　In everlasting silence have I sealed.

If in my fantasy I leant awhile
　　To those first follies, penitence indeed
　　Removes the grief, leaving the fault revealed." [1]

" O thou sole glory of our century,
　　Lady most admirable, wise, divine,
　　To whom to-day do reverently incline
　　All who deserve a place in history.
Immortal here shall be your memory;
　　Time, that dooms all to ruinous decay,
　　Shall make of your fair name no impious prey,
　　But unto you shall be the victory.
To Pallas and to Phœbus shrines of old
　　Were reared, and such to you our sex should raise
　　Of richest marble and of finest gold.
And, since in you is found all excellence,
　　In equal measure I would give you praise,
　　Lady, with worship, love, and reverence." [2]

---

[1] " Mentre da vaghi e giovenil pensieri
　　　Fui nodrita, or temendo, ora sperando,
　　　Piangendo or trista, ed or lieta cantando,
　　　Da desir combattuta or falsi, or veri,
　　Con accenti sfogai pietosi e feri
　　　I concetti del cor, che spesso amando
　　　Il suo male assai più che 'l ben cercando,
　　　Consumava dogliosa i giorni interi.
　　Or che d' altri pensieri e d' altre voglie
　　　Pasco la mente, a le già care rime
　　　Ho posto ed a lo stil silenzio eterno.
　　E, se allor, vaneggiando, a quelle prime
　　　Sciocchezze intesi, ora il pentirmi toglie,
　　　Palesando la colpa, il duolo interno."

[2] " O de la nostra etade unica gloria,
　　　Donna saggia, leggiadra, anzi divina,
　　　A la qual riverente oggi s' inchina
　　　Chiunque è degno di famosa istoria,

M

It is not from her poems that we get the clearest view of Veronica; to become really acquainted with her, we must read her clever, worldly letters, which reveal the woman of many tastes and whims. There we can note her ambition, and gauge the things that appeared to her worth striving after; at the same time, there is a lightness of touch and a playing upon the surface which give a sense of rest and attractiveness. After her letters to Bembo, which bear the palm for interest, those to Rosso and Ercolani, both Bolognese worthies, are far the pleasantest, while those to Aretino are fulsomely flattering; Veronica, no less than finer spirits of her time, was completely taken in by him, and her adulation of him is almost past belief. No doubt he played up to it sufficiently. One remark of hers is amusing: "You honour me too much in saying that my letters are better than those of the Signora the Marchesa di Pescara, to whom I give place in everything in the world; nevertheless, I cannot help being glad at hearing this said by the divine Aretino."

The following long letter (without date) is to Lodovico Rosso:—

"I will not say how many days or months it is since

> Ben fia eterna di voi qua giù memoria,
> 　Nè potrà 'l tempo con la sua ruina
> 　Far del bel nome vostro empia rapina,
> 　Ma di lui porterete ampia vittoria.
> Il sesso nostro un sacro e nobil tempio
> 　Dovria, come già a Palla e a Febo, alzarvi
> 　Di ricchi marmi e di finissim' oro.
> E, poichè di virtù siete l' esempio,
> 　Vorrei, Donna, poter tanto lodarvi,
> 　Quanto io vi riverisco, amo ed adoro."

I wrote to you, my Signor Lodovico, and certainly it is not from failure of memory or from want of love, but on account of the numberless cares that have occupied and still occupy me. I am engrossed with everything that is most contrary to my natural inclination, so that I have come to the conclusion that there is not a happier or quieter way of life than that of a little country-girl, who, taking care of her sheep, remains under the shade of a chestnut-tree, letting the world go as it pleases, content with her solitary life, eating poor food which yet is sweeter and more agreeable to her than ambrosia or Jove's nectar would be. O most happy life ! O most happy lot ! How often have I desired to be one of these ! However, here we are and here we must remain, and, returning to my first subject, I say again that the only cause of my not having written to you is the reason which you have heard, and which I would explain willingly, only it would take too much time. I hope, however, to see you one day before I die, so I will reserve the explanation till then. I live desiring to serve you, and let that be enough. The time of the election to the *ruota* is drawing near. I very much want a place in it for Messer Giberto Gatti, and so I should like you to leave no stone unturned for him to obtain it. You know how much I have the affairs of my friends and patrons at heart, so, without ceremony, do all that is in your power, and more if it be possible, so that he and I may be gratified. Then let me know what your hopes are. Henceforth I will be more regular about writing to you, and please be the same, remembering that I am always yours. I pray God to bless and preserve you, and you to keep me in your memory."[1]

These two letters to Agostino Ercolani are amusing as showing the light-hearted way in which Veronica regarded public affairs :—

"I saw by your letter that, after so many trials and labours, Pope Clement has had to die, destroying so many plans and hopes. Now we must have patience. As for me, I will laugh at this ill-fortune and enjoy life. God preserve all our friends, and then let the world go as it pleases. As soon as a pope has been made, and the affairs of Bologna have been settled, I shall expect you at once ; it seems five years until I see you."[2]

A little later she writes : " Now that we know for certain of the creation of Pope Paul, I think that arms will be laid down at Bologna, and that everything will be quiet, so I expect nothing else than to see you. Do please come, for everyone of us is longing for you more than the Jews long for their Messiah. This pontiff pleases me from every point of view, and particularly because he is, as you write me word, a friend of the Cardinal. I wish him all good ; but I fear he will have a short life, because I should like him to have a very long one."[3]

The following letter to Rosso, of a much later date, is curiously modern in its requirements :—

"My Messer Lodovico, I am obliged to go to Mantua, summoned by the Signora Duchessa, and to take my daughter-in-law there. I have not been able to avoid making this journey, as much out of obedi-

---

[1] Letter LIV.   [2] Letter LXIII.   [3] Letter LXV.

ence to the honoured princess, who has such great claims upon me, as in order to give a little amusement to my said daughter-in-law. You know well that I should not take this trouble for myself, as I belong to the world no longer. But I was born to please others and to help in every situation. My daughter-in-law is very well provided with jewels and gold ornaments, but, because at this wedding there will be great doings and the ornaments will be wonderful, I, being rather proud about such things, should like the jewellery of this girl of mine to surpass that of all the others. Wherefore I beg you with your usual fidelity and trustworthiness to ask Count Girolamo Pepoli and the Signora his wife if they would do me the favour of lending me a pearl necklace, which I hear is very beautiful, promising them that it shall be kept with such care as is due to beautiful things, and that I will return it in a fortnight. And if, besides, they had a garland of pearls or of jewels, or even another necklace, it would be most acceptable to me, in order to be able to change frequently. I do not use ceremony, knowing that with you it is enough for me to express my desire ; I will only say that I shall remain greatly obliged to these lords and others if they will comply with my request, as I hope. Let me know, then, when I may send to fetch the ornaments ; and, if they require a receipt or anything else, whatever is wanted shall be done. Remember that I am always yours, and on my return, if the time permits, pray come and see me, and I commend myself to you."[1]

Our short survey of Veronica's life had brought us

---

[1] Letter LV.

down to 1532, the time of the Emperor's second visit to Correggio ; the last letter, given above, was written in 1549, and, between those two dates, the writer had to pass through many troublous events, before she could settle down in the calm of age and write of herself as " non essendo omai più del mondo."   In the autumn of 1532, Veronica made an excursion into the province of Brescia, and this seems to have revived her old love of the country, and was the occasion of her composing some very pretty stanzas in the manner of Virgil ; her famous lines to Cosimo I, afterwards Grand-duke of Tuscany, are in the same form.

In 1538, great danger threatened Correggio in the person of Galeotto Pico della Mirandola, who invaded the territory.   Veronica, acting with great courage and presence of mind, called her people together, made a gallant defence and saved the city ; but plague and famine followed hard on the averted disaster, and Veronica faithfully ministered to the wants of her subjects.   Thanks to her efforts, prosperity returned, and in 1541 we find brighter days had dawned, and the town was keeping festival for the marriage of Ippolito, Veronica's eldest son, with his cousin, Chiara da Correggio.

Two years later, in 1543, that prodigy of genius, Rinaldo Corso, brought out his commentary on the second part of the *Rime* of Vittoria Colonna, he being then only seventeen, and inscribed it " alla molto illustrissima Madonna Veronica Gambara da Correggio et alle Donne gentili."[1]   This Rinaldo was born in 1525 at Correggio ; at fifteen he distinguished himself by

---

[1] See below, Chapter xi, p. 284.

publicly arguing theses of philosophy, and thus brought himself into Veronica's notice, for she never failed to recognise native-born talent.   He then went to Bologna and applied himself to the study of jurisprudence, remaining still devoted to poetry, history, and abstract science.   On his return to Correggio, he always stood high in the favour of Veronica, being one of the greatest ornaments of her learned circle ; in 1546 he became her auditor, and subsequently wrote her life and that of her husband.

The closing years of Veronica's life seem to have been given over to study and to religious observances ; she lived in her beloved Casino, and does not appear to have left Correggio except in 1549, when she went with her daughter-in-law to Mantua for the wedding festivities of the Duke Francesco III, who married Caterina, daughter of Ferdinand of Austria.   It was on this occasion that she wrote the letter, quoted above, to Lodovico Rosso.   Returning to Correggio, Veronica died in the following June at the age of sixty-four, immensely regretted by the people she had served so faithfully.   She was buried with great pomp and honour in the Church of San Domenico, beside her husband, a branch of laurel and of olive being placed on her coffin, to signify the benevolence of her rule and the fame that was rightly hers.   Nothing, however, remains of her tomb or of her favourite dwelling, for both were destroyed in 1556 by the Spaniards, when they were holding the town against the attacks of the Pope and his allies.   There is something more than the irony of fate in the fact that it was Spain that wrought this destruction, when we recall how assiduously Veronica had courted the Emperor, and how he, in his turn, had praised and flattered her, and, in acknowledgment of his royal reception at Correggio, had granted the town a safeguard which should ensure its protection against the Spanish soldiery.

Veronica's memory is enshrined in her letters and poems, the former, as it seems to us, giving a far more favourable impression of the woman. Her poetical genius was prostituted to private ambition, which narrows and dulls its expression, and introduces a perpetual element of vulgarity. Neither is there in her verses any of the spontaneity which makes her correspondence agreeable. When we think of the brilliant circle she attracted, and the magic of her voice and conversation, we wonder that a greater impression of charm is not left upon us. The fact remains that, with all her wit, readiness, talent, and solid devotion to study, there was, yet in her character a deep vein of that unlovely quality of worldliness, which, oddly enough, seems to damn the possessor of it as effectually for this world as for the next. There is something about her that is too obvious; her best qualities are those that make for popularity, and what we miss in her is that sense of the unknown and the unfathomable which is, in fact, the soul's attraction.

CHAPTER VII

GASPARA STAMPA

Ah Love! could thou and I with fate conspire
To grasp this sorry scheme of things entire,
    Would we not shatter it to bits—and then
Re-mould it nearer to the Heart's Desire!
                    FitzGerald's *Omar Khayyám.*

In passing from the study of the life of Vittoria
Colonna to that of Veronica Gambara, despite the
similarity of position, of tastes, and of circumstances,
it seemed as though we had descended to a distinctly
lower plane: but to study Gaspara Stampa, we must go
into a lower sphere. There we shall look in vain for
the dignity and order which characterised the mind of
Veronica, and we shall be still further removed from
the loftiness and mysticism which flowered in the soul
of Vittoria : we shall find nothing noble, nothing ideal,
only an intensely passionate human heart ; and yet, had
the lot fallen to her in another ground, she might have
had a different life-record.

Very little seems to be known certainly of Gaspara's
family. She was born in Padua in 1523, but is said
to have belonged to a noble Milanese family—a fact
which is borne out by the existence of a letter written
to her by Paola Antonia de' Negri, the daughter of
Lazzaro Negri, public professor of letters at Milan, who

was a religious in the newly founded order of the
Angeliche of San Paolo in that city. Gaspara had one
sister, Cassandra, and one brother, Baldassare, both of
whom were tenderly devoted to her, and the latter was
also a poet.

The possessor of any great gift can hardly fail to be
interesting, but endowments like Gaspara's must be so
in the highest degree. From a child, her intellect was
the wonder and admiration of all her teachers; all
testify to her ardour for study, the breadth and grasp
of her mind, and her unerring taste; while to personal
beauty of no common order—that beauty which com-
bines perfection of feature with variety of expression—
she added the accomplishments of poetry, music, and
singing. Her education was as complete as the high
standard of the age exacted, so that none can ever
have stood forth more splendidly equipped for life in
its widest and most intellectual meaning, and, if she
had remained in the cultivated, sober, and critical
society of Padua, it is probable that her story would
not have been so unsatisfying in the living and so sad
in the writing. But, on the death of her father, which
took place when Gaspara was only a child, the family
moved to Venice, and it would be hard to conceive of
surroundings which demanded a steadier head and a
more balanced judgment.

It has been thought by some that a parallel might be
drawn between the Venice of the sixteenth century and
the England of to-day, each being a mercantile nation.
The aristocracy of Venice was chiefly an aristocracy
of wealth; money was a necessity to that gay and
expensive community, and consequently counted for

much. The spirit of commerce reigned supreme there, as with us to-day, and, perhaps, this can never be the case without a certain lowering of standard and coarsening of taste ; but, apart from this, it would be difficult to push the comparison further. For Venice had at least a great tradition, " whose merchants are princes, whose traffickers are the honourable of the earth " ; if she was more rich and more corrupt than any other state in Italy, she was also more cultivated, more elegant, and more artistic. Nor was this mere dilettanteism ; it was a serious devotion to art and letters, recognising in them the business, as well as the pleasure, of life.

It is honourable alike to Gaspara and to the society which opened its arms to welcome her that, if she quickly became its idol, she owed her reception not only or chiefly to her beauty and wealth, but infinitely more to the gifts of her mind. The great world found its recreation then in every sort of intellectual reunion. Poet and musician, Gaspara's success is easy to understand, and her singing captivated all hearts and drew tears from many eyes, as no doubt it would have done in London to-day. But the side of Venetian society to which we find no parallel consists in those more serious séances which, while meeting in gorgeous palaces and enchanting gardens, yet concerned themselves with questions of scholarship, grammar, language, and style, and produced translations, glossaries, and commentaries without end. The house of Domenico Veniero, poet and senator, was the most famous place for these gatherings, being the rendezvous for all that was wise, noble, and learned ; it was, indeed, the cradle of the celebrated *Accademia dei Pellegrini* of which Doni was the secretary, and his account of it, which we have in a letter to the organist of San Marco, is interesting enough to be given in full.

"Your Lordship will forgive me if I do not tell you, or write you, the names of the *Signori Accademici Pellegrini*, but only their cognomens, for so I am instructed to do, and, if I were to fail, I promise you I should not be safe on the top of Mount Sinai. I will, therefore, explain to you the manner, order, and customs, the foundations, and all the remaining things concerning the Academy, only excepting the proper names. It happened that six honourable, virtuous, and influential gentlemen, meeting at a famous house here in Venice, began to wonder that so many Academies had been created in Italy and had so quickly come to nothing. And a memorable argument took place about this, and ultimately the members of these were excused for true and efficacious reasons. Now, having a desire to form a new one, many names were proposed ; one wished that it should be called the Academy of Apollo, another of the Nobles, but they could not find the crests, mottoes, works, names, and places that would go well together. At last one gentleman said: ' It seems that we six ought to include in our congregation the most illustrious and learned spirits that there are in Italy and abroad, but with this compact and condition, that those who accept our company and whose we embrace must never be made known to anyone, and that this should be the promise.' And so this beginning found favour, and immediately they elected the most learned men in

France, in Germany, and in Italy, but all Italians, dispersed in divers countries. From this arose the name *Pilgrim*, because it is the essence of a Pilgrim to go over the world, to be found in all places, to talk with all sorts of men, to know how to discourse about the nature of all things, and to discuss every subject. And this arrangement was confirmed, all the more that in this world we are like pilgrims ; and at once the general crest suggested itself to put over the shield of the Academy—a Peregrine Falcon with a Diamond in its claw. And I said: ' Gentlemen, the motto that will go perfectly with it is wanting, and this is a very important thing.' And there came into my mind this saying, which was accepted: *Naturæ et Artis Opus ;* because the Peregrine Falcon is excellent when art has trained him, while the Diamond, which is natural, as soon as art polishes and cuts it, becomes perfect. To which one of the members added that there could not be a motto more appropriate to the Pilgrim-Academy, because the natural powers of speech and understanding must be tempered with the art of letters and the exercise of the virtues. The arms were designed thus: a shield, in the middle of which was depicted a staff, a hat, shells, a winding-sheet, and other things with which one goes on pilgrimage ; and a short inscription round it with these words, *Finiunt Pariter, Renovantque Labores,* because every evening the pilgrim lies down and his labours come to an end, and every morning he begins his journey anew. And, because in this miserable world we are now bewildered by fears, now lost in happiness or in sorrow, now ill-content to live, thirsty, hungry, drowsy, slothful, swift, devout, and other things as occasion offers, it seemed that such cognomens as *Devout, Vexed, Wandered, Lost, Weary, Foot-sore,* and such-like, were very suitable to the Pilgrim-Academicians, who are now twenty-five in number. The gentleman who was the originator of the idea is called the *Staff,* and he has appointed three Councillors, that is, the *Palmer,* the *Pilgrim,* and the *Traveller.* All these offices are in being, as also the Chancellor, which am I, and I shall now and always keep silence about my cognomen given me by the Academicians. The special seal of all the members is a pilgrim with the motto as I have written it in the discourse of Niccolò Martelli at page 37.[1] Each Academician produces his works by himself and sends them to these gentlemen, and, according to their judgment, the titles are given, and they are sent to be printed ; and we have some in print already as I have written (in the letter I addressed to the *Staff* at the request of the Academicians). . . . You will see what a fine thing it will be to see the styles clearly differentiated in the lives of poets that we know ; at Naples a Pilgrim-Academician is doing the life of Sannazzaro, another at Ferrara that of Ariosto, here that of Bembo, that of Aretino, that of the Signora Vittoria Colonna, and others as you will see. Such and so much information I can give you and no more."[2]

In spite of Doni's discretion, we do know the names of many members of this attractive assembly. Veniero

---

[1] " Il suggello, che portono particularmente gl' Accademici nostri Pellegrini, ha un viandante pellegrino che camina, con questo motto atorno: *Tentanda via est* " (*La Libreria del Doni,* p. 37).

[2] *Ibid.,* pp. 63, 64.

(who was probably the *Staff*) is specially interesting in
that, in the chronic ill-health into which he fell, which
obliged him to give up all public offices, his love of
study never abated, and in his acute suffering his chief
solace was to cultivate poetry, and to surround himself
with learned men, with whom he would discuss questions of scholarship.

Another member was Girolamo Parabosco, poet and
musician, who in his book of *Lettere amorose* includes
one to Gaspara, of which the end runs thus: "O Lady
loved above measure and favoured by the stars, this is
that fire which shall never burn in me less fiercely,
owing to your great virtues. Who ever saw elsewhere
such beauty? Or such graces, or such sweet ways?
And who ever heard such sweet and gentle words, or
listened to such high ideas? And what shall I say of
that angelic voice, which, whenever it penetrates the air
with its divine accents, makes such sweet harmony that
it does not merely, like the Siren, make everyone who
is worthy of hearing it thrall to the brother of death,
but infuses spirit and life into the coldest stones,
making them weep for sovran sweetness. You may
then rest assured, most beautiful and most gracious
Lady Gasparina, that every man who sees you is bound
to remain your servant for ever. Of which number,
albeit I may be the most unworthy in virtues, yet I
shall not be so in love, and from henceforth, in everything that I know will please you, I shall show it you
by most evident tokens."[1]

The other poet-members were Benzone and Molino;
the latter resembles Galeazzo di Tarsia in that his

---

[1] *Lettere amorose*, Lib. i. p. 32.

extreme modesty prevented the publication of his poems until after his death; in his lifetime, he was chiefly known for his excellent taste in literature, and his liberality towards literary men. Other well-known names are those of Lodovico Dolce and Francesco Sansovino, the last-named being also a member of the celebrated *Accademia degl' Infiammati* at Padua. He was only two years older than Gaspara, and was a prolific, but not very discerning, author and compiler; with him we find Gaspara disputing on the merits of the styles of Boccaccio and Castiglione, and he dedicated to her his reprint of Boccaccio's *Ameto*, his *Ragionamento d' Amore*, and the *Lettura di Messer Benedetto Varchi sopra un Sonetto della Gelosia di Monsignor Della Casa*. In the *Ragionamento*, which is extremely rare, the prefatory letter to Gaspara, containing many allusions to her brother, Baldassare, to whom it is evident that the author was much attached, runs thus :—

"Many times, gracious damosel, while Messer Baldassare was alive, whom I cannot remember without grief (your brother and a part of my very soul), I heard him, in telling over to me the blessings given him by the supreme grace of God, mention you as the chief, and the one which he esteemed most highly. Many times did he describe to me the excellence of your intellect and the steadfastness of your mind. . . . And because, being somewhat the elder, I remember that, as though he had made me his father, I rebuked, admonished, counselled that most gentle nature of his which begged me for advice, instruction, and restraint; proceeding with you in the same manner, because I am bound to do so, you being his very self, I send you this little sketch which I have made as a relaxation from graver studies, to remind you that by its means you may learn to shun the deceptions which perverse men practise on pure and innocent maidens, such as you are. And herewith I instruct and advise you to proceed with your glorious studies, shunning every occasion which might distract you from your undertaking. I know that I am too bold, but the memory of your virtues, and the extreme affection that I bear to you and to Madonna Cassandra, your honoured sister, and the duty to which I am bound, constrain me to this, and so I hope for your forgiveness. . . ."[1]

The dedication of the *Ameto* shows great respect for Gaspara's judgment and scholarship, as does that of the *Lettura*, which Sansovino says he desires to bring out under her most sweet and dear name; and he further assures her that both Varchi and della Casa will consider themselves highly honoured " when they know that their works have been read and prized by you, who are most worthy of all commendation, because your worth and your most admirable judgment so far exceed common praise."

Other honourable friendships were with Trifone Gabrielli, a very learned old man, called the " Socrates of his time," and with Monsignor Giovanni della Casa, to whom Cassandra Stampa dedicated her sister's collected works after her death. Della Casa was Archbishop of Benevento and Nuncio at Venice in 1544. He takes rank as one of the most original poets of his

---

[1] *Lettera di prefazione al Ragionamento di M. Francesco Sansovino, nel quale brevemente s' insegna a' giovani uomini la bell' Arte d' Amore.* Venice, January 3, 1545 (*i.e.* 1546).

N

time, but is probably better known to us as the author of the *Galateo*, a little book on manners and good breeding, full of wise and charming things.   The writer says it was designed to show "what manner of countenance and grace behoveth a man to use, that he may be able in communication and familiar acquaintance with men to show himself pleasant, courteous, and gentle : which, nevertheless, is either a virtue or the thing that comes very near virtue."

The rather illusive Mirtilla must have been a very great friend of the poetess, to judge from the sixth Capitolo which is addressed to her.   It is generally thought that Mirtilla was the academical name which hid the personality of Ippolita Roma, a Paduan poetess, with whose family Gaspara is known to have been intimate, for Sansovino, in the dedication of the *Ameto*, begs her to show it to Messer Giovanni Roma, and refers to a day on which they all disputed together a question of style.   The wonderfully interesting series of thirty-five letters, published by Luigi Carrer, purports to have been written to Mirtilla by Gaspara, but the general opinion seems to be that the letters are not genuine, but that in them Carrer has woven a true romance, and, utilising every known detail of the life of Gaspara, and following the lines of her own sonnets, has presented a very faithful delineation of her character.

In Sansovino's letter, given above, we have evidence of the anxiety felt for so beautiful and talented a girl in the *milieu* in which she was placed, and this finds still clearer expression in the noble letter written to her by the Angelica Paola Antonia de' Negri.   Paola Antonia was a wonderful woman ; she would have been remarkable in any position of life, for her insight and force of character would always have made her a power ; but, far above these, she was distinguished by her great sanctity, which drew men and women to consult her, many of whom owed their conversion to her, while no small number, attracted by her example, left the world for a life of penitence and prayer. To her high spirituality, her letters bear eloquent testimony. It was on August 20, 1544, that she wrote as follows to Gaspara from her convent of San Paolo in Milan.

"Why should you wonder, O soul most sweet to me, and most dear in the most pure Blood of Jesus Christ, that I should love you in Him who has loved you so much that, through excess of love, He gave Himself to so bitter and painful a death ? If the Creator loves you so much, why should not I, a miserable creature, love you ? If He took such pleasure in you as to adorn you with His abundant graces in order that He might better be able to take delight in you, why should not I also take delight in the wonderful works that He has wrought in you ? Ah ! if it might please His goodness to make me worthy to see the beautiful work which He has begun in you brought to perfection ; and this I am sure He will do, you being willing, as I trust you will be. For, if you are possessed of that noble spirit that is announced to me by many, I cannot believe that you would wish to imitate the folly of those who, arrogating to themselves the gifts and graces bestowed on them, are so charmed with themselves and become so proud that, making an idol of such graces, they desire for themselves the praises that belong to God. They want to be worshipped and praised, and they make it their whole study to please the world and men, and to gratify themselves, their own senses and sensual impulses, and other abominable desires. They only use the favours which God has bestowed on them to offend and revile Him, and, if they could, they would choose that there should be neither God nor soul, so that they might serve their unbridled desires, ambitions, and vices more unrestrainedly. I pray earnestly that this may never happen in your sweet soul, but I know that you are grateful for the graces that you have received, so that you may become worthy of greater ones. Remember, most sweet sister, that the graces you have were given to you in order that you might make yourself all spirit, and an angel in the flesh. Now what an evil it would be if, with so many gifts and graces, you were to turn away from God who created you and re-created you in the most precious Blood of His Son, to give yourself to the world, to its frivolities, ambitions, vanity, and luxury? Recognise, recognise, the beauty, and the dignity, and excellence of your spirit, and strive to increase its worth by making it all divine with holy virtues. Remember that all these good gifts pass away with the wind, and, after death, nothing remains of them but sorrow and torment, if we have not made good use of them. Those virtues which the world honours give nothing to the soul but that small and momentary content which springs from the praises of flatterers; and, when these eyes are closed in their last sleep, those also will be dead; but true virtues, holy virtues,

Christian virtues, divine virtues, adorn the soul, illu-
minate it, enrich it, ornament it, glorify it both in the
present life and in that which is to come.   What is
the worth of that virtue which, when we die, dies with
us ?   How much more useful and more desirable is
that virtue which always accompanies the soul, and
never leaves it, but brings it always new crowns, new
palms, new triumphs ?   O God, shall I believe that
my sweet Madonna Gasparina will have so little
insight that she will not know how to choose ?   Will
she refuse heavenly good for earthly ?   O but, someone will say to me, I wish to have both.   And I
answer (nay, not I, but the Lord) : One can only serve
two masters badly.   Paul answers : 'The unmarried
woman and the virgin thinketh on the things of the
Lord that she may be holy both in body and in spirit.
But she that is married thinketh on the things of the
world how she may please her husband.'   Ah ! dear
soul, make it your study to be truly pure, humble,
patient, and full of all other holy virtues, so that you
may indeed be pleasing to your celestial Spouse, whose
chaste embraces give more joy to the soul than all the
pleasures that can be had apart from Him.   And you,
to whom He has given such favours, can you not,
with the help of His grace, prepare yourself to enjoy
Him for ever ?   Would you then refuse such a great
good ?   Ah ! no, for the love of God, no, no, blessed
soul, redeemed at so great a price ; nay, leaving all
others, embrace Him alone.   Do not be sorry to dis-
appoint the world in what it expects of you, and do
not believe in flatterers, those who love you according
to the flesh.   Do not deceive yourself, I pray you, but

cut off all those intimacies and conversations which separate you from Christ and put you in peril, or which might bring a breath of suspicion upon that beautiful chastity which shines forth in you, besides all your other virtues, on account of which I said that you must not wonder if I love you. I love you and will love you always, if you will love Him who loves you so much ; and not only with letters, but with my blood, my life, my soul. I shall be content—and I will not go back from my word—I shall be content if I am able to help you in the virtuous course which He who has begun it in you gives you to make perfect. I pray you to familiarise yourself by constant thought with the pains and torments that have been suffered for you. Take some time from your other occupations to spend it at the feet of your Saviour. Pray do this, so that you may be made worthy to receive true light and real knowledge of the will of God in you, so that you may be able to perform it, and pray for me. Salute your mother and sister whom I consider mine ; our Lady Abbess salutes you. Farewell, spirit created in Paradise in order that there might be your conversation and hereafter your eternal habitation.

"From the holy place of St. Paul the Apostle in Milan, August 20, 1544.

"Yours wholly in Jesus Christ,

"A. P. A."[1]

Yet, in spite of the band of lovers and flatterers by whom Gaspara was always surrounded, it was not until she was six-and-twenty that fate, in the person of

---

[1] *Lettere spirituali della devota religiosa Angelica Paola Antonia de' Negri*, pp. 619–623.

Collaltino, Count of Collalto and a nobleman of Tre-
viso, overtook her.   He was one of the Pilgrims, his
academical name being Virgiliano Coridone ; Gaspara
calls him by it only once, but constantly uses her own
of Anassilla, which she had adopted as signifying the
nymph-goddess of Anasso, a river which ran through
part of the Count's territory.   Outwardly, Collaltino
promised everything to attract the fancy : young, hand-
some, gallant, cultivated ; a poet at a time when everyone poetised, and a soldier in an age when war was the
noblest art.   He was, no doubt, conquered by the
striking beauty and the manifold talents of Gaspara,
but whether her transports and her jealousy wore him
out, or whether he had never meant to do anything
but pass away the time with her, it is difficult to say.
It is most likely that he never really loved her ; his
seems to have been a cold and selfish nature ; hers,
though absolutely self-centred, was passionately loving.

It would be difficult to picture to ourselves anything
more out of keeping with the tastes of the present
day than the world in which these two moved.   Now,
when conversation is a series of snap-shots and an
opinion of any kind is to seek ; when no one wants to
think, and only a very limited number of people want
their thinking done for them, the formal and learned
coteries which made up the fashionable society of
Venice would be things impossible and incomprehensible.   And yet Gaspara Stampa, the centre and the
idol of these, stands before us essentially as the modern
woman, the sister of Marie Bashkirtseff, the woman
who has done with conventions, and who has the
courage of her own egotism.   Hers is the first literary

autobiography ; we do not need to go beyond her
verses to know her whole history ; she is alike without
conventional modesty and without reticence, but she
has the grace of being natural.   Subjective to the last
degree, she has no outlook ; she only writes true
history, but it is written with a fire and fervour which
compels attention and defies oblivion.   Her literary
output is the story of a three years' passion, and
strikes the varying notes of joy, transport, jealousy,
and reproach, returning to the height of ecstasy only to
sink down in desolation and despair ; it is a love-record,
in fact, of everything except nobleness, for the love of
passion is never an unselfish love, being fulfilled with
the desire of getting ; whereas love in its purest aspect
means giving, not receiving.

According to Sonnet 11, it was at Christmas-time that
Gaspara first met the Count ; he began the acquaintance
by writing her a sonnet, after which their intimacy pro-
gressed rapidly.   Her first poems are occupied with the
personal charms and attractions of her lover, whom all
the stars of heaven dowered with their gifts,

> " That he might be the only perfect one."

We get the same well-worn comparisons between his
face and the sun, his eyes and the stars, yet her praises
are not as wholly conventional as those of her sister-
poets.

> " Ladies, let who desires to know my lord
> Picture a lord of fair and sweet aspèct,
> Though young in years mature in intellect." [1]

---

[1] " Chi vuol conoscer, donne, il mio signore,
   Miri un signor di vago e dolce aspetto,
   Giovane d' anni e vecchio d' intelletto."

And again,

> "In that angelic beauty I behold
> Ever new miracles and new effects." [1]

But it is not long before these notes of doubt make themselves heard, as in Sonnets XVIII and XXIV.

> "Whene'er I see my beauteous ray appear,
> It is as though I saw the sun arise,
> And when he makes sweet stay he, to my eyes,
> Is like the sun that on his course doth fare.
> Pleasure and strength then cause my heart to wear
> An aspect gracious as green fields display
> At high noon in the loveliest time of May,
> When by the sunshine they are coloured clear.
> But when my sun departs from me at last,
> I seem to see the other's swift descent
> Into the west, leaving the earth o'ercast.
> But he will come with life and light once more,
> While of my dear and shining orient
> Return is doubtful and departure sure." [2]

---

[1] " E veggo in quel angelica beltate
    Sempre nuovi miracoli ed effetti."

[2] " Quando io veggo apparire il mio bel raggio,
    Parmi vedere il sol quando esce fuora ;
    Quando fa meco poi dolce dimora,
    Assembra il sol che faccia suo viaggio.
    E tanta nel cor gioia e vigore aggio,
    Tanta ne mostro nel sembiante allora,
    Quanta l' erba, che il sol pinge e colora
    A mezzo giorno nel più vago maggio.
    Quando poi parte il mio sol finalmente,
    Parmi l' altro veder, che scolorita
    Lasci la terra andando in occidente.
    Ma l' altro torna, e rende luce e vita ;
    E del mio chiaro e lucido oriente
    È il tornar dubbio e certa la partita."

" Let all speech come, and all intelligence,
    As many as e'er wrote in prose and verse,
    As many as in times and lands diverse
    Were spirits worthy of our reverence ;
Yet there were none of all could make pretence
    To tell Love's trouble, anger, loss, and scorn ;
    Since in true Love so many things are borne,
    Love's fancy at its side is impotence.
Nor shall there ever yet be one to prove
    The legion of delights, untold, unguessed,
    Love, of his courtesy, doth make me know.
You, who by favour are elect to love,
    Do not bewail the griefs you undergo,
    Because the sufferings of Love are blest." [1]

Also, from the very first, she complains of his coldness :—

    " Since I am made of fire and you of ice,
      You are in liberty and I in chains." [2]

---

[1] " Vengan quante fur mai lingue ed ingegni,
    Quanti fur stili in prosa e quanti in versi,
    E quanti in tempi e paesi diversi
    Spirti di riverenza e d' onor degni ;
Non fia mai che descrivan l' ire e i sdegni,
    Le noie e i danni, che in amor soffersi ;
    Perchè nel vero tanti e tali fersi,
    Che passan tutti gli amorosi segni.
E non fia anche alcun che possa dire,
    Anzi adombrar la schiera de' diletti
    Che Amor, la sua mercè, mi fa sentire.
Voi, che ad amar per grazia siete eletti,
    Non vi dolete dunque di patire,
    Perchè i martir d' amor son benedetti."

[2] " Ma, perch' io son di foco e voi di ghiaccio,
    Voi siete in libertate ed io in catena."

And, in Sonnet XLIII :—

> " My star is cruel, but more cruelty
>   I suffer from my Count ; from me he flies,
>   I follow ; some on me cast longing eyes ;
>   No loveliness but his can I descry.
> I hate who loves, love who despitefully
>   Regards me ; 'gainst the humble cries my heart ;
>   To him who scorns I play a humble part ;
>   Such the strange food my soul is nourished by.
> Fresh cause for anger doth he ever bring,
>   While others seek to give me peace and rest ;
>   But, leaving them, I am by him possest.
> Thus in thy school, O Love, is ever done
>   The contrary of each deservèd thing ;
>   Not humbleness but pride the day hath won."[1]

But these vague sorrows suddenly assume an objective form when she is confronted with her lover's proposed departure to take service under the French king, Henry II ; she implores him to delay his going :—

---

[1] " Dura è la stella mia, maggior durezza
        È quella del mio Conte ; egli mi fugge,
        Io seguo lui ; altri per me si strugge,
        Io non posso mirare altra bellezza.
    Odio chi m' ama, ed amo chi mi sprezza ;
        Verso chi m' è umíle il mio cor rugge ;
        Io sono umíl con chi mia speme adugge ;
        A così strano cibo ho l' alma avvezza.
    Egli ognor dà cagione a nuovo sdegno,
        Essi mi cercan dar conforto e pace ;
        Io lascio questi, ed a quell' un m' attegno.
    Così nella tua scola, Amor, si face
        Sempre il contrario di quel ch' egli è degno ;
        L' umíl si sprezza, e l' empio si compiace."

"Alas! for some few hours at least defer
  Your obstinate departure, till such time
  As I am used such heavy grief to bear."[1]

And, when he is gone, she thus invokes the breezes of
France :—

"Tell him in accents sad, in woful wise,
  That, if he will not bring my heart relief
  By coming or by writing, few and brief
  The hours ere light be quenched within my eyes."[2]

She reproaches him with having changed his thought
and will as soon as he reached France ; she complains
that he no longer cares for her and for her love, and
that he has not deigned to write one word to his
"misera Anassilla." At least forty sonnets form one
long lament over her lover's absence and the surpassing
greatness of her own grief.

"Dear Ladies, you who haply like to me
  Have trod the pathway steep and amorous,
  And who have sometime seen and provèd thus
  How sore that cruel archer's wounds can be.
Tell me the truth then, of your courtesy,
  If there are any griefs, or ever were,
  That with my bitter sorrows can compare,
  Or equal one of mine in agony."[3]

---

[1] "Deh prolungate almen per alcune ore
      Questa vostra ostinata dipartita,
      Fin che m' usi a portar tanto dolore."

[2] "E ditegli con tristi e mesti accenti
      Che s' ei non move a dar soccorso al core,
      O tornando o scrivendo, fra poche ore
      Resteran gli occhi miei di luce spenti."

[3] "Voi, che per l' amoroso, aspro sentiero,
      Donne care, come io, forse passate,
      Ed avete talor viste e provate

It was during this first absence, when she could get no word from the Count, that she wrote him a touching letter sending therewith all her collected poems, and wrote at the same time to his brother, Vinciguerra, to beg him to gain some response for her. To Collaltino she wrote thus :—

"To my illustrious Lord.

"Since the pains which I suffer for love of your Lordship, written in divers letters and verses, have not been able singly to make your Lordship pitiful towards me, nor even to make you courteous enough to write me one word, I have resolved to write them all in this book, in order to see whether all together they will be able to effect this. Here, then, your Lordship will see, not the depths of my passions, my tears, and my torments, for that is a bottomless ocean, but only a little rivulet therefrom. Nor must you think I have done this in order to convict you of cruelty, because one cannot talk of cruelty where is no obligation ; nor yet to make you sad ; but rather to make you conscious of your own greatness and to make you rejoice over it. Because, seeing these fruits are the outcome of your harshness towards me, you will be able to guess what would result from your compassion, if it should ever happen that heaven should make you compassionate towards me, O noble, illustrious, and divine one, since by torturing me you bring aid and fruitful-

---

Quante pene può dar quel crudo arciero ;
Dite per cortesia, ma dite il vero,
  Se quante ne son or, quante son state,
  All' aspre pene mie paragonate,
  Agguaglian un de' miei martiri intero."

ness.   When you have a truce from your greater and dearer cares, let your Lordship read these records of the grave and tender ones of your most loving and unhappy Anassilla, and infer from this shadow how she must experience and feel them in her mind.   For, certainly, if it should ever happen that my poor mournful house should be found worthy to receive its great guest, who is your Lordship, I am sure that the beds, the rooms, the halls, and everything would recount the laments, the sobs, the sighs, and the tears which I have shed day and night calling on your name.   Nevertheless, in my worst torments, I have ever blest heaven and my good fortune for the cause of them, because it is far better, Count, to die for you than to rejoice for any other whomsoever.   But what am I doing ?   Why am I troubling your Lordship needlessly and at too great length, and injuring even my verses thereby, as though these did not know how to tell their own reasons, and wanted help from others ?   Referring myself then to these, I will make an end, praying your Lordship, as the greatest reward of my most faithful service, that, on receiving this poor little book, you will grant me only a sigh, which from afar will revive the memory of your forgotten and abandoned Anassilla. And you, my little book, depositary of my tears, present yourself before our Lord, in the humblest fashion that you can, in company with my pure faith.   And if, when he receives you, you shall see that those my fatal and eternal lights grow gentle, even a little, then blessed be all our labours, and most happy all our hopes.   And so remain with him in peace for ever." [1]

---

[1] Dedicatory letter prefixed to various editions of Gaspara's *Rime*.

But even this obtained no recognition. Then came to her the news of his approaching return, and all was transport for a brief while :—

"What words and welcomes can be worthy found
    With which to greet my longed-for lover, he
    Who comes with so great glories back to me."[1]

And in her present joy she will make light of past sufferings :—

"I bless thee, Love, for all the griefs and fears,
    For all the injuries and weariness;
    All new and old vexations now I bless
    Which thou hast made me bear so many years.
I bless the frauds with which thy followers
    Thou dost deceive, the errors manifold,
    Since, now that I my two dear stars behold,
    All trace of sorrow straightway disappears."[2]

But she is too soon troubled by jealousy :—

"Love, speak with me a little, tell me this,
    With thy two sisters what have I to do,
    With fear and jealousy? I would I knew
    Why ever in my heart their dwelling is."[3]

---

[1] "Con quai degne accoglienze o quai parole
        Raccorrò io il mio gradito amante,
        Che torna a me con tante glorie e tante."

[2] "Io benedico, Amor, tutti gli affanni,
        Tutte le ingiurie e tutte le fatiche,
        Tutte le noie novelle ed antiche,
        Che m' hai fatto provar tante e tanti anni.
    Benedico le frodi e i tanti inganni,
        Con che convien che i tuoi seguaci intriche;
        Poi che tornando le due stelle amiche
        M' hanno in un tratto ristorati i danni."

[3] "Vorrei che mi dicessi un poco, Amore,
        Che ho a far io con queste tue sorelle,
        Temenza e gelosia? ed ond' è ch' elle
        Non sanno star se non dentro il mio core?"

And, if her lover really read the long tirade of fear,
torment, and recrimination which she poured forth,
one can hardly wonder that he wearied of her ; but, at
the same time, there is never wanting a touching accent
of humility in all she writes. Her sorrow breaks forth
still more bitterly when the Count will return to the
French army :—

> " Since life departs from me, lo ! I shall die,
>   For, lacking life, can I remain alive ?
>   That were a new and strange alternative,
>   O Love, and this thou knowest certainly.
> And since by death the weary history
>   Will close for ever of my bitter cries,
>   My sorrows, and my sufferings, and sighs,
>   I feel it will not greatly trouble me.
> Only for Love's sake will I grieve, that thou
>   Henceforth shalt never find so firm a heart
>   Or one so constant to receive thy dart.
> And all thy glories and thy victories,
>   So many and so great, shall lose their prize
>   When this so faithful lover is laid low."[1]

---

[1] " Ecco, Amore, io morrò, perchè la vita
        Si partirà da me, e senza lei
        Tu sei certo ch' io viver non potrei,
        Chè saria cosa nuova ed inaudita.
    Quanto a me, ne sarò poco pentita,
        Perchè la lunga istoria degli omei,
        De' sospir, de' martir, de' dolor miei
        Sarà per questo mezzo almen finita.
    Mi dorrà sol per conto tuo, che poi
        Non avrai cor sì saldo e sì costante,
        Dove possi avventar gli strali tuoi ;
    E le vittorie tue, le tante e tante
        Tue glorie perderanno i pregi suoi
        Al cader di sì fida e salda amante."

This separation was final, and the remainder of her
writings, the *Rime di vario argomento*, has a different
tone.   There have been few traces of religious feeling
in Gaspara's work hitherto ; human love had claimed
too large a part of her life ; but, as that goes from her,
she turns with humility and penitence to God.   Her
religious sonnets, if not strong, have in them at least a
note of sincerity, and witness to the struggle through
which she had passed.

> " Repentant now, over my sins I grieve,
>   Over my wild and foolish fantasies,
>   That in vain loves I should have wasted this
>   Brief time of mortal life so fugitive.
> To Thee, O Lord, who tenderness dost give
>   To human hearts, and melt'st the frozen snow,
>   And makest heavy burdens easy grow
>   To those in whom Thy holy fervours live ;
> To Thee I turn, and pray that Thou afford
>   Thine aid to draw me forth from the deep place,
>   Whence I to free myself should vainly try.
> It was Thy will, O Lord, for us to die,
>   And so to ransom all the human race ;
>   Then do not let me perish, dearest Lord."[1]

---

[1] " Mesta e pentita de' miei gravi errori
>   E del mio vaneggiar tanto e sì lieve,
>   E d' aver speso questo tempo breve
>   Della vita fugace in vani amori,
> A te, Signor, che intenerisci i cori,
>   E rendi calda la gelata neve,
>   E fai soave ogni aspro peso e greve
>   A chiunque accendi de' tuoi santi ardori,
> Ricorro, e prego che mi porghi mano
>   A trarmi fuor del pelago, onde uscire,
>   S' io tentassi da me, sarebbe vano.

o

There are also a few sonnets addressed to a new lover ; they are infinitely paler in colour than any that have gone before, but they show that a new hope was springing up in her heart. Whether any happiness could ultimately have come of this is an unsolved question, for Gaspara had felt and suffered too much ; she had literally worn herself out, and died in April, 1554, when only thirty-one. Two stories were at one time current concerning her death : first, that she was poisoned by Collaltino ; secondly, that she died of grief on hearing of his marriage. Both tales have long since been discredited, and the date of Collaltino's marriage has been fixed at 1557, three years after Gaspara's death.

Her sister, Cassandra, who evidently regarded her with overpowering love and admiration, caused her poems to be published immediately after her death, and dedicated them in the following letter to della Casa, the learned and famous Archbishop of Benevento, who had been the friend of both sisters.

" Since it has pleased our Lord God to call to Himself, as one may say in the flower of her age, my very dear and much-loved sister, and she, departing, has taken with her all my hopes and consolations and life itself, I have tried to put all her things away out of sight, so that seeing them and dealing with them should not renew the bitter memory of her in my mind, or reopen the grievous wound made by the loss of so excellent a sister. And while I was wishing and

Tu volesti per noi, Signor, morire,
Tu ricomprasti tutto il seme umano ;
Dolce Signor, non mi lasciar perire."

intending to act in the same manner with these poems
of hers, composed by her, partly to exercise her talent,
great as ever woman had, if my sisterly affection does
not deceive me ; partly to express some of her amorous
ideas ; many talented gentlemen who loved her while
she was alive, have dissuaded me, against my will, from
this resolve, and have constrained me to collect all
those that could be found, showing me that, for the
sake of my own peace, I neither could nor ought to
hinder the glory of my sister by concealing her honourable labours. This then is why I have had them published, and the reason why I have preferred to dedicate
them to your most reverend Lordship rather than to
anyone else is this. . . . I am sure that in this I
shall also please the blessed soul of my beloved sister,
if yonder she has any sense or memory of the things
of this world, for, while she was alive, she always looked
up to your most reverend Lordship as to one of the
most shining lights of Italy, and had destined her
labours for you, always reverencing your name, and
bowing to your critical insight, whenever she discoursed
about it, which was very often, and praising to the
skies your most learned, graceful, and weighty writings,
to the level of all the ancients and moderns that are
read. Let not your most reverend Lordship then
disdain to receive, with that great kindness of heart
which God has given you, these few fruits of the
talent of my most lamented sister, by whom, while she
lived, you were so much honoured and revered ; being
glad that under the shadow of your most celebrated
name should repose also the pen, the study, the art,
and the amorous and fervent desires of a woman, with

so many other most divine works of the highest and most exquisite spirits of our age ; and with this, kissing your learned and holy hands, I make an end." [1]

Reviewing the work of Gaspara Stampa as a whole, though it cannot be said that her sonnets are free from convention (the same similes and illustrations being brought perpetually into play), there is a directness of treatment and often a very great simplicity which, at that time, were an originality in themselves. The *Capitoli* are, perhaps, her best work, giving her more scope than the sonnet form, and one or two of the madrigals are charming : the following has always been considered the most perfect :—

> " My heart with you would be,
>   My lord, as forth you fare,
>   Had it remained with me
>   Since with your eyes Love made me prisoner.
> Therefore with you shall go my sighs
>   Which only tarry here,
>   Faithful companions dear,
>   These and my words and cries;
>   And should you ever find your escort fled,
>   Then think that I am dead." [2]

---

[1] Letter prefaced to most editions of Gaspara's poems.

[2] " Il cor verrebbe teco,
>   Nel tuo partir, signore,
>   S' egli fosse più meco,
>   Poi che con gli occhi tuoi mi prese Amore.
> Dunque verranno teco i sospir miei,
>   Che sol mi son restati,
>   Fidi compagni e grati,
>   E le voci e gli omei ;
>   E, se vedi mancarti la lor scorta,
>   Pensa ch' io sarò morta."

It is, of course, evident that Gaspara was not a great artist ; yet, with her brilliant classical education and her ripe judgment, it is astonishing that she has not given us more thoughtful work ; but her unhappy passion for Collaltino wasted the powers of her heart and mind, and it is with immense sorrow and pity that we close the record of so much genius and beauty.

CHAPTER VIII

THE BEGINNING OF A TRAGEDY

> Let knowledge grow from more to more,
>   But more of reverence in us dwell ;
>   That mind and soul, according well,
> May make one music as before,
> But vaster.   TENNYSON.

IT is refreshing to pass from the weary, passion-tossed life of Gaspara Stampa to breathe again the loftier atmosphere which belongs to Vittoria Colonna. As a poet, one would hardly hesitate to give Gaspara the higher place : as a woman, no comparison would be possible.

For seven years Vittoria elected to sing her sorrow and her loss, and it is probable that the greater part of this time was passed by her at Ischia, where the circle in which she then found herself had very far-reaching effects on her later life and writings, and so it is to the realisation of this circle that the present chapter will be devoted.

The central figure of the Neapolitan group was certainly the Spaniard, Juan de Valdès. The names of the twin-brothers, Alfonso and Juan, have become strangely confused, so much so that some authors have contended that they were one and the same ; this controversy, however, has been finally laid to rest by the

Alinari.

Vittoria Colonna.
by Girolamo Muziano.
(Palazzo Colonna. Rome.)

discovery of a letter from Juan to Erasmus, dated January 12, 1533, in which he deplores Alfonso's death ; yet, from a literary standpoint, the latter remains a shadow, for the work which passed muster as his is now thought to have been chiefly his brother's. The two de Valdès, like most of the young Spanish nobles of the time, were educated by Pietro Martire d'Anghiera, an Italian who had come to Spain in the train of Mendoza, and was by him presented to Ferdinand and Isabella, with whom his influence became paramount.   At d'Anghiera's suggestion, Alfonso was subsequently made Latin Secretary to the Emperor Charles V, and it was he who, being present at the burning of Luther's books at Worms, said that it was " not the end but the beginning of a tragedy."   Both brothers were the warm friends of Erasmus, with whom their turn of mind had much similarity, and who had a boundless admiration for their scholarship.

There is some doubt whether Alfonso was an ecclesiastic, but Juan was certainly a layman, and occupied various posts at court.   When Adrian of Utrecht, the former tutor of Charles V, became Pope as Adrian VI in 1522, Juan was made one of his chamberlains. The appointment was of short duration, owing to the death of the Pope, but this residence at the papal court may have supplied copy for the Dialogues of *Mercury and Charon* and the *Sack of Rome*, which were published after the latter event and raised a storm of controversy.   The Dialogue on the Sack of Rome was written to prove that the whole blame attached to the Pope, and was a direct visitation of Providence for the crimes of the Papacy ; it was answered by Castiglione, who was then the papal envoy in Spain, with some dignity, but both documents are as violent and unrepaying as religio-political controversy never fails to be. Alfonso alone acknowledged the authorship of this work, probably feeling that his position as state-secretary was a sufficient protection for him, and if Juan had a hand in it, it is strangely unlike any of his subsequent writings.

The *Mercury and Charon* was always attributed to Juan, who states in the preface that the chief reason which had induced him to write it was his great desire to manifest to the world the justice of Charles V, and the iniquity of those who had provoked and betrayed him into war. This statement might lead us to expect a wholly political document, but, while a very remarkable knowledge of contemporary politics is shown and very clear-sighted judgments pronounced, the conversation, which purports to take place between the boatman of the Styx and Mercury, the messenger of the gods, and many passing souls, deals with domestic life, religion, and education from an original point of view. The author did not feel himself safe in Spain after its publication, but went to Naples, where there was no Inquisition, in 1530; the two following years he was in Rome and Bologna, but in the autumn of 1533 he returned to Naples and did not leave it again, becoming secretary to the Viceroy, Don Pedro de Toledo, and it is from this point that for us the interest of his life dates.

There will always be those who thrive on controversy, of whom it will be said that they are "subtle at tierce and quart of mind with mind," and who thoroughly enjoy the process, but such are not the most lovable, nor, perhaps, the most influential characters: anything of the kind was quite foreign to the gentle, contemplative nature of Juan. Like the men of his time—and surely of every time—he could not but bewail the shortcomings of the rulers of the Church, but he had no desire for reformation from without: the saving qualities of loyalty and humility preserved him from this. Certainly he never incited anyone to leave the Church, or thought of doing so himself, nor did he imagine himself to be a leader of men ; his teaching was always of a private character, he never expected, or probably desired, to influence the masses, but simply applied himself to helping those immediately around him, striving rather to build up than to destroy, and, by simplifying religion, to make it at once attractive and attainable. A scholar, though not a theologian, he felt, along with Erasmus, that we cannot afford to turn our back upon the wisdom of the ages ; modesty and humility breathe through all that he wrote, and it would have seemed to him the merest foolishness that men should engage without a guide in the most complicated, the most intricate study to which the human mind can ever apply itself.

Whatever else there was in what is known as the Reformation, there was in it this crude folly, that the fabric built up laboriously by wisdom and patience, the truth which many errors had chiselled out, was placed at the mercy of the immature and the untrained: in particular, it was left to the caprice and the idiosyncrasy of individual opinion, and so the history of Protestantism inevitably tends to become a mere history of sects.

But though the mind of Valdès exhibited points of resemblance with that of Erasmus, in the main the two men were conspicuously different. To the latter, classical learning was the chief attraction, but the Greek speculative spirit found no response in him ; he was neither a philosopher nor a mystic. None has ever seen more clearly than he the value of scholarship, none pursued it with more devotion, or was more instrumental in throwing open the doors of knowledge to his own and succeeding generations. His object was the union of the classical and the Christian, and, by grafting the one upon the other, to set mankind on the way to a sounder, saner progress : it was a new aim and a high one, but perhaps a trifle superficial, containing only such elements as made it rather a noble idea than a noble ideal. Juan de Valdès, taking rank far below Erasmus as a scholar, yet saw other and higher things than he. He lived among the realities that cannot be uttered, and realised, as all mystics do, the futility of words, which, far from being the embodiment of our thoughts, are scarcely the similitudes of them, and barely even the symbols.

It is this which sharply divides the mystic from the theologian and the scholar, that, soaring so far into the suprasensible, all outward things lose their actuality, and forms, from their very inadequacy, hardly seem worth preserving. In this, as in all things, there is a golden mean, but, while materialism has its votaries, how would it be with us if the mystics ceased to exist ?

Grouped around Valdès, the names of Carnesecchi and Pietro Martire Vermigli, and of Ochino (with whom Vittoria Colonna and Caterina Cibo were specially connected), make a confused picture in our mind ; while the great ladies, Isabella Manriquez, the Duchessa Costanza d'Avalos of Amalfi, and Giulia Gonzaga, float no less vaguely before our eyes, and we need to arrange and focus them before they can really mean anything to us.   Of these, Giulia Gonzaga and Pietro Carnesecchi were particularly the disciples of Valdès.

Born in 1499, Giulia Gonzaga was the daughter of Lodovico di Gian Francesco Gonzaga, Signor of Sabbioneta, and when only thirteen was married to Vespasiano Colonna, a widower of forty with one daughter, Isabella.   Vespasiano, dying in 1528, left all his estates to his wife, but two claimants arose for them, one being Ascanio Colonna, Vittoria's brother ; it is greatly to the credit of both ladies that this circumstance never interrupted the friendly relations that existed between them.   Clement VII substantiated Giulia's rights, and, when put into possession of her domains, she took up her residence at Fondi.   In the meantime her stepdaughter, by marrying Luigi " Rodomonte " Gonzaga, had become her sister-in-law, and many family complications ensued and much weary litigation took place.   Isabella questioned her stepmother's right to the income of her father's estates, and also refused to give up many valuable heirlooms. Giulia seems to have acted throughout with great judgment and forbearance, and a compromise was at last effected.

Sung by Ariosto as the fairest woman of her time,[1] and celebrated in contemporary letters and poems as a beauty and a poetess, the fame of Giulia Gonzaga caused her a very terrifying experience in 1534 when the African corsair, Khair-ed-din Barbarossa, attempted to carry her off. Coming to Fondi, he disembarked at midnight; the inhabitants of the little town, alarmed and surprised, could make small resistance, but fortunately the uproar aroused the castle, and Giulia escaped by a secret passage and rode to Vallecorsa, while the corsair, disappointed of his object, only plundered the town and retired. Among the many who flocked to Giulia's assistance was Cardinal Ippolito de' Medici, a former suitor for her hand; the enemy having departed, there was nothing for him to do, but he took the opportunity of begging the lady to allow him to send the painter, Sebastiano del Piombo, to paint her portrait for himself. We gather from Vasari that he was a month doing it and that, owing to the celestial beauty of the subject, it was one of the painter's most successful pictures. It is strange to find it said that this is the portrait now in the National Gallery.

It is not surprising that, after this episode, Giulia elected to leave Fondi and live in Naples, where she established herself in the Convent of S. Chiara, using her own beautiful house for business and for the reception of her friends. Knowing what we do of her family troubles, we can imagine that, in spite of her charms, her cultivation, and her resources, she can have had but a weary life, and this gives us special light to understand her intercourse with Valdès and

[1] *Orl. Fur.*, XLVI. 8.

the position he held on her horizon. She was his
devoted disciple : Isabella Manriquez, the wife of Don
Garzia Manriquez, the governor of Piacenza ; Vittoria's
aunt and cousin, the Principessa of Francavilla and the
Duchessa of Amalfi ; Vittoria herself ; all were notable
figures in the circle of Valdès, but with none was his
influence so supreme as with Giulia Gonzaga.   And it
was to her that he owed his most noted follower of the
other sex, Pietro Carnesecchi ; it is true they had met
in Rome, at the court of Clement VII, but Carnesecchi
says he had never known him as a theologian until the
time of their intercourse in Naples, and that it was to
Giulia that he was indebted for this intimate knowledge.

Belonging to a Florentine family of high rank that
had always followed the fortunes of the Medici, Pietro
Carnesecchi was appointed secretary by Clement VII
when he became Pope, and was not only loaded with
honours, being presented with two abbeys, one in the
kingdom of Naples and one in France, but was so
much consulted and deferred to that it became a
popular saying that the Church was controlled more by
Carnesecchi than by Clement.   Poet, orator, and scholar,
Carnesecchi numbered among his friends Cardinals
Pole, Sadoleto, and Bembo, and also Flaminio and
Vittoria Colonna.   He made the acquaintance of the
latter in Rome in 1534, when she and Caterina Cibo
hastened thither simultaneously to intercede with the
Pope for the newly founded order of the Cappuccini,
which Clement, incited thereto by the jealousy of the
parent-order, the Osservanti, had just banished from the
city.   Ochino is sometimes erroneously said to have

founded the Cappuccini, but the real founder was Fra
Matteo da Bassi who, together with Lodovico da
Fossombrone, left the Osservanti in 1526, desiring to
keep a stricter rule. Their earliest patron was Caterina
Cibo, Duchessa of Camerino, who allowed them to
settle near Camerino, and offered to build them a
convent, but they contented themselves with a little
church and a house near it, with which Caterina presented them, and she was instrumental in obtaining
from the Pope the confirmation of their order, which at
first constantly suffered persecution. To her and to
Vittoria Colonna this revival of the soul of St. Francis
seemed a cause worth championing, and Vittoria wrote
long letters on its behalf to Cardinals Contarini and
Ercole Gonzaga, and in 1534 helped to obtain from
Clement the revocation of the edict of their banishment from Rome.

But to us the chief interest of the new-born order
centres in one remarkable man, whose career is full of
interest and excitement and, whether regarded as a
triumph or a failure, is at all events a tragedy. Bernardino Ochino was born in Siena in 1487, and his
name is probably derived from the contrada of the city
which he inhabited, which had for its ensign a white
goose (*oca*) ; to this district St. Catherine had belonged,
and while he lived in sight of her house, walked the
same streets, saw the same sights, how much did he
know of the desires of her heart ? How much, too,
had he in common with his own namesake and spiritual
father, San Bernardino ? For a while, at any rate, their
feet were set on the same path ; where and how did
the road divide ?

Little is known of his early life ; he is thought to
have been a page of Pandolfo Petrucci, then a great
power in Siena, and this idea is favoured by the fact of
his joining the Osservanza, a convent specially endowed
and protected by Petrucci. There he was both General
and Provincial, but he left it in 1534 to join the stricter
order of the Cappuccini, six years after it had been
confirmed by the Pope. Going to Rome with the
other members of the order, one and fifty in all, he
passed through the crisis of their banishment and
recall, and there, no doubt for the first time, came into
contact with Caterina Cibo and Vittoria Colonna.
The Marchesa was then residing with the Sisters of
San Silvestro, and Agostino Gonzaga writes of her to
the Marchesa Isabella, that she does not wish to be
visited by anyone, and likes to go about Rome unrecognised and in the poorest clothes. He also says
that she is attending the sermons in San Lorenzo in
Damaso where the preacher is Fra Bernardino of Siena,
a very learned man of most holy life, who has wonderful fervour and a most perfect voice.[1] There was then
a rumour, which Agostino mentions, that Vittoria and
Caterina Cibo were thinking of entering a convent of
the rule of Santa Chiara, recently founded in Naples
by a Spanish lady, Maria Longa, but the project, if it
had existed, was never carried out. Vittoria, however,
continued to wear her " abito abietissimo," and seems
to have imposed the same on the ladies who accompanied her to Ferrara.

In 1535, Ochino was again preaching in Rome, and
appealed to Vittoria on behalf of the order, when Fra

---

[1] Luzio, *Vittoria Colonna*, p. 26.

Lodovico refused to convene the General Chapter.
The Marchesa, keenly interested in the fortunes of the
Cappuccini, made an appeal to Paul III, and obtained a
direct command from him, which resulted in Bernardino
of Asti being made Vicar-General and Ochino one of
the four generals.   From this period Ochino's fame as
a preacher grew rapidly, and he was so much sought
after that the Pope reserved to himself the right of
sending him where he would.   Every city in Italy
clamoured for him, while Siena pressed a special claim.
And so he climbed to the most perilous of all positions,
that of being a great popular preacher; for there is no
influence so personal as that of an orator; from a ruler,
a statesman, or a soldier, we demand something more
than mere words, but the spell of the orator lies in his
voice and in his speech; with these he has to captivate,
to mould, and to master: it is a most insidious power,
making the largest demands on the truthfulness of a
man's nature and the balance of his mind.

In the Lent of 1536, Ochino was preaching at Naples,
in San Giovanni Maggiore, and Charles V went to hear
him several times, and is reported to have said that such
a spirit and devotion would make the stones weep.
The Emperor left Naples in the spring for Rome, and
accepted the hospitality of Ascanio Colonna at Marino
for a night, making from thence a triumphal entry into
the city, and being received with great ceremony and
festivities.   He remained twelve days and found time
to make formal visits to the wife of Ascanio, and to
her sister-in-law, Vittoria Colonna.   His interview with
the latter is interesting as being the occasion on which
she implored him to make peace at home and turn his

arms against the infidel, pressing on him the glory of undertaking a Crusade : it seems to link her to the best period of history to know that she lived at a time when such a hope was even possible, although alas ! never realised. Even her cherished idea of going on pilgrimage to the Holy Land, for which the Pope gave her facilities, never came to pass, although it was with great reluctance that she finally abandoned it, owing to her delicate health and to the apprehension felt on her account by her brother and del Vasto.

The plan was still in her mind when she journeyed to Ferrara in the following year ; she meant to proceed to Venice and to embark from thence, but the difficulties in the way were too great for her, and the result was that she remained at Ferrara for ten months, living a most austere life in the Convent of Santa Caterina, and worshipped by the whole city for her charity and good works. We say " the whole city " advisedly, for it was not to one kind or one class that Vittoria was acceptable. At the invitation of Duke Ercole II, the most learned men in Venetia and Lombardy hastened to Ferrara to do her honour, while Cardinal Gonzaga tried to induce her to come to Mantua, and her old friend, Giberti, despatched his secretary, Francesco della Torre, to bring her to Verona, on which account the latter was in danger of rough handling from the Ferrarese, who said he wished to rob them of their greatest treasure.

A special interest attaches to this Ferrarese Convent of Santa Caterina. It was built in 1499 by Ercole I for the Beata Lucia of Narni when, after many fruitless attempts and prolonged struggles, he at length

P

succeeded in procuring her presence in his capital.   In
her honour the convent was planned, and it was on
account of the visions she had during its erection that
it was dedicated to St. Catherine of Siena.   Nothing
of it now stands, though the site is still known,
and happily some details remain to us of the decora-
tion of the building.   There were two frescoes of St.
Catherine outside the convent, and several scenes
from her life were depicted in the cortile ; also the
Duke ordered many pictures to be executed for
the interior, two of which had St. Catherine for their
subject.   It is strange, indeed, that all should have
vanished, but stranger far is the history of her for
whom it was raised.

Born at Narni in 1476, Lucia was forced into marriage by her uncles at an early age, but left her
husband when she was only eighteen, and became a
Dominican nun.   In 1496, she was sent by the General
of the Order to Viterbo, to direct a house of Dominican tertiaries, and there she received the Stigmata, had
wonderful visions, and was a living miracle.   All the
details of these marvels were sent to Duke Ercole by
his nephew, who was then Governor of Viterbo, and
the Duke used every effort to persuade the holy nun
to come and live at Ferrara.   Lucia herself made no
opposition, but the people of Viterbo were so determined not to part with her that it was some time
before Ercole could accomplish his purpose.   However, the transfer was effected at last, and Lucia became the trusted friend and adviser of the Duke,
besides being placed at the head of the convent, and
having special rules and privileges granted to her.   It

is not astonishing to find that this did not produce harmony; Lucia was too young to enforce her authority, and jealousies ensued. During the Duke's lifetime, his favour and support were sufficient to maintain his favourite in her position, though not to ensure peace, but the sequel to the story is the saddest and strangest part of all.

Lucia was only twenty-nine at the time of Ercole's death; as soon as she was deprived of his countenance, the members of the convent took from her all authority and every privilege that had been hers, and for nearly forty years—until her death in 1544—they kept her a prisoner. It is terrible to think what she must have suffered during those years, but she is said to have borne everything with the utmost humility and patience, still comforted by visions of St. Catherine.

The dictum of St. Philip Neri about the wonder-working nun, who refused to pull off his boots, is well known : "here is no miracle, for here is no humility." In the case of Lucia, we might well think that the greatness of the second miracle is sufficient to vouch for the truth of the first, for verily the second is the greater, since humility is the steepest, furthest height that human nature ever attains. But the story does not end here : with that extraordinary revulsion of feeling of which history furnishes so many examples, no sooner was the despised nun dead than all the members of the community hailed her as a saint, and made fruitless reparation by preserving her body as a sacred relic.[1]

---

[1] See Mr. Edmund Gardner's *Dukes and Poets in Ferrara*, from which this account is taken.

Now it is evident that Lucia must have been alive
and shut up in the convent during Vittoria's residence
there, and it seems unlikely that the Marchesa should
not have been aware of this, for Lucia's advent in
Ferrara was an event which had made some stir, and
was not very ancient history ; moreover, it was history of a nature that was particularly interesting to
Vittoria ; still, there is no record of any intercourse
having taken place between them, though it is certain
that the Ferrarese convent possessed a very great
attraction for the illustrious visitor, who recurs to it
again and again.

The ostensible reason for the Marchesa's visit to
Ferrara seems to have been Ochino's request that she
would obtain leave for him to found a convent there ;
this the Duke readily granted, making over to him a
piece of land and a house, so that he and some of his
companions established themselves there in August,
and, in Advent, Fra Bernardino preached before the
court. It is also said that Ercole had warmly welcomed
Vittoria in hopes of relieving the strained relations
which existed between him and his wife, the Duchessa
Renata, who was thought to favour the reformed
opinions, and had been entertaining Calvin under an
assumed name. If this were so, Renata could hardly
have fallen into better hands than Vittoria's, whose
tact, sympathy, and supreme and intelligent interest
in religion were strong enough to draw together two
women so completely different, and from this time
dated the better conditions of court-life at Ferrara; the
Marchesa was godmother to Renata's daughter, Leonora,
whose name Torquato Tasso was to make famous.

Vittoria was evidently well-content from one point of view with her life at Ferrara, for she thus writes of it to Cardinal Ercole Gonzaga : " It has pleased God that I should find much quiet and consolation in Ferrara. Thanks be to God, his Excellence the Duke and all of them leave me the liberty that I desire to attend only to true acts of charity, and not to such mixed ones as are produced by conversation. May it please the Divine Goodness that all my time here may be so spent that none of it may be mine but all Christ's." Unfortunately, the place was not good for her health, as we see from her letters to Trissino and Aretino. Her charities must have been considerable, as she tells the latter that she cannot afford to go " to a little place in the Bolognese I go to for change of air."

On the other hand, the Marchesa was no stranger to the life of the court, and was present at several of the great entertainments. In particular, the evening before her departure, we hear of her assisting at a farewell festival, organised by the Marchesa Isabella d'Este, who had arrived the week before, and whose incomparable ladies contributed the dancing and the music, while Vittoria recited five of her own sonnets, to the admiration of the company. She always retained a pleasant memory of Ferrara, and always hoped to return there. Once, when writing from the Convent of Santa Caterina in Viterbo, she says : " Not that most beautiful one in Ferrara"; and, in a letter to the Duke, she writes that she will be sure to pray to God to let her return to his most sweet Ferrara.[1] Taking her departure in February, 1538, the Mar-

---

[1] Letters LXXXV, LXXXVIII, CLXII, CVIII.

chesa went to the above-mentioned Castello in the Bolognese, and stayed there a month. After this, her movements seem to have been guided by those of Ochino, who certainly had acquired a great influence over her. She proceeds first to Florence and then to Lucca, in both which places he is preaching, and here he has also Cardinal Pole and Pietro Carnesecchi for his attentive listeners. The latter, who had known him previously in Rome, went to visit him two or three times, and also became more intimate with Vittoria. Guidiccioni, writing at this date to Annibale Caro, says : "A few days ago, I heard in Lucca Fra Bernardino of Siena—a truly wonderful man, and he pleased me so much that I addressed two sonnets to him." [1]

Ochino's sermons, as usual, were much in request ; early in the year, Bembo had written from Venice to beg the Marchesa to use her influence to get him to preach there during the following Lent, which he did, and it was then that Fra Bonaventura, a former Minorite, presented him with a church and house, thus enabling him to found his first convent in Venice. Meanwhile, Ochino had been appointed apostolic missionary by the Pope, and had also been elected Vicar-General of his Order, and under him the Cappuccini spread and flourished. He sent Fra Marino to Corsica, and others to found new convents in many Italian towns, while he devoted his own energies to preaching. Vittoria, recalled to Rome by Pope Paul III, settled there towards the end of 1538, and it is in the follow-

---

[1] Letter xxvii (undated) in *Opere di Monsignor G. Guidiccioni*, ed. Minutoli. The sonnets are those numbered 72 and 73 in this edition.

ing year that we have the fullest account of her intercourse with Michelangelo, as reported in the conversations of Francisco d'Ollanda, already quoted. It is strange that the course of sermons of which he tells us, that the Marchesa was attending in San Silvestro, should have been preached by the man who was afterwards the bitter enemy of Ochino. This was the Dominican friar, Ambrogio Politi, whom we have already met, also a native of Siena, who was deputed to write an answer to the letter Ochino addressed to the magistracy of that city in 1542, and who subsequently wrote a long epistle against his "pestilential doctrine."

That Ochino had no less success in Venice than elsewhere we learn from Bembo's letters to Vittoria. Writing first on February 23, 1539, he says : " I send your most illustrious Ladyship the particulars of our very reverend Frate Bernardino, whom I have heard all the few days of this present Lent with such great pleasure as I cannot adequately describe. I confess that I never heard anyone preach more usefully or devoutly than he. Neither do I wonder that your Ladyship loves him as much as you do. He is very different from all the others who have occupied the pulpit in my time ; he speaks in a more Christian manner, and with a more lively charity, and of better and more profitable things. He pleases everybody beyond measure, and I believe, when he goes, he will carry away with him the heart of all this city. For all this we owe undying thanks to your Ladyship, who sent him to us, and I, more than others, feel eternally obliged to you." Two other letters, dealing chiefly with Bembo's elevation to the purple, follow this, and in both the Frate is mentioned. "I am speaking to your Ladyship as I spoke this morning to the reverend father, Frate Bernardino, to whom I opened all my heart and mind as I would have opened them to Jesus Christ, to Whom I believe him to be most dear and acceptable, nor do I think I ever spoke with a holier man than he." And again: "Our Frate Bernardino— whom henceforth I will call *mine* in speaking to you— is now adored in this city; there is neither man nor woman here who does not praise him to the skies. O how great his influence is, how he pleases, how much he helps! But I will wait to speak of him to your Ladyship face to face. And yet I have thought of begging the Pope to order his life in such a manner that it may last longer for the honour of God and the profit of man than it can do, living as austerely as he does."[1]

In view of Ochino's enormous popularity as a preacher, one would like to form some idea of the reason of his attractiveness. There was first of all his reputation for holiness and mortification, which was borne out by his remarkable appearance—his spiritual cast of countenance and long venerable beard; his voice, too, was distinguished for sweetness and penetration, and he had the gift of sympathy, while for his matter he had certainly struck out a new line, treating the Scriptures in an original way, not contradicting, but disregarding, accepted interpretations. Even on the burning question of justification by faith he had not, up till now, excited any suspicions of unorthodoxy, for this, though (like all best things)

---

[1] Bembo, *Opere*, Vol. VIII, pp. 109–113.

peculiarly capable of being "confused to ill," is a completely Catholic doctrine when it is understood to mean *operative* faith, and in this sense Ochino appeared to preach it at this time, and was so understood by his constant disciples and admirers, Vittoria Colonna and Caterina Cibo, neither of whom ever followed him to his later conclusions.

After his Lent sermons in Venice, Ochino must have returned to Florence, as it is to the year 1539 that the *Seven Dialogues* are attributed. These were conversations which took place chiefly between himself and the Duchessa of Camerino on a variety of religious subjects. They are strictly orthodox, but, for the most part, dry ; there is nothing spontaneous about them, as in the dialogue between Valdès and Giulia Gonzaga which we shall presently consider. There is, indeed, one singularly naive remark of Caterina's, who, when the Frate is urging upon her the duty of striving after perfection, replies : "I should like to be perfect, only it must not give me too much trouble" ;[1] but this is curiously out of character with the didactic tone of the rest, which appears to consist of set-pieces designed to show off the erudition of the lady and the skill of Ochino as a dialectician.

Passing through Rome, where he most probably visited the Marchesa, Ochino went to preach in Naples during Advent. He must have felt singularly at home in the Valdessian circle, where life lived on a high plane offered such facilities for the attainment of the true ends of existence. We think of the group as a

---

[1] K. Benrath, *Bernardino Ochino*, English translation, pp. 71–84. These *Dialogues* are not in the British Museum.

learned, leisured, little community, not narrow or self-
centred, but looking out with interested eyes for the
best that was to be had in religion, in literature, and in
language, and eagerly welcoming every new mind, and
everything that promised an idea. Their number had
been augmented by Pietro Martire Vermigli, a Florentine of very remarkable talents, who had entered the
Augustinian convent at Fiesole in 1516, but had left
it to complete his studies at Padua, and was a proficient
Greek and Hebrew scholar. He was made Abbot of
Spoleto and visitor-general of the Order, and later
was Prior of San Pietro ad Aram in Naples, where
he preached on St. Paul's Epistles, and his sermons
attracted great attention. Carnesecchi and Marcantonio Flaminio also came south together about this
time, on account of the latter's health. These were
eminently fitted to form a part of such a society ;
Flaminio probably had most in common with Valdès,
combining, as he did, profound scholarship with great
refinement of taste ; while Carnesecchi, as we have
noticed, was the special friend of Giulia Gonzaga, and
was by her presented to Valdès, an introduction which
must have availed him much. Ochino consulted
Valdès about the matter of his sermons, and was sometimes indebted to him for a subject, but the two men
were of different mould ; holding, as it might seem on
the surface, the same opinions, each carried them to
a very different conclusion. The genius of Valdès'
mind would rather have inclined him never to come to
a crisis, nor to put into words that which is beyond
words ; while to Ochino's more direct intelligence it
was a necessity to crystallise ; neither was his intellect

sufficiently strong, nor his vision sufficiently wide, to show him exactly where he was tending, so that he was rather the victim of a surprise than of a decision. Meantime he preached, and out of one of his sermons grew the most charming of Valdès' writings.

This was the *Alfabeto Cristiano*, a conversation which took place between Valdès and Giulia Gonzaga, after listening to a discourse of Fra Bernardino's on heaven and hell.[1] The principal charm of the dialogue lies in its absolute naturalness ; we can quite understand that two friends did talk together like this, and, as it is entirely natural, so it is in no wise out of date ; a woman of the present day might, and no doubt does, say and feel the same, and might, if fate were kind to her, receive the same gentle reproof : " You want me to show you some royal and august road by which you may get to God without forsaking the world." She begs Valdès not to press too many mortifications on her " lest everything should become indifferent to me "—surely a natural protest, for that is the real test of what we are willing to forego : few are so poor-spirited as not to be able to make some great renunciation and bear the pain of it ; but to renounce little by little, and come to feel not pain but indifference, and so despoil life of outward loveliness, this is heroism ; but Valdès did not lead his pupil so far.

Other works he wrote for her—a translation of and commentary on the Psalms and St. Paul's Epistles, and a translation of St. Matthew's Gospel.

---

[1] *Alphabeto Christiano, che insegna la vera via d' acquistare il lume dello Spirito Santo,* printed without indication of place or publisher, in 1546.

At his country-house near Chiaja, Valdès was accustomed to assemble a select circle of his friends, Sunday after Sunday ; here they breakfasted with him, walked in the garden, and read portions of Scripture on which he commented.   In the afternoon, the tables were turned, and the master, having employed his disciples according to his own pleasure all the morning, now gave himself up to obey theirs, and placed his vast culture at their disposal, and in this manner the *Dialogo de la Lengua*, a disquisition on the Spanish language, something on the plan of Bembo's *Prose della Volgar Lingua*, is said to have originated.   Questioned on the difference between genius and judgment, Valdès replied : "Genius discovers what may be said, and Judgment selects from what Genius discovers.   Had I to choose, I should prefer a man with but moderate genius and good judgment, because men of great genius lose themselves through want of judgment. Man has no jewel to compare with a sound judgment."[1]   Probably, this was where Ochino fell short.

Such of the Commentaries as remain to us do not seem much more illuminating than that kind of literature usually is.   The *Hundred and Ten Considerations* are far more original, and have an additional interest for us from the fact that they were translated into English by Nicholas Ferrar, and submitted by him to his friend, George Herbert, who returned them with a few comments and the following letter :—

"My deare and deserving Brother, your Valdesso I now returne with many thanks, and some notes, in

---

[1] Cf. Wiffen, *Life and Writings of Juan de Valdès*, p. 99.

which perhaps you will discover some care, which
I forbare not in the midst of my griefes ; First, for
your sake because I would doe nothing negligently that
you commit unto mee ; Secondly, for the Author's
sake, whom I conceive to have been a true servant of
God ; and to such, and all that is theirs, I owe diligence ; Thirdly, for the Churches sake, to whom, by
printing it, I would have you consecrate it. You owe
the Church a debt and God hath put this into your
hands (as he sent the fish with money to St. Peter) to
discharge it : happily also with this (as his thoughts
are fruitfull) intending the honour of his servant the
Author, who being obscured in his own country he
would have to flourish in this land of light, and region
of the Gospell, among his chosen. It is true, there are
some things which I like not in him, as my fragments
will expresse, when you read them ; neverthelesse I
wish you by all meanes to publish it, for these three
eminent things observable therein : First, that God in
the midst of Popery should open the eyes of one to
understand and expresse so clearly and excellently the
intent of the Gospell in the acceptation of Christ's
righteousnesse (as he showeth through all his considerations), a thing strangely buried and darkened
by the Adversaries, and their great stumbling-block.
Secondly, the great honour and reverence which he
everywhere beares towards our deare Master and Lord,
concluding every Consideration almost with his holy
Name, and setting his merit forth so piously, for which
I doe so love him, that were there nothing else I would
print it, that with it the honour of my Lord might be
published. Thirdly, the many pious rules of ordering

our life, about mortification, and observation of God's Kingdome within us, and the working thereof, of which he was a very diligent observer. These three things are very eminent in the Author, and overweigh the defects (as I conceive) towards the publishing thereof, etc.

" Benmorton, Sept. 29."

Of Considerations III and XXXII, which regard the use of the Scriptures, Herbert says in his notes : "I like none of it"; and in another place : "His opinion of the Scriptures is unsufferable." The Publisher also seems to have had qualms, for he thus addresses the Reader : " It is certain that the book containeth many very worthy discourses of experimental and practical Divinity, well expressed and elegantly illustrated ; especially concerning the doctrine of justification and mortification, and yet, notwithstanding, there be some few expressions and similitudes in it, at which not only the weak reader may stumble, and the curious quarrell, but also the wise and charitable reader may justly blame. . . . It hath been thought fit to print the book, according to the Author's own copy, but withal to give particular notice of some suspicious places and of some manifest errors."[1]

These *Hundred and Ten Considerations* are thought to have been the substance of Valdès' Sunday-morning conversations for about two years, and they were also

---

[1] *The Hundred and Ten Considerations of Signior John Valdesso : treating of those things which are most profitable, most necessary, and most perfect in our Christian Profession.*   Oxford, 1638.

circulated as meditations. Another book, *Del beneficio di Cristo*, much read and talked of, was at one time attributed to Valdès, but it is now generally believed to have been the work of a Benedictine monk, Don Benedetto of Mantua, who wrote it in a monastery of his Order near Mount Etna, and asked his friend, Flaminio, to polish and improve it, an embellishment to which it probably owed its immense success. It dealt, of course, with the question of justification by faith, on which, we must always remember, no pronouncement had yet been made. The *Alfabeto* establishes Valdès' orthodoxy on this point, for he expressly states in it that a lively faith cannot fail to work deeds of charity, any more than a fire can fail to warm.

These tranquil years at Naples, however, were drawing to a close, for the storm was soon to break, and death was indeed kind to the master-mover. We have no particulars of the death of Valdès, except that the Archbishop of Otranto was one of those who were with him ; we only know that he died very peacefully in 1541 ; he could not have been more than fifty. Few men could have left a larger circle of intimate friends to mourn them. The historian Bonfadio, writing to Carnesecchi, says : " Where shall we go now Signor Valdès is dead ? This has been a great loss for us and for the world, because Signor Valdès was one of the exceptional men of Europe, and those writings which he has left on the Epistles of St. Paul and the Psalms of David are the fullest testimony to it. He was without doubt in his deeds, his words, and all his counsels, a perfect man. He governed his frail, feeble body with a particle of his mind ; with the greater part, and by sheer intellect, as though out of the body, he raised himself to the contemplation of truth and of divine things."[1]

Happily, the mantle of Valdès had fallen on Flaminio, and the same way of life was to be reproduced at Viterbo.

---

[1] *Lettere famigliari di Jacopo Bonfadio* (Brescia, 1746), p. 22.

CHAPTER IX

IN THE STORM

For hers, in peace or strife,
  Was a Queen's life.
                    D. G. ROSSETTI.

VITTORIA must often have wished herself one of that
peaceful Valdessian circle during the political storms
of 1540 and 1541. Pope Paul III, dominated by the
ignoble desire of enriching his family, and not averse
to humbling the power of the great houses, had imposed many taxes from time to time, and in particular
in 1540 had increased the duty on salt, at the same
time compelling all the cities and provinces to receive
it from Rome. Perugia resisted this arbitrary decree,
but only to her own destruction. Ascanio Colonna
should have been warned by her example, more especially as his sister was then living in Rome and, being
in contact with the papal court, was able to know
something of the mind of the Pope. The Marchesa
had already endeavoured to strengthen the Colonnese
position by trying to arrange a marriage between Vittoria Farnese, the Pope's granddaughter, and Fabrizio
Colonna, Ascanio's eldest son ; but the project fell
through because the Farnese really desired a more
powerful alliance, and Ascanio's well-known avarice
prevented his making a suitable settlement.

In the present instance of the salt-tax, Ascanio determined to contest the point, all the more that some
of his subjects, being in Rome and refusing to comply
with the decree, had been thrown into prison.   Ascanio,
roused to fury by this insult, made sundry raids from
his two castles of Paliano and Rocca di Papa, coming
right up to the walls of Rome, carrying off cattle, and
doing damage, in consequence of which the Pope commanded him to appear before him, to which the refractory noble made no answer except that he was a loyal
vassal of the Church.   It is probable that Ascanio, with
all his Spanish and Neapolitan connections, counted too
surely on the support of the Emperor and of the Viceroy of Naples ; but they only urgently advised him to
come to terms with the Pope.   Charles V had recently
united himself with the Farnese by giving the hand of
his widowed daughter, Margaret of Austria, to Ottavio,
the son of Pier Luigi Farnese, and was in no mind to
involve himself in a papal quarrel : Vittoria, at any
rate, expected no active help from him.

The real greatness of the Marchesa is nowhere more
clearly shown than now, when she held aloof from all
petty intrigues and jealousies, trusted and respected by
all.   Several letters were exchanged between the brother
and sister in the early days of March, 1541, and they
are interesting as showing the place Vittoria occupied
in the eyes of all concerned.   She was corresponding
with the Emperor at Ratisbon, and constantly inter-
viewing the imperial ambassador, the Marqués de Agui-
lar, and his secretary, Conciano.   Leading, as she no
doubt did at the Convent of San Silvestro, that life
"troppo dismessamente", on account of which it is said

that the Pope had recalled her to Rome, she did not forget that she was a Roman Princess : "Casa Colonna sempre è la prima." At the same time, her anxious desire is for a peaceful settlement; she tells her brother that " there was no need for so much war about thirty cows," and presses on him the Emperor's advice to arrive at a compromise, now urging him to one surrender, now to another, though probably too well acquainted with his wilful, impracticable temper to entertain any hopes of peace.[1]

The whole burden of the negotiations fell upon the Marchesa, who was the only one who acted in entire good faith ; for the Pope, under the pretext of reducing an unruly vassal to submission, was really seeking to despoil the House of Colonna ; the Emperor, on account of his newly-made alliance with the Farnese, was but half-hearted in his support of those who had been uniformly faithful to him, while the rashness and procrastinations of Ascanio made it impossible to act with or for him.

Vittoria elected to remain in Rome as long as there seemed to be the slenderest chance of peace, and then chose to retire to Orvieto, the papal city *par excellence* (Pope Paul had been its Arch-priest and had always shown it special favour), that she might be at hand to watch events, and, while she allowed her vassals to bear arms in her brother's cause, she managed, at the same time, to keep up friendly relations with the Farnese. Before leaving Rome, she sustained the loss of her devoted companion, and secretary, Innocenza Gualteruzzi, whom she had brought up and educated,

---

[1] *Carteggio*, Letters cxxviii to cxxxv.

and who now took the veil at San Silvestro. Parting
from her must have been an additional trial to the
Marchesa, when she left Rome at such a gloomy
moment for the fortunes of her House.

It was on March 17 that she proceeded to Orvieto,
and it is characteristic of her that she again selected
a Dominican convent for her residence. The Convent
of San Paolo, originally an offshoot of the Benedictine
San Paolo in Rome, was given over to the rule of
St. Dominic by Benedict XI in 1303, and was always
noted for the holy lives of its inmates. One of these
had been Suora Daniella, the friend of St. Catherine, who
addressed several letters to her. Also this convent
was one of the first to be imbued with the spirit of
reform inculcated by Savonarola, and from it reformers
were sent forth to found other houses.

We like to think, as we see her moving from one
Dominican convent to another, that some spark of the
spirit of St. Catherine was alight in her—that spirit
which ennobled the sordid and the tortuous, and was
never brought low by what it dealt with, thereby
witnessing to the truth that it is not the events or the
possessions of our lives which can elevate or lower,
but that their meaning for us depends wholly on the
height to which we can raise them. In these months
of petty, inglorious warfare, the one beautiful thing is
the life of Vittoria, which commanded the admiration
of friends and enemies alike ; for, indeed, she was surrounded, if not with enemies, at least with spies, all
her doings were noted and reported, her visitors
chronicled, her letters read, and under this search-light
there was nothing but what was blameless to be revealed.

All her biographers say that the breath of scandal never touched her, and assuredly this does not mean that she lived only among the charitable and the uncensorious, but rather that, hedged in by dignity and reserve, she chose for herself a way of watchfulness and perpetual renunciation.

It would seem that the Marchesa's arrival at Orvieto was an unexpected thing, as the people were not at first aware of her presence, so that no special reception was accorded to her ; but two days afterwards, the governor, Brunamonte de' Rossi, called a council at which it was agreed that, owing to the rank and importance of the illustrious guest, and considering the honour in which she was held by the Pope and Cardinal Farnese, it would be fitting that the Signori Conservatori and the principal citizens should wait upon her and present her with a gift, which was to consist of four couples of fowls, thirty pounds of fish, and fourteen pounds and a half of marchpane; to Vittoria, with her limited retinue, one wonders if this was not a rather overpowering present !

This same governor, a servile tool of the Farnese, constituted himself the spy of all her actions throughout her residence in Orvieto, and we are not sorry to find that, in spite of his cringing servility, he fell into disgrace in the ensuing year and was superseded, and that the same ill-fortune attended him in his next appointment. The following letters of his to Cardinal Farnese[1] show both the nature of the man, and the

---

1 Published by Domenico Tordi, *Vittoria Colonna in Orvieto durante la Guerra del Sale*, pp. 522 et seq.

dangers which beset Vittoria's path, and which would surely have entrapped a less wary traveller.

" I have not failed, nor will I fail, to visit the Signora Marchesa di Pescara continually, with the greatest assiduity possible, in the name of your most reverend Lordship, and both in word and deed she shows herself as devoted and attached as words can say to his Holiness and to your most reverend and most illustrious Lordship. Her Excellence has shut herself up in the Monastery of San Paolo, alone with two servants, and keeps two serving-men outside, who provide her with what she needs ; she lives as devoutly as persons of holy and pure life are wont to do, and she shows that it is very acceptable to her that I should visit her on behalf of your most reverend and most illustrious Lordship, which I do with that assiduity which is fitting."

" Seeing how much your most reverend and most illustrious Lordship has written to me concerning the Signora Marchesa di Pescara in your letter of the 8th instant, I have not failed to carry out and satisfy your desire; in short, I have cautiously found out and heard from the Bishop of Orvieto that, about a week ago, a retainer, secretary or servant of the most reverend Cardinal Fregoso, came here and spoke with the said Marchesa, and stopped and lodged one evening with her servants, and only brought one other horse with him ; and the Bishop tells me that he came solely to inform her Excellence about the war. Having obtained this information, as I was going to the citadel, passing in front of the Monastery of San Paolo, where the said Signora is living, I found a gentleman with sword and

spurs on, who had just arrived and was speaking with
the said above-mentioned Signora at the grating.   I
asked him cleverly, and under pretence of being anxious
to pick up any news, who he was and whence he came,
and he replied that he was Messer Berardino de Lassis
of Loreto, and that he came from Naples and from
Rome, sent by the Signora Duchessa of Tagliacozzo
and the Signora Principessa of Ischia to her Excellence.
And I saw when he gave her a packet which he put
through the grating, about as high as two little boxes
one on the top of the other, and sewn up in some sort
of linen.   What was inside I know not, because one
could not see, and he put it through the grating as
soon as I arrived there.   There was someone else
with this gentleman, I think his servant.   The gentleman is tall, with a big beard, and growing very grey.
I cannot hear of anyone else who has been there to
speak to her ; any person, I mean, of note ; however,
I shall not fail to investigate.   This I have immediately done on the receipt of your most reverend and
most illustrious Lordship's letter, and for the future
I shall not fail to use all diligence, and to have myself
informed as much as possible so that I may be able to
keep an eye on all those who come to speak with
her Excellence, I mean important persons, and I will
immediately advise you of everything."

"In another letter of mine, in answer to your most
reverend and most illustrious Lordship's, I advised
you of the two persons who had spoken with the
Signora Marchesa di Pescara and had come on purpose ; and, in order that I may not fail in my service
and duty of satisfying fully the mind of his Holiness

and of your most reverend and most illustrious Lordship in everything that I can, I write to inform you that, when I was in conversation with the Bishop of Orvieto a few days ago, I wormed out of him that the aforesaid Signora Marchesa, who seems to repose great confidence in his most reverend Lordship, has shown him two letters ; one was from his Cæsarian Majesty the Emperor, and the other from the Marchese del Vasto. This was the substance of the Emperor's letter ; he exhorted her Excellence to keep up her courage, because, having written to Signor Ascanio to do all that his Beatitude wished, and to his Holiness begging his favour for Signor Ascanio, his Majesty hoped that things would come to a good end and that arms would be suspended ; for her Excellence must consider that it would be impossible for his Majesty to fail her House. The Marchese del Vasto's letter also contained in substance that her Excellence should be of good heart, because he hoped that the war between the Pope and Signor Ascanio would soon terminate, seeing that his Majesty had written to Signor Ascanio that he should do everything that our Lord might reasonably require of him. And this his Majesty had done in order to take away from his Holiness every occasion for remaining under arms, because it did not please him and he was not willing that his Beatitude should thus make war and keep an army in Italy. This is the substance of the two letters. I have not seen them, but so much was told me by the aforesaid Monsignor of Orvieto, who has seen them. It seemed to me that I ought not to fail to advise you of it, in order that if, in any way, it came to the point, the opportunity might not be lost, *sin autem transeat.*"

"This will be to inform your most reverend and most illustrious Lordship that yesterday, which was April 28, a groom of the most reverend Cardinal Fregoso came here, sent to the Signora Marchesa di Pescara by the aforesaid Cardinal, with letters from his most reverend Lordship and from the most reverend Cardinal of England—according to what I have heard—from the most reverend Fregoso I am certain. I have not yet been able to find out the contents of the letters, but I shall not fail to use diligence, and, if I can find out about it, I shall not fail in that service which I owe, and, if I think it is of some little moment, I shall advise you immediately. Since the departure of Messer Berardo, of whom I wrote to you in my other letter, I have not heard of any other person of account coming to speak with her Excellence."

"To-day, which is the 14th instant, a Spanish gentleman, named Don Diego Mandrigal, sent by the Signor Marchese del Vasto, has taken leave of the Signora Marchesa di Pescara. So far as I can hear, he is governor of certain towns of his Excellence, and stayed in Orvieto one evening, coming to speak with the aforesaid Marchesa. Great satisfaction is universally felt at the taking of Paliano, which I immediately made known and published everywhere, and may it please God that the same may follow of the Rocca. Nor did I fail to report the news to the Signora Marchesa, who replied : 'Possessions may come and go, so long as persons are safe.'"[1]

---

[1] Letters of April 1, 9, 20, 29, May 14, respectively, 1541.

War must always be accompanied by its own horrors, for which a righteous cause is the only justification, and there are no woes so unrepaying as those of an unwarrantable contest. Vittoria's friend, Giovanni Guidiccioni, was Commissary-General for the Pope during the Salt War, and has left a complete account of it in his official letters, which are immensely interesting. He never fails to impress upon his master the miseries entailed upon the numbers of innocent people by the unquiet state of the country, and by the oppression of the soldiery, and he repeatedly implores that more officers may be sent to restrain the violence and put a stop to the depredations of which these are guilty. He would fain have had the Pope agree to some compromise and urged him to bring the war to an end, but his appeals were in vain ; in vain, too, did Vittoria address him in prose and in verse, and Giovanna d'Aragona, the wife of Ascanio, write to him with touching humility, on behalf of his poor people and vassals, to desist from so much ruin.[1] The Colonna castles, commanding as they did all the heights round Rome, appeared to Pope Paul to be a danger constantly threatening the city, and nothing would satisfy him but the possession of all of them. Genazzano, Cave, Ciciliano, and many others fell, but Paliano and Rocca di Papa still held out, and it was these two strongholds of which the Pope was most avaricious ; so the affair went on to the bitter end till, with the final surrender of Rocca, the whole Colonna states had passed to the Pope, till no shred of power remained to that mighty House, and its lord was an exile in Naples.

---

[1] See Guidiccioni, *Opere*, ed. cit., Vol. II, p. 395 *n.*

Pope Paul III and the Farnese
By Titian
(Picture Gallery, Naples.)

Cardinal Farnese, writing to the Bishop of Aquila at the end of May, said sententiously : "Here in Rome there is no news since the total capture of the States of Signor Ascanio, including Paliano and la Rocca, which last, seeing itself at length hemmed in and the citadel taken by force, surrendered at discretion, for the fulfilment of justice, and for an example to anyone who should wish to do an injury to this holy See and to his Holiness."[1]

In a letter from Cardinal Pole to Cardinal Contarini, written in April, we find : "As to the most illustrious Marchesa di Pescara . . . she is now in Orvieto, where she has retired to a convent of nuns with whose mode of life and conversation, she has since written to me, she is so delighted that she imagines she is conversing with so many angels. O happy souls whose business it is to know these things!"[2] And Vittoria, writing to the Duke of Ferrara, says : "Your Excellence must know that I am immensely consoled in these misfortunes, and I thank God that by the loss of the goods of fortune He should give me the occasion of acquiring those of the soul, and I am in a holy place."[3] We cannot but admire the detachment and recollection of her mind : surrounded by dangers, overwhelmed by misfortunes public and private, she yet led a life of holy calm, capable of thought, of study, and even of enjoyment. She carried on, as usual, a vast correspondence, and wrote a great many poems ; the

---

[1] Guidiccioni, *Opere*, II, p. 437 *n*.
[2] Pole, *Epistolæ*, Pars III, p. 18.
[3] *Carteggio*, Letter cxxxviii.

capitolo, *Del Trionfo di Cristo*, is believed to have been written here.

The questions of Free Will and Justification by Faith were still being earnestly debated, and, in May, Cardinal Contarini published his *Epistola de Justificatione* at Ratisbon, and Bembo immediately sent it to the Marchesa. In the same month, a great affliction fell upon Cardinal Pole, for his aged mother, the Countess of Salisbury, was put to death on the scaffold, after two years' imprisonment; Vittoria wrote him a letter of condolence which has unfortunately been lost, but we have his answer, which begins thus : " As there are so few things in these days which I read or hear from the speech of others that can give me pleasure or comfort, the letter of your Excellence was all the more acceptable to me, for it gave me great comfort and pleasure also. Though it was not the letter (for, to speak sooth, I do not ascribe so much to it, however elegantly written and well-calculated to console) that lifted me— destitute of all human consolation and well-nigh prostrate in soul—to a better hope, but He who did this was that Spirit Who spoke in it, Who, since He is the fountain of all true and solid consolation, exercising this power then especially when we seem most destitute, hath the name of Comforter and is called Paraclete, Whom I see that your Excellence has as guide of your actions and master of your writings ";[1] and he goes on to tell her that he has chosen her for his mother, a statement which he repeats subsequently in a letter to Cardinal Cervini, and they lived henceforth in the spirit of this relationship.

---

[1] *Carteggio*, Letter cxxxix.

In July, Vittoria's friend and cousin, Cardinal Fregoso, paid her a visit, and received the homage of the city ; he was already in very bad health and died at the end of the month, greatly regretted by Vittoria, who wrote thus about him to Eleonora Gonzaga : " I know the very great love and reverence that our Cardinal of blessed memory bore to your Ladyship, and, therefore, that your grief will not differ from mine, which is immense. Only we ought to rejoice at his glory, and the true peace anticipated by him, which Our dear Lord had assured to him by a thousand experiences and visions, by faith and graces."[1]

Leaving Orvieto in August, the Marchesa proceeded to Rome, by way of Bagnaja, where Cardinal Pole and Gualteruzzi came to visit her, and from whence she courteously wrote to Cardinal Farnese, thanking him for all the civility she had received at Orvieto, though one thinks she must have felt as if she had just escaped from a dangerous prison ; however, she always thought of the convent with special affection and remembered it in her will. Proceeding to Rome, she returned to San Silvestro, and remained there until her departure for Viterbo in October. Rome must have been a melancholy residence for her —the glory of her House departed, and all her own people in exile. A letter to Conte Ettore di Carpegna, from Luca Contile, who visited Vittoria at this time, gives an interesting picture of her.

---

[1] Letter LIII, dated August 1. The Editors of the *Carteggio* and Reumont are clearly in error in assigning this to the year 1532 and taking Pompeo Colonna as the Cardinal in question. Cf. Domenico Tordi, *op. cit.*, p. 510.

"I have been visiting the Signora Marchesa di Pescara, and I could not leave her under four hours. She showed with such charming graciousness that my staying was pleasant to her, and I, being tolerably presumptuous, did not mind if I never went away. She questioned me closely about the Marchese and the Marchesa and the little Pescara. Having seen and visited the Marchese del Vasto, I was able to tell her that I had left him well and cheerful, but meaning to go to Piedmont, and that the Marchesa was on the point of going to Naples, and would take the Marchese di Pescara with her, of whom they have small hope that his foot will get well. She sighed, and asked after Fra Bernardino of Siena. I answered that he was gone, and that he had left such a good name, and such universal contrition in the city of Milan, that everyone considered him a man verily Christian. May it please God, she replied, that he persevere. She then asked me after your Lordship; I told her what I could, and then she entered upon the excellencies of Conte Ettore, and how, as an exemplary gentleman, she knew few like him. And, because her Excellence had known me formerly (I do not exactly know how many times I visited her with the Abbot Giulio), she began to ask me if I had completed the spiritual banquets, and I replied that I had not been able to finish those banquets of which I had not deserved to taste the viands. Nevertheless, in order not merely to chatter, I said that God would soon help me to finish them. She wished me to talk with her about the first, which treats of the existence of God, and how He is Three in One. So, although it was my part to answer, in saying what I knew, I learned from her what I needed. In short, I hold it for a most certain thing that the spirit quickeneth and the letter killeth, and I see how a Christian mind, that has a good judgment to work with, is able to make others walk on the road to salvation. If your Lordship should wish to write to her, as she appears greatly to desire, do me the favour to direct your letter to me, in order that by this means I may give pleasure to this so honoured lady, whom I call the Queen of Sheba, full of courtesy and learning, rather infused than acquired by art, according to my belief. Remember, then, not to avail yourself of any other than me, directing your letter to the house of Cardinal Trivulzio, and I commend myself to you.

"From Rome, August 9, 1541."[1]

The "banquets" referred to in this letter were a series of conversations which, under the name of *Dialoghi Spirituali*, were only printed in February, 1542, though they were evidently begun a good while before. The book is extremely rare ; it takes the form, as was the fashion of those days, of conversations between eight people, three gentlemen and five ladies, all friends of the author. They are supposed to be assembled in the house of Lodovica Trivulzio, Marchesa Pallavicino, at the beginning of Lent, and the Marchesa suggests that, the Carnival being over, they shall enter "nel ballo della divinità," and discuss the most difficult points of the Christian Faith. The conversations took place on five consecutive evenings, and the subjects

---

[1] Luca Contile, *Lettere*, pp. 23 v–24 v.

were as follows : Of the existence of God, and how
He is Three and One ; if the Christian Faith can
show itself to be, among all others, the only true one ;
why the Jews remain in their obstinacy ; the nature
of the lives of the lost and of the blessed ; the way
to ascend to Heaven.[1]

After the publication of the book, Claudio Tolomei
wrote the following appreciative letter to his friend,
informing him, however, that the grammar of the
Dialoghi was not at all to his taste :—

"I have read your Spiritual Banquets and have
found them full of learning, full of tenderness, full of
unction, full of holiness, and, in reading them, I felt
myself inflamed and kindled with the true love of
Christ. . . . In this little book you have collected so
many and such profound and difficult articles of
Christian theology, and you have discussed and resolved them so learnedly, that, indeed, he must be of
a perverse and stubborn mind who, in reading them,
does not feel himself moved, rapt, and, as it were,
transformed into Christ. . . . Would to God, Messer
Luca, that such discourses as you fashion and invent
were always, or often, or sometimes, held by gentlemen
of our time.   For, certainly, the world would become
more virtuous and more well-regulated thereby, and
would also be more happy and more fortunate.   Because, from such frequent discussions, they would little
by little fashion their souls to the likeness of those
things of which they spoke, whence the mind, being
full of those holy ideas and divine instructions, would
bring forth flowers perpetually, and would produce

---

[1] See A. Salza, *Luca Contile, uomo di lettere e di negozii del secolo xvi.*

fruits proper to a plant of such virtue. And then we should be able to say with Plato that that city is truly happy where either the princes philosophise or the philosophers are princes. For, if that appeared to him to be true of mundane and worldly philosophy, what ought we to think of that which is Christian and divine ?"[1]

It is evident that these discourses owed something to Vittoria, and from Contile's letter we should say that he had laid her under deliberate contribution.

Another friend of hers, Fortunato Martinengo, who used often to visit her in Rome, wrote of her in exactly the same strain. "She is a wonderful and unique woman, and, from what I have been able to understand, on fire with the love of Christ, of which she always speaks not less with the heart than with the mouth. What humility is hers, and what unexampled goodness! And the manner of a princess, as indeed she is! I visited her often, and, if I had not been afraid of being troublesome to her, I should never have taken leave of her."[2]

The Marchesa's affectionate inquiries after del Vasto, who was something between a son and a brother to her, afford a fitting opportunity for giving a sketch of his life, since he can never be dissociated from her. As we have already seen, he owed his earliest training and education to her, and she was wont to say that, remembering him, she could not call herself childless. In later years, her relations with him became more sisterly than maternal, and she addresses him in all her

---

[1] Claudio Tolomei, *Lettere*, Lib. I, p. 41.
[2] Reumont, p. 261.

R

letters as "fratello amantissimo." Del Vasto was as devoted to Spanish interests as Pescara had been, and was in high favour with the Emperor, by whom he was sent on many difficult expeditions. After the campaign in Hungary, Charles made him a Knight of the Golden Fleece, and, after taking part in the brilliant affair of Tunis, he was made Captain-General of the imperial troops in Italy. Accompanying the Emperor to Naples in 1535, he was attracted by the preaching of Ochino (whom he was destined to meet later in Milan), and, proceeding to Rome, he would have been in communication with Vittoria, to whom the Emperor made special visits at that time, and it was owing to del Vasto's entreaties that the Marchesa abandoned her favourite project of going to the Holy Land.

In that age, del Vasto's great courage and warlike exploits would have been sufficient to win him popularity, but, besides this, he was famed for his culture, wit, and readiness in conversation, and was no less remarkable for his personal beauty, and the splendour of his dress and appointments. That he wrote verses goes without saying at the epoch in which he lived, but he seems also to have had great literary taste and a wonderful memory for poetry, and also a faculty for making impromptu sonnets. We get a spirited description of his turn for this kind of pastime in a letter from Girolamo Muzio, who was taking a journey of some days with him : " Since our departure from Vigevano, the Signor Marchese has always kept the Muses in his company, and has made as many as twelve sonnets, and one letter of a hundred lines in blank verse, in answer to one of mine, and he obliged me to make

something every day. We competed with each other
as we rode along, for he and I held aloof from our
companions. As soon as I had made a sonnet, I went
to recite it to him, and he did the same to me, having
me summoned. Then, in the evening, when we had
arrived at our quarters, I wrote down what I had composed in the day and took it to him, and he, with his
own hand, wrote down his things, and either sent them,
or gave them to me when I went to him."[1]

Two other letters about the Marchese, written by
Luca Contile, serve to show how his contemporaries
regarded him. The first is to the Bishop of Tolone,
who had apparently asked whether " the magnificence,
courtesy, and prudence " of the Marchese were as great
as they were reported to be. Contile replied : " Believe
me, the virtues of this Prince are greater than his fame;
nay, verily, both by reason of his singular beauty of
form, and of the charm which makes him seem divine,
and by reason of his natural eloquence, on account of
which no one departs from him ill-satisfied, the mind
of everyone who associates with him is overpowered
by as many ideas as there are wonders issuing from all
his actions in every time and place."[2]

And writing to another friend on the varied habits
and tastes of Princes, how he who has a taste for
letters surrounds himself with those who are literary,
artistic, musical, and so forth, Contile says : " In
particular, the Signor Marchese del Vasto takes comfort

---

[1] Letter to Francesco Calvo, dated Monreale (Mondovi), October 31,
1543. *Lettere del Mutio Justinopolitano*, Venice, 1551, pp. 48 *v*, 49.

[2] Letter, dated Milan, April 22, 1542. Luca Contile, *Lettere*.

daily in inquiring now from one and now from another; occupying himself now with history, now with cosmography, now with Sacred Scripture, and, for the most part, with poetry, in which he has shown the finest talent as certain of his things bear witness."[1]

In 1538, the Marchese was made Governor of Milan, and he seems to have become a great light of the cultivated society there; it is probable that he was a member of the Pilgrim-Academy, as we learn that he often bore for a device the motto *Finiunt pariter, renovantque labores*, which was that of the Pilgrims, as we know from Doni. Del Vasto had climbed to the pinnacle of court-favour, and this governorship was his latest reward—an honourable and important position, but one full of difficulties and temptations. And so he seems to have found it, for it appears from a passage in the life of the Angelica, Paola Antonia de' Negri (whose letter to Gaspara Stampa we have already quoted), that, up till now, the Marchese, being engrossed with his military profession and with worldly cares, and constant change of place and occupation, had thought little of spiritual things; but that during his sojourn at Milan, owing to the burden of his office, and the hatred of the people over whom he was set, and finding himself more and more out of favour with the Emperor, he became a prey to melancholy. It was just at this time that he was brought into contact with the Angelica, and she " with that grace which was given her by Our Lord to convert souls . . . did so draw him to the knowledge of virtue and the contempt of the world, that all those who had known him before

---

[1] Letter to Federigo Orlandini, dated Milan, June 9, 1543. *Ibid.*

were amazed to see him so changed, so calm, and so glad."[1]

Thus light is thrown on a deeper and more attractive side of his character by two letters addressed to him, the one by Ochino, the other by the nun. Del Vasto, who had heard Ochino in Naples, must have fallen under his influence again in Milan in 1541, when the Frate was preaching there; the following letter is dated from Venice :—

" MOST ILLUSTRIOUS SIGNOR,

" There never was nor will be a more valiant captain than Christ, because, while other warriors conquer with powerful hosts, by force of arms and artillery, and many by deceit, cunning, or favour of fortune, Christ, coming into this world, began His battle all alone. Despoiled of all earthly power and favour, naked upon the Cross, clothed only with truth, humility, patience, charity, and all His other divine virtues, by the impetus of love in one sole combat He has overcome for ever, not human beings, but infernal spirits, death, vice, and all the enemies of God, and won the most goodly and rich booty that ever was or could be won—the souls that for many centuries had been in so miserable a servitude. It is true, indeed, that He died, but this makes His triumph and His glory the more wonderful. Being, then, such a divine captain, your Excellence will have no cause to be ashamed, but will rather feel honoured in being of the number of His valorous knights, especially as the palms, crowns,

---

[1] *Vita dell' Angelica Paola Antonia de' Negri* prefixed to the *Lettere Spirituali*, pp. 28–29.

victories, trophies, and triumphs of His soldiers are, without comparison, greater than those of the world. And remember that you were enrolled in the militia of Christ or ever you were in that of Cæsar (that is, in holy Baptism), and to fail in loyalty to Christ is so much the more vile as Christ is more rich, generous, powerful, compassionate, holy, and just, and more full of love than all other lords. And just as the words of the crowd, *We have no King but Cæsar*, were impious, equally divine were those of Christ: *Render to Cæsar the things that are Cæsar's and to God the things that are God's*. And now all the more as one does not serve but injure Cæsar every time an offence is done against God, on whose favour depend the emperors and empires of the world. This I have written, not because I do not think that your Excellence has the honour of God always before you, for that I am constrained to believe, both on account of your virtues, and because of the love I bear you. But I behold you in the high places of the world, where the violent winds of human respect are most powerful, to conquer which one needs to be most perfect. Nevertheless, the attempt is proper to the greatness and nobility of your mind. Your other friends will extol and rejoice over your victories in the world; but my joy will be when you conquer yourself, and do not make an idol of human respect, but show yourself superior to it by greatness of soul; and when you do not serve the world, but rather use it for the honour of God. I have been more than long, and I have not satisfied my desire, but I have exercised it. Therefore I make an end, in order not to weary you, and to increase my wish. Perhaps someday I shall come to see you again. Meanwhile and always I will pray the Lord to prosper you with your wife and children in all that is according to His will.

" From Venice, February 10, 1542.

" FRATE BERNARDINO DA SIENA."[1]

The nun's letter is even more interesting.

" O most excellent Signor, O soul beloved in the most pure Blood of Jesus Christ, and observed with reverence, what are you doing? Are you sleeping that I hear nothing from you? Whence does this proceed? Are you perhaps offended by my presumption, and therefore keep silence? Or are those living desires grown cold in you, which were inspired by that Spirit, Who, like a sharp cutting knife, penetrates and divides; or are you shrinking back in order not to feel the stroke of such a division? If this has happened because I have given you offence by my presumption, at any rate tell me, so that I may draw back; and tell me what you wish me to do, for I will do everything, except cease to desire and procure the good of your soul, and that I will never leave off doing as long as I live. . . . Ah, most excellent Signor, pray let us not allow our affections to be so inebriated with the things of this world, that we forsake that which is so necessary to us. Alas, do not let us become so hard, so rebellious to our own good, so contemptuous of holy calls, that our heart may grow impenitent, and wrath may be laid up for us in the

---

[1] *Lettere volgari di diversi nobilissimi huomini et eccellentissimi ingegni*, Venice, 1551, II, p. 96 v.

tremendous Day.   Let us open our eyes, Signor, let
us open them for the love of God, for it is not time
to sleep.   Time is flying, the years of our age fly
from us in numbers, and every hour we are nearer
death. . . . Lift your eyes ; raise up your mind, do
not let it remain behind in the earth.   Remember the
gift you have received, the graces given you.   Do not
throw them away, do not trample on them, do not
despise them. . . . You have my most affectionate
and most excellent Signora Marchesa, who is of so
Christian a heart that she will be a great help to you in
the way of God, and will bear you company, which
is a most happy thing.   Of how many men set in
authority do we read who led a holy life !   I cannot
persuade myself that it is so difficult a thing for such
as you to be good and faithful Christians ; nay, you
are appointed over subjects to govern them, to rule
them, to make them keep the laws and commandments
rather of God than of men.   What is there, then, to
hinder you more than others ?   Are you perhaps less
skilful, less adapted for this office ?   O God, think
a little of the fair graces, of the many gifts and endowments of your souls ; will you not employ them in
honour of Him who gave them to you ?   If the
earthly Emperor, whom you serve so faithfully, were
to give you more cities and castles than those you have,
would you by chance use them to his dishonour, to
make war or rebel against him ?   Would you not
rather seek, as faithful vassals, to honour him more, the
more generosity he showed you ?   O why not thus
with God ?   Does He deserve less gratitude than a
man ?   And does man give you anything that is not

from God, or without the will of God? What can there be in the world more exemplary, more pleasing and dear to everybody, than to see two such princes of one mind and inflamed with the love of God? Would this, perhaps, be derogatory to your reputation, and make you less acceptable to the great ones of the world? Even if this were so, you should not desist from it on that account, for we ought to esteem God and the true good above men and transitory and vain goods. If we had not got to die, if we were not all obliged to appear before the judgment-seat of Christ, if there were not to be such a strict examination, if we had not to do with Him who scrutinises our hearts and reins; if grandeur, emperies, soldiers, horses, arms, nobleness of blood, great friendships and favour of men, could defend us from death and from judgment, then we might indeed close our eyes and persevere in our ingratitude towards God. But alas! nothing avails; alas! all these things will only condemn us more, if we have not used them as we ought. I say too much and shall only weary you; forgive my presumption, but wake, I pray you. You are so loving; love that Christ a little Who loves you so much; consider what an excess of love He has shown for you. Make a firm and steadfast resolution to be faithful to Him. You, most excellent Signor, are about to depart; do not depart without Him; go to confession and communion, and then bear Him good company, and, as you go, do not let your heart be ensnared by these ways of the world. Do what you have to do in a Christian manner, and with elevation of mind. Do not let yourself be captured by men and favours, or enslaved by hatred, contradictions, and hardships, and God be with you always and accompany you. I shall be with you always in heart ; meanwhile, we shall enjoy your most excellent Signora, and we shall see that she outstrips you on the spiritual road so that, when you return, you will find her so advanced that you will have a holy envy of her. Madonna Giulia and I and all the others greet you both, and commend ourselves to you. From your holy place of San Paolo,

"June 10, 1545.

"Your Excellence's most faithful servant
in Jesus Christ." [1]

In the life of this nun, it is stated that del Vasto wrote her many letters, full of divine fervour and recognising the gifts which he received through her. In 1541, the shadow of an inexplicable crime hung over him : two French ambassadors, who had been despatched, one to Venice the other to Constantinople, were assassinated near Pavia, and their bodies flung into the river. Suspicion attached to the Governor of Milan, and, though he constantly denied the charge, it was never disproved ; yet no motive could be alleged for it, and it must have seriously displeased the Emperor as supplying Francis I with a legitimate pretext for renewing the war, the chief event of which was the disastrous day of Ceresole. It is said that del Vasto made so sure of victory that he was provided with four thousand pairs of fetters with which to secure

---

[1] *Lettere Spirituali*, pp. 593–599.

his prisoners, but the tide of fortune turned against him, and, being severely wounded, he fled to Asti, having lost eight thousand men.

Little can be argued from the fact that the Milanese accused him of extorting money from the State and spending it with lavish extravagance, because these accusations were made against every governor in turn, and, in del Vasto's case, they followed hard on his defeat, after which he had fallen out of favour with the Emperor. Summoned to an interview with Charles, he was ordered to return to Milan and appear before the Corte there, but he was already in a desperate condition of health, and died of fever at Vigevano on his way back. After his death, nothing was remembered but his wonderful career of brilliant exploits, while the letters of his friends testify to his high-mindedness and nobility of character.

Luca Contile, writing to Claudio Tolomei, who was tutor to the young Marchese di Pescara, says : " I wrote to you of the illness of the Signor Marchese, and now I tell you with the greatest grief of his death, which took place yesterday at four o'clock, on the last day of last month. He is dead, having left the example of a good Christian, and having been the most excellent of Princes and Knights while alive." [1]

Del Vasto died on March 31, 1546, so we are anticipating by some few years this last great sorrow of Vittoria's life.

The Marchesa remained in Rome till the October of 1541, when she proceeded to Viterbo, and three quiet years now followed the turbulent one through which

---

[1] Letter dated Milan, March 2, 1546. Luca Contile, *Lettere*.

she had just passed. But neither peace nor strife, fortune nor humiliation, could alter the abiding impression that Vittoria always created : it was like the breath of the softest wind of summer, or like a friend who comes to meet us with his hands full of roses.

CHAPTER X

VITERBO

Myself when young did eagerly frequent
Doctor and Saint, and heard great Argument
  About it and about : but evermore
Came out by the same Door as in I went.
              FitzGerald's *Omar Khayyám.*

WE have already heard a note of doubt struck in the
mind of Vittoria as to the man she had trusted so
implicitly, and who had been her guide for several
years. "May it please God that he persevere!" she
had said to Luca Contile, and, with this doubt before
her, she must have passed an anxious year at Viterbo,
until the news of Ochino's flight reached her in the
August of 1542. The year before that, he had been
preaching with his usual success in Milan, where
the Governor, del Vasto, was one of his friends and
most eager listeners ; at Pentecost he was at Naples,
where he was again elected to the dignity of Vicar-
General of his Order, and, proceeding to Florence, he
fell ill and remained at the convent about three miles
out of the city, until the following February, when he
went to Venice for Lent. Siena had begged hard for
him, but the Pope had granted him to Venice, where-
upon the Sienese implored him to come to them in
Advent ; but he was then too ill. It is said that when

he began his Lenten preaching in Venice, the Nuncio, Fabio Mignatelli, had instructions to observe him narrowly. These may have emanated from Cardinal Caraffa, who had already had him watched by the Theatines at Naples, though nothing had come of it. Now it chanced that Giulio Terenziano, a friend of Ochino's, had just been condemned for preaching heresy, and the Frate took the opportunity of making a strong protest : "What will it lead to, O men of Venice, if such things may happen ? O Queen of the Sea, if thou castest the heralds of truth into dungeons and chains, and condemnest them to the galleys, what rest-ing-place shall remain for the truth ?"[1] On this the Nuncio immediately forbade Ochino to preach, but he had to give way before the unanimous outcry of the city, and Fra Bernardino finished his Lenten course, after which he withdrew to the Capuchin Convent in Verona, and remained there in cordial relations with the Bishop, Giberti, whose complete confidence he still possessed.

In the life of Paola Antonia de' Negri, to which reference has already been made, we read that she, having been invited to Verona by the Bishop, who was a great friend of hers, was present at a sermon of Fra Bernardino's, after which she foretold his fall into heresy, which Giberti could in no wise believe or accept ; but he remembered it later.[2]

It was in the early summer that Ochino received a summons to Rome ; it came from Cardinal Farnese and was couched in most friendly terms, asking him to

---

[1] Benrath, *Bernardino Ochino*, Eng. ed., pp. 94, 95.
[2] *Vita dell' Angelica*, pp. 88, 89.

come and discuss "matters of some importance"; but, notwithstanding the tone, the Frate was filled with apprehension, and was doubtful whether to respond. Giberti, however, exhorted him to absolute obedience, though at the same time he endeavoured to obtain a delay, making the great heat an excuse. At the Bishop's request, Ochino repaired to Bologna to consult with Cardinal Contarini, who had recently been appointed legate there, and who had been almost immediately seized with a mortal illness, on which account poison (as was usual in such cases) was suspected, Contarini having given offence to many by dealing, as was thought, too leniently with the Lutherans at Ratisbon. The Cardinal was in a dying condition when Ochino arrived, and accounts differ as to the precise nature of the interview, for, while Ochino would have us believe that Contarini warned him against going to Rome, Muzio and Beccadelli state that the Cardinal was too ill to see him for more than a minute, and that his only words were: "Father, you see my condition; have pity on me, and pray to God for me, and I wish you a good journey."[1]

However this may have been, Ochino proceeded to Florence where he found his old friend, Pietro Martire Vermigli, and we have no doubt of the advice given by the latter, as he was himself resolved on flight. From Florence, Ochino wrote to Vittoria :—

"I find myself here on the outskirts of Florence in no small trouble of mind, having come here with the

---

[1] *Vita del Cardinale Gasparo Contarini da Lodovico Beccatello,* Brescia, 1746, p. 40.

intention of going to Rome, although many people dissuaded me from doing so before I arrived. But, understanding better every day the way things are going on, I am most particularly persuaded by Don Pietro Martire and others not to go ; because I could not but deny Christ or be crucified. The first I will not do ; the second, yes, but with His grace, and when it shall be His will. I have not now the spirit to go voluntarily to death. When God requires me, He will know how to find me anywhere. Christ several times taught us to fly, by His flight into Egypt, and to Samaria, and so Paul tells me when I am not received in one city to go to another. After this, what could I do more in Italy ? Preach doubts and preach Christ disguised in jargon ? It is often necessary to blaspheme Him in order to satisfy the superstition of the world, and that is not enough, for every seeker of favour would be ready to write to Rome and harass me : and so we should return at once to the same confusion. And still less in writing could I throw light on anything. For these and other reasons I choose to depart, and especially because I see things going in such a manner as makes me think that, in the end, they would want to examine me, and make me deny Christ or kill me. I think, if Paul were in my place, he would not act otherwise. I may truly say that I passed through Bologna as by miracle, and was not detained there both on account of the willingness I showed to go to Rome, and also by the kindness and prudence of Cardinal Contarini, of which I had evident tokens. Since then, I have heard that Farnese says I am summoned be-cause I have preached heresy and scandalous things.

From the information that I have received it seems that the Theatine, Puccio, and others whom I do not wish to name, speak of me in such a manner that, if I had crucified Christ, I do not know if they could have made so much noise. I am such as your Ladyship knows, and anyone who has heard me can give an account of my doctrine. Never have I preached with more reserve or more moderation than this year, and yet, without hearing me, they have declared me to be a heretic. I am glad that they begin to reform the Church with me. . . . On the other hand, think if it is not hard for me in all respects ! I know you will think so. The flesh recoils from leaving everything behind and thinking what will be said. Christ has permitted and willed that I should be compelled to this for some good reason. It would be more than welcome to me to speak with you, and to have your opinion and that of the reverend Monsignor Pole, or to have a letter from you ; but it is more than a month since I heard from you. Pray to Our Lord for me ; I desire more than ever to serve Him with His grace. Salute everybody.

"From Florence, August 22, 1542."[1]

On the day following, Ochino set out, being supplied with a horse and a servant by Ascanio Colonna. The account of his flight is full of discrepancies ; some say that he went to Ferrara, where the Duchessa Renata helped him with clothes and money. From a letter of Giberti's to del Vasto, it would seem that he went to Milan and there saw the Marchese, who endeavoured to

---

[1] *Carteggio*, Letter CXLVI.

S

dissuade him from his purpose, but there is no other mention of this digression, and it does not appear likely. It is more probable that he struck across the plain of Lombardy, directing his way to Geneva through Chiavenna and Zurich. He took with him a lay-brother of his Order, Fra Mariano, a man who had been a soldier, and who had a practical knowledge of French and German. The annalist, Boverius, states that three Brothers went with him, and he gives a graphic account of Ochino's farewell to Italy, almost too circumstantial to be true, except that it accords well with what we know of the man's character.

Boverius writes thus : " He had reached the summit of the Alps which shuts out the last view of beautiful Italy, when, turning his face towards her, softened by a certain natural love which aroused in his heart tender affections towards the country which he had no hopes of seeing again, reviewing in his mind the honours and the applause which he had received . . . he began to be grievously afflicted in his mind and to shed many tears ; and broke into these words : ' O Italy, most happy land in all the world, my most sweet country, land of my birth, and, in time now passed, of my delights. With what tears and sighs must I take leave of thee, since such a sad and perpetual exile separates me from thee as deprives me of all hope of ever see-ing thee again. Henceforth shall I no more enjoy thine honours, nor see the crowds of the people, nor the vast assemblage of the nobles who applauded me ? Will they never more hear me speak from the pulpits, or receive me with acclamations of joy when I return from preaching ? My departure deprives me of all this happiness. Alas! Order of the Cappuccini, so dear erewhile, my sweet hostess, my sweet daughter! With how many kind offices and with what courtesy didst thou receive me! With what benefits didst thou load me, and with how many honours didst thou distinguish me! Ought I not, on every account, to have given back to thee benefits like to those I received, or, at any rate, I ought to have rendered thee due thanks. In what calamity and disaster I see thee plunged by my flight. Thou didst nourish and bring up a son that he might be to thee a Benjamin, the son of thy right hand, but he is changed into Benoni, the son of thy sorrow.'"[1]

Vermigli followed Ochino two days later. With the subsequent career of these men we are hardly concerned here, except in so far as it may interest English readers to know that they both came to England, and were entertained by Cranmer at Lambeth, that Vermigli became Dean of Christ Church, Oxford, and that Ochino held a prebend in Canterbury Cathedral : both were regarded as factors in the spread of the reformed doctrines in England. Some have said that different treatment would have preserved Ochino to the Church, that if he had been made much of at Rome, and been created a cardinal, he would have remained faithful ; to which the only answer seems to be that, if this were so, his faith must have been of so poor an order as not to have been worth preserving. But there are some clear indications that Ochino was on the wrong road. If he had been alive to the peril of his really great position,

---

[1] *Annales Minorum Capucinorum*, Tom. I (Lyons, 1632), pp. 316, 317.

he must have been before all things a man of prayer
and retirement ; whereas, on the contrary, we find it
asserted, as freely by his friends as by his enemies,
that he had almost left off saying Mass, that he rarely
appeared in choir, and had asked to be dispensed from
saying his office, on the plea that more important things
were occupying his time : one does not need to be a
prophet to foretell the fall of such a man, in one way or
another.   In Italy his defection could not but be pro-
ductive of grave results ; his voice had been heard
through the length and breadth of the land, and he
had an immense following both inside and outside his
Order.   Two letters from his contemporaries give us
some idea of the consternation induced.

In October, Claudio Tolomei writes : " Returning
to Rome yesterday from the country, a piece of news
was suddenly communicated to me, but wild, incredible,
dreadful news.   I was told that you, I know not by
what strange counsel, have passed out of the camp of
the Catholics into the quarters of the Lutherans, consecrating yourself to that wicked and heretical sect.   I
was absolutely horror-stricken, as one says, and I made
the sign of the Cross.   Since then, as the tidings were
confirmed first by four, and then by six people, and
finally by everyone, I was constrained to believe it against
my will.   It seemed to me that I had heard stranger
news than if I had been told that doves had turned
into serpents, or that kids had become panthers... Truly
I am reduced to this, that whereas formerly (as you
know) I asked you many times to pray to God for me,
at the present moment, knowing the contrary need, I
can do nothing but pray to God for you : and now

again I humbly beg Him that He may please to enlighten and help you." [1]

The second letter is from Girolamo Muzio, of
whom mention has already been made in connection
with del Vasto, in whose service he was. Vittoria
appears to have handed over to him Ochino's letter of
August 22. Muzio was an unwearied writer on all
subjects, and published many books against heretics,
but he was wanting in point and judgment ; not being
much of a theologian, his arguments here are long-
winded and commonplace, but what he says is not
wanting in sense.

"If I have more than once listened to your sermons
and arguments, I am now all the more grieved, having
seen a letter of yours, written a few days ago, to the
no less worthy than illustrious Marchesa di Pescara.
Truly the cause of my grief is that you have abandoned your religion, that Italy will be for ever deprived of your voice . . . and this is not so much
mine as a universal grief, as is also the scandal that
you have given by your departure." Ochino's correspondent then goes on to tell him that he has stated
his reasons in such a confused and obscure fashion
that they sound more like excuses. He asks him
whether he should not have gone to Rome to justify
himself, seeing that his doctrine had been valued there.
If he had changed his views, he ought to have gone to
explain the cause. Or, if he would not go to Rome,
why on that account should he have left Italy ? Was
Geneva the only place open to him ? And then
Muzio pertinently asks : "Is this the humility and

---

[1] *Lettere di M. Claudio Tolomei*, Vol. II, p. 209.

patience you have preached so often, and that we have
praised so much ?　Your life henceforward can only be
one of extreme unhappiness. . . . You have made
shipwreck of the doctrine of Christ." He ends by
exhorting him to repent like Peter, that so, like him,
he may be forgiven, and then he will arrive at that
" buon fine " which he mentions in his letter.[1]

To Tolomei, Ochino replied in a long rambling
epistle, which was indeed but a tissue of excuses. A
more reasoned document was sent to the Council of
his native city, Siena, and answered by Fra Ambrogio
Politi, first by a short letter, and subsequently by a
treatise entitled *Remedy against the Pestilential Doctrine
of Fra Bernardino Ochino.*　Ochino then busied himself
with drawing up his *Prediche,* which were published at
intervals, in three parts ; they are not sermons, but
theological discussions, and were composed with the
view of justifying his resolution before the world. The
first set were sent by him to Muzio, as an answer to
his letter, and it is probably a copy of these that was despatched with a second letter to Vittoria from Geneva,
and which she immediately sent on to Cardinal Cervini,
with the accompanying letter :—

" Most illustrious and most reverend,
　　　　　most worshipful Monsignor,

　　　" The more opportunity I have had of observing the actions of the most reverend Monsignor of
England, the more he seems to me a true and most
sincere servant of God.　So, when in his charity he

---

[1] Letter from Muzio to Ochino.　*Le Mentite Ochiniane del Mutio
Justinopolitano,* Venice, 1551.

condescends to answer any question of mine, I think I
am secure from error in following his advice. And
since he told me that, in his opinion, if a letter or anything else should come to me from Fra Bernardino, I
had better send it to your most reverend Lordship
without answering it, having to-day received the en-
closed with the little book which you will see, I send
them to you. The whole was in one packet, without
any other writing inside, and was sent by an express-
courier who came from Bologna, and I have chosen to
send it on to you by one of my servants. I beg your
Lordship will pardon my giving you this trouble,
although, as you see, it is in print. And Our Lord
God preserve your most reverend Lordship's person
in that happy life which all your servants desire for
you.

"From Santa Caterina di Viterbo, December 4.

"Your most reverend and most
illustrious Lordship's servant,
"THE MARCHESA DI PESCARA.

"It grieves me exceedingly that, the more he thinks
to excuse himself, the more he accuses himself, and, the
more he thinks to save others from shipwreck, the more
he exposes them to the deluge, being himself outside
that Ark which secures and saves."[1]

It was no doubt owing to Cardinal Pole's advice
that Vittoria had vouchsafed no answer to Ochino's
first letter, but an additional reason may have been
that she must have received it at the very moment of
Cardinal Contarini's death, which would have been a

---

[1] *Carteggio*, Letter CXLIX.

grievous loss and sorrow to her. The Cardinal died on
August 24, and towards the end of September the
Marchesa wrote the following letter to his sister, Suora
Serafina, who was a nun at Santa Chiara at Murano.

"Reverend sister and most honoured

mother in Christ,

      "If I did not know that your Reverence is
armed with all those divine shields which do not suffer
the points of human arrows to pierce too deeply, I
should not have ventured to write to you on such a
sorrowful and bitter occasion. But, remembering your
pious and sweet letters, when you invited that most
beloved brother to desire to be with you in the true
celestial country, and the request that you made to him
to explain certain psalms which showed that you had
the death, passion, and resurrection of Christ always
impressed upon your heart, I have dared to rejoice in
spirit over that which, in the sense, supremely grieves
me, and to beg you to consider, with that supernatural
light which God bestows on you, that we have no
cause to sorrow nor to desire that this so worthy and
Christian life should have been prolonged. And
speaking of lesser things, such as are justly little prized
by you, I will say that he was already so loaded with
worldly honours, which came to seek him out as their
proper resting-place, that it is rather he who laid them
down as a painful weight, than that they would have
at any time abandoned him. And these honours he
carried so devoutly and uprightly, having for his first
object and his last end God, Who gave them to him,
and so satisfied both spiritual and temporal expecta-

tions that, rejoicing his true friends, he never gave others any just cause of complaint. His doctrine, prudence, and wisdom had come to be held in such admiration by the good and in such envy by the world, that either he must strip himself of them, or all others would seem to be despoiled and stripped by him. As for the excellent and divine example which he gave to everyone, and as for his most important usefulness to the Church and to our peace and quiet living, we must be assured by lively faith that the infallible disposition of the King, Lord, and Head of us all, knows the best and most auspicious time in which to draw His members to Himself. There remains, then, only the loss of his most sweet conversation, and the profit of his most holy instructions, for which your Reverence and myself would be greatly to be pitied if it had not been that his journeyings and your seclusion did not allow us to enjoy them. So that I do not see much reason for us to be sorrowful, but rather to be comforted, and to rejoice greatly in seeing, with the eyes of the mind, his peaceful spirit united with that true eternal peace, and his most humble soul made great and glorious by Him, Who, with such loftiness of intellect, made him such a model of humility that he clearly showed how he surpassed all human reason with the divine spirit. Now your Reverence can speak to him without absence hindering you from being heard. Now you will not have the sorrow of going far from your true brother according to the flesh, but, thanking God, you will rejoice in Him at your brother's weal at once, with one sole imagination and one same light, as I am sure you will experience in your soul ; since I am only trying to draw it with my pen for one who by long experience knows all the colours, the lights, and the shades of that holy picture. But I have done it in order to beg you affectionately to fix your inward eyes firmly on this alone, as I hope surely that God will help you to do ; and to pray you to command me, as the most true and obliged servant of that most perfect brother of yours and lord of mine, now that no other spiritual service remains to me than that of the most illustrious and most reverend Monsignor of England, his singular, intimate, and most true friend, and more than son and brother, who feels this loss so much that his strong pious mind, unvanquished by so many varied troubles, seems to have given itself over to grief more than it has ever done on any other occasion. It is as though the Spirit of consolation, who dwells ever in his Lordship, has willed to allow him to be thus grieved as a proof that this loss only effects the good. So you alone must supply my need, as a soul already freed from earthly things, since in you that may be attributed to natural sorrow which in that Signor is imputed to spiritual charity. So may you be confirmed for very many years in the embraces of your celestial Spouse, and may He grant us to find ourselves all together in eternal felicity.

    " From Santa Caterina at Viterbo.

" Your Reverence's sister and
obedient daughter in Christ,
" The Marchesa di Pescara." [1]

---

[1] *Carteggio*, Letter CXLVII.

Cardinal Contarini was indeed a grievous loss to the Church at large, and especially to that small band of reformers within the fold, whose elusive hopes were fading rapidly away.

We have already glanced at the Oratory of Divine Love, established with the avowed object of spiritualising the hierarchy. Almost a direct offshoot of the Oratory was the Valdessian community at Naples, with this difference, that it was chiefly composed of laity, and that it confined itself to the reform of the individual : yet another development was the circle at Viterbo which was just now taking shape. But in the ecclesiastical world the Oratory had also borne fruit. Paul III on his accession had his thoughts wholesomely turned in the direction of reform. Having created Contarini a cardinal, he ordered him to reside in Rome, and asked him to name the men he thought most fitting to report on existing abuses and to devise remedies. Among those chosen were Fregoso, Giberti, Sadoleto, and Pole, all great friends of the Marchesa's, and also Cardinal Caraffa, a man of stern and harsh nature, who worked in a spirit very alien from that which influenced his colleagues. His cry was always : Let us stamp out these heretics ; while Giberti's was : Let our lives be such that they will have nothing wherewith to reproach us. All these men were imbued with the necessity for reform ; they met daily in Contarini's house, and their discussions extended over a period of two years, after which a report was drawn up by Caraffa and presented to the Pope. But, after this long delay, Paul's interest had evaporated ; the report was laid by, and the scheme suffered to come to nothing. Yet the men who had been engaged upon it did not desist from their purpose ; each in his own place carried out what amendments and improvements he could, and who can say how many souls were thus saved to the Church ?

But, as years went on and the spread of heresy became alarming, the Pope turned, not to his first band of counsellors, but to one among them, Cardinal Caraffa, and asked how the evil was to be combated. Caraffa, who had always been in favour of extreme measures, suggested establishing a universal office of the Inquisition in Rome, and so the Holy Office was created with the bull *Licet ab initio*, July 21, 1542.

The situation was certainly sufficiently grave, but from this time forth a sort of stage-fright seems to have seized on the rulers of the Church. They scented heresy everywhere, the most saintly men were accused, and in a few years suspicions attached to all the leading Catholics. Giulia Gonzaga, Caterina Cibo, and Vittoria herself were suspected and watched ; the harass and distress caused to the first-mentioned lady are said to have shortened her life. Little was ever proved against Caterina, though she is thought to have aided Ochino in his flight, and she corresponded with him afterwards.

Against the Marchesa, though she was watched for a short time, no single charge was ever substantiated. Although her name appears in the *Compendium Processuum Sancti Officii*, and many questions were asked concerning her in the processes instituted against Carnesecchi and Morone long after her death, it would be absurd to cast any doubt on her orthodoxy on

account of transactions which took place when she was
no longer living, and because of her friendship with
men who, in her lifetime, were held to be above suspicion.   In the trial of Carnesecchi, the only thing that
could be mentioned to her discredit was that she had
received a copy of Valdès' Commentary on St. Paul's
Epistle to the Romans, and that she had read Luther's
exposition of one of the Psalms, being ignorant that
he was the author of it.[1]   Of Valdès' book we have
the following mention, in the only letter of Vittoria's
to Giulia Gonzaga which has come down to us.   It
was written from Viterbo in December, 1541.

"It would assuredly be fitting that your Ladyship
should revisit your country in Lombardy for a little,
now that you are so well instructed about the celestial
country, for it would be very beneficial to you, and,
as you pass by here, you could stay a couple of
months. . . . I understand that your Ladyship has
sent the Commentary on St. Paul, which was very
much wanted, and especially by me who have most
need of it, wherefore I thank you the most, and will
thank you more when I see you, God willing."[2]

On the other hand, the Marchesa's position in Rome
in 1546 is attested by a letter of Cardinal Gonzaga's in
which he relates that Paul III had been to visit her
and had conversed with her about his possible successor, informing her that he greatly wished that
Sfondrato should be chosen, and charging her to
repeat this to all the cardinals who came to her
house.[3]   This fact alone goes far to disprove the

---

[1] *Estratto del processo di Pietro Carnesecchi*, pp. 498, 550.
[2] *Carteggio*, Letter cxlii.   [3] Luzio, *op. cit.*, p. 49.

assertion that Vittoria was suspected of Protestant tendencies. Certainly, she was happy in not living on into the darker days which were coming, when was seen that spectacle which has been seen many times since, and will no doubt be repeated to the end of time, of faith strong enough, humility deep enough, to engender that loyalty to authority which can cry out :—

> "I am no courtier of thee sober-suited,
>   Who loves a little for a little pay.
>   Me not thy winds nor storms nor thrones disrooted
>   Nor molten crowns nor thine own sins dismay."[1]

It has been asked in a fine novel recently published : "What sort of sons are you who talk of forsaking your mother because her dress is not to your taste ? Is her maternal bosom, forsooth, altered by a dress ? When leaning upon it, weeping, you tell Christ of your sins and Christ heals you, do you think of the authenticity of a passage in St. John, of the real author of the fourth Gospel, or of the two Isaiahs ? When sheltered upon it you unite yourself to Christ in the Blessed Sacrament, are you disturbed by the decrees of the Index or the Holy Office ? When abandoned upon it you enter into the shadow of death, is the peace which is breathed upon you less sweet because a Pope is adverse to Christian democracy ?"[2]

And this is a twofold testimony : we cannot be loyal to nothing ; the questionings, the differences, the bitternesses may all be there, but underneath there is

---

[1] A. C. Swinburne, *Songs before Sunrise.*
[2] Antonio Fogazzaro, *Il Santo.*

something that admits of no question, that is eternally the same, the "great rock in a weary land," under whose shadow we sit down "with great delight."

Learned leisure is undoubtedly speculative, and the most favourite theme for discussion in the sixteenth century was Justification by Faith. It is difficult to understand why this took hold of men's minds as if it had been a new proposition. Whether it was a re-action from formalism, from a bondage to rules and observances ; or whether mysticism, as is its wont, so emphasised the essential inwardness of religion as first to minimise, and then almost to obliterate, the value of outward forms, it is hard to decide. But certain it is that this was a fruitful subject for dispute, opening up many and unexpected problems, and there is little doubt that, in its inception, few of those who adopted the formula realised what could be deduced from it, and very many entirely rejected these deductions. Valdès, as we have seen, only recognised "operative faith"; Ochino seems to have held the same view for some time, though his later utterances are more doubtful ; Flaminio allowed himself greater latitude ; Carnesecchi's mind was so unsystematic that one can hardly fasten him down to anything; while Cardinal Pole, whose acute intellect was thoroughly alive to the interest of a dialectical point, very evidently kept himself and Vittoria in the right road, and had the honour of bringing Flaminio back to it.

Of Pole's dealings with Flaminio, Cardinal Querini has given us the following account : " When Messer Marcantonio Flaminio returned from Naples, his old and dear friend (Cardinal Pole) finding him tinctured

with some not very safe opinions which he had derived
from the conversation of Valdès in Naples, in order to
help his friend, whom he knew to be of good life and
excellent understanding, without saying anything of
this, invited him to stay with him in that ease of
Viterbo where he then was.   And living together,
talking sometimes of humanistic studies, in which
Messer Marcantonio was proficient, and sometimes
of sacred things, the Cardinal proceeded with so
much cleverness that in process of time, without
any dispute arising, he convinced him of Catholic
truth, so that his doctrine remained sound and
pure ; and continuing therein, and writing sacred
poems, he died as a good Christian in the house of his
most reverend Lordship, who was wont to say that,
besides the benefit to his friend, he had rendered no
small service to Catholics in having retained Flaminio
and not suffered him to rush headlong with the
heretics, as he might easily have done, amongst whom
he would have been very dangerous, because of the
easy and accurate way he had of writing Latin and the
vernacular."[1]   In fact, Flaminio died in Cardinal Pole's
house in February, 1550, aged fifty-two.   The Cardinal had him buried in the English Church, and all
Italy mourned for him.   Still it can hardly be denied
that Flaminio was, as might be said, " temerarissimus "
in his study of heretical books, and some of his own
works were prohibited by Paul IV in 1559, though the
prohibition was subsequently removed.

From all details that have come down to us, the life
at Viterbo seems to have been no less attractive than

---

[1] *Vita del Cardinale Reginaldo Polo da Lodovico Beccatello.*

that at Naples ; it was on a smaller scale, but, perhaps, for that reason it was all the more intimate and perfect. The Pope had appointed Cardinal Pole Legate at Viterbo, "governo piacevole e d' ozio," as Beccadelli calls it, and it was on this account that the Marchesa went to live there, residing as was her custom in a convent, in the Dominican house of Santa Caterina. The church and convent stand in a quiet and secluded piazza of Viterbo, out of the stream of the life of the town. There is a fine old mediæval fountain in front of the convent, which is dedicated to St. Catherine of Alexandria. The church is decorated with pictures in honour of the two Saints Catherine, and there is a frescoed apotheosis of St. Catherine of Siena on the ceiling, but these are all of a later epoch. The only painting that could have been there in Vittoria's time is an old picture of St. Dominic. The Marchesa refers to this convent in the letter already cited to the Duke of Ferrara, dating "from Santa Caterina, but not now that most beautiful one at Ferrara, but this indifferent one at Viterbo." No doubt the society was sufficient compensation for other things that were wanting.

Pole may be regarded as the embodiment of that spirit of piety which was the most effectual protest against the laxity of the times ; and, in addition to his piety, he had great natural gifts—wit, readiness in conversation, and unfailing tact ; also a wide knowledge of the worlds of society and of books : he could not fail to be an attractive companion, and from henceforth he became Vittoria's guide and mainstay. Carnesecchi says in the *Processo* that these two often had long discourses on spiritual things, "because both of them

T

took more pleasure in this than in any other subject."
From the same source we learn that Flaminio and
Priuli frequently visited the Marchesa and also in-
dulged in religious arguments, but that, in their case,
the discourse was intermixed with profane and ordinary
topics.[1]

Reunions for study, preaching, and discussion were
held every day at the Cardinal's house, and we get an
idea of them in certain letters written to Contarini.
Having explained how he passes the morning in study
and in the transaction of a few hours' business, Pole
continues : " The rest of the day I spend in the holy
and profitable society of Signor Carnesecchi and our
Monsignor Marcantonio Flaminio.   I call it profitable
because, in the evenings, Monsignor Flaminio feeds me
and the greater part of our household with that meat
which does not perish, and in such a manner that I do
not know when I have felt greater consolation or greater
edification."

In another letter he writes : " As to the passage in
St. Bernard noticed by your most reverend Lordship,
where he speaks so explicitly of the Justice of Christ,
we have found and read it with our friends here, with
the greatest satisfaction to all of us.   And considering
afterwards on what the doctrine of this holy man was
founded, together with his life, it does not seem
wonderful to me if he speaks more clearly than others.
For all his doctrine was formed and founded upon the
Holy Scriptures (which in their inward meaning
proclaim naught else but this Justice), and he had therewith such a goodly commentary to explain what he read

---

[1] *Estratto del processo di Pietro Carnesecchi*, p. 269.

—I mean, the conformity of his life thereto, which gave him continual experience of the truth learned; and on this account he must needs have been most steadfast. And if the other adversaries of this truth would set themselves to examine how it is established in this way, to wit, by the two rules of Scripture and experience, without doubt all controversy would cease. They, therefore, do err, not knowing the Scripture and the power of God, which is hid in Christ, to whom be glory for ever, Who has begun to reveal this holy truth, and one so salutary and necessary to be known, using for instrument your most reverend Lordship. Therefore, we are all continually constrained to pray His Divine Majesty that He will strengthen what is wrought to His glory and the benefit of the whole Church ; as indeed we do, and especially the Signora Marchesa, who unceasingly commends herself to you." [1]

While Flaminio was the mouthpiece and might seem to be the leader of the little circle, Pole was its most virile member and its real head ; he was probably also the only one who saw clearly to what length doctrines might be drawn out. Flaminio was too purely a mystic to carry out premises to their logical conclusions, and so, like many people, he often found himself adhering to wholly incompatible beliefs. That he held the Catholic doctrine of the Mass and the Holy Eucharist, we know from a letter of his to Carnesecchi, and this one to Carlo Gualteruzzi is interesting as giving us his view of a devotional book as popular in our days as in his. He writes : " I could not recommend you any

---

[1] *Epistolarum Reginaldi Poli*, Pars III, Letters xxiii, xxx.

more useful book (not speaking of the Holy Scriptures) than that little work *De Imitatione Christi*, if you will read it not from curiosity, nor in order to know how to argue and dispute about points of Christian doctrine, but in order to edify your soul and to attend to the practice of a Christian life, in which lies the whole matter, as soon as man has accepted the grace of the Gospel, that is Justification by Faith. . . . If you were to read the aforesaid book carefully and with attention, and with the desire to put what it teaches you into practice, I am sure that you would find it most useful, as all those do who read it thus . . . and the further the book is from worldly eloquence and learning, the more worthy it is of being read as something more Christian and more spiritual ; and it is more like Holy Scripture, and consequently more perfect." [1]

We have already spoken of the great influence which Cardinal Pole had over the Marchesa, and we get the following particulars from Carnesecchi : "Before the Signora Marchesa contracted her friendship with the Cardinal, she used to afflict herself so much with fasts, sackcloth, and other mortifications of the flesh that she had reduced herself to skin and bone, and this she did, perhaps, because she placed too much confidence in such works, imagining that true piety and religion, and consequently the salvation of one's soul, consisted in these things.　But after being advised by the Cardinal that she rather offended God than otherwise by treating her body with such austerity and rigour . . . the aforesaid Signora began to desist from that very austere mode of life, reducing her mortifications little by little

---

[1] *Lettere volgari*, p. 124.

to a just and reasonable mean." Speaking of Justification by Faith, Carnesecchi says : " I could not exactly say in what special way she held it, but it is enough that she attributed a great deal to grace and to faith in her discourses, and, on the other hand, by her life and actions she showed that she set great store by works, giving large alms and showing universal charity to everyone ; thereby observing and following the advice which she said the Cardinal (whom she trusted as an oracle) had given her, to wit, that she ought to set herself to believe as though she must be saved by faith alone, and to act as though she must be saved by works alone. She referred to this one day when talking to me, saying that she had implored the Cardinal to tell her his opinion about that article of Justification, and had not been able to get any other pronouncement out of him but this. Nor had she dared to ask him anything further about it, or about any other dogma relating to faith, being afraid of offending him by too great curiosity." [1]

Cardinal Morone, who became the Marchesa's special friend after Contarini's death, says that she once told him that she owed her salvation to Cardinal Pole, because he had strengthened her, and detached her from many vain fancies ; " her mind was entirely his." And Vittoria writes in one of her letters to Morone : " I confess to your Lordship that I was never under such obligations to anyone as to Pole." [2]

It seems likely that, during the earlier part of her

---

[1] *Estratto del processo di Pietro Carnesecchi,* pp. 499, 269, 270. Cf. Corvisieri, *Compendio de' processi del S. Officio,* pp. 279, 280.

[2] Corvisieri, *op. cit.,* p. 280.

sojourn at Viterbo, the Marchesa threw herself heart
and soul into the interminable discussions on Justification by Faith, from which no thoughtful mind at that
moment seemed to be able to free itself, and which
was a perfectly legitimate subject for debate, no pronouncement having as yet been made upon it. But it
is evident that, before her visit came to an end, she
had wearied of an atmosphere of polemics, which
never could have been congenial to one at the same
time so simple and so devout. Guided by Pole, she
had broken off all communication with Ochino, and,
further influenced by him, she desisted from controversy, while remaining ever more keenly alive to the
interest of spiritual things, and her later poems, which
we shall shortly consider, bear ample witness to the
fact that her faith had deepened and strengthened.

In the spring of 1543, the Marchesa had a long and
dangerous illness, which caused much anxiety to her
friends. When the news reached Rome, Claudio
Tolomei wrote thus to Giuseppe Cincio, a celebrated
doctor then at Viterbo : "I am exceedingly distressed
about the illness of the Marchesa di Pescara of which
you write to me, as she is one of the women who
ought to be reverenced by the whole world, because
there is in her so much virtue, and goodness, and
worth, and, above all, because in these corrupt times
she has done so many good works in the service of
Christ. But I do not wish to enter into her merits
now, because, perhaps, in another place I shall leave a
testimony to those who shall come after us, although
her life is such that it will shine forth at all times like
a sun newly arisen, and will renew itself like the

phœnix. You have, indeed, done towards me the contrary to what doctors are wont to do, for they temper the bitterness of their medicines with something sweet, while you have spoilt all the sweetness that was in your letter by the bitterness of this news. I beg you, Messer Giuseppe, do everything in your power for the health of so noble a lady, who gives more profit to the world by the teaching of her example than others do by their sermons and erudition. Expend your utmost care, use all your knowledge, for if she were to die, to our great disaster, Italy might say :

'Spento il primo valor, qual fia il secondo?'[1]

But I think that the most high God, pitiful rather to us than to her, has sent you now to Viterbo that you may be His instrument to restore that virtuous and unique lady to perfect health. . . .

"Rome, June 28, 1543."[2]

Cincio must have answered this, and provoked a further effusion from Tolomei : "What you have written to me about the Marchesa di Pescara has both pleased and displeased me at the same time. I am glad that she is pleased to accept the reverence I bear her ; but that she should be astonished at my reverencing her, that I cannot hear without much displeasure. Because to say that is nothing else than to accuse me of extreme ignorance, as though I were reduced to the last stage of stupidity, if I did not understand or recognise her most shining and singular virtues, which

[1] Petrarca, Sonnet cccxxxviii.
[2] *Lettere di M. Claudio Tolomei*, Vol. I, p. 167.

are so illustrious and so evident to the world, that one may well say with the poet :

         ‘In tutto è orbo chi non vede il sole.’[1]

Let us take it for granted that she well knows for how many years I have honoured her as my lady, not allured by other loveliness, nor bound by any other tie than that of her most noble virtue. But I know very well that these words were born of her incredible modesty, on which account she would always far rather do things worthy of praise and admiration than hear the praises and wonder to which her works give rise. Also, she is always more eager to help others than to receive any fruits of gratitude and honour, which, however, follow her all the more, the more one knows that she is far from desiring them. I am delighted to find from your letters that she is gradually recovering from her illness, for let me remind you, Messer Giuseppe, that in her life is bound up that of many others, who are continually sustained by her both in body and soul.

     “Rome, August 7, 1543.”[2]

Yet another most interesting letter was the outcome of the Marchesa’s illness; this was from Giberti’s friend, the Veronese physician and humanist, Girolamo Fracastoro, to Carlo Gualteruzzi, Vittoria’s faithful friend and secretary, and runs thus : “Concerning the state of the most illustrious Marchesa di Pescara . . . this, as you know, is my opinion, that as the body when it tyrannises over the mind ruins and destroys all its

---

[1] Petrarca, *Trionfo d’ Amore*, Cap. ii.
[2] *Lettere di M. Claudio Tolomei*, Vol. I, p. 179.

Alinari.

Viterbo from the Giardino Pubblico.

soundness, so in the same way when the mind becomes
the tyrant, and not merely the true lord, it wastes and
destroys the soundness of the body first, and then
their common bond of union . . . and sins against
prudence and charity. For God wills that, while we
are on this pilgrimage and wayfarers, this companion
and minister should be necessary to us. So we ought
to take care of it and behave to it like a true master,
who does not deprive his servant of that which is due
to him. God alone knows the end of things, and
when and how it will be good for us to be delivered
from this. It does not belong to us to bring it about,
or to be the cause of it by our want of care, contrary
to the example that God, our true Lord and Master,
showed us in Himself. I have put forward this little
discourse, my Lord, because I fancy that all the
Marchesa's sufferings had their origin in this. Not
that I do not think that so much intellect will not
know and recognise this better than I do, but that the
error does not arise in general things, which can be
clearly seen and known, but in particular things, and
there lies all the difficulty : not in things in which one
sees a great departure from the right, but in those
where the departure is small and insensible, and,
because one does not see it, one does not heed it.
Which little, repeated over and over again, becomes
great and perceptible, yet, as we do not perceive it
ourselves, we go on little by little to our hurt, so
difficult is it to find that just mean and balance which
is fitting between the master and the servant. On
which account, Signor Messer Carlo, I should wish for
a physician of the mind to be found, who should

minutely calculate and justly balance all the Marchesa's actions, giving to the master what is his and to the servant what belongs to him. And this physician must be wise, and of so much authority that her Ladyship would believe and obey him, like the most illustrious and most reverend Cardinal of England. And this beginning once put right, I do not doubt that all the rest will follow. Otherwise, I see that the most beautiful light of this world in some strange way will be extinguished and removed from our eyes, which God avert of His goodness. . . .

"Verona, August 12, 1544."[1]

Under the direction of Cardinal Pole, Vittoria no doubt achieved that "giusta misura e bilancia," and, before the end of 1544, she returned to Rome.

---

[1] Letter dated Verona, August 12, 1544. Pino, *Nuova Scelta di Lettere*, Lib. I, p. 263.

CHAPTER XI

LATER WRITINGS

The true and principall ornament of the minde in everye manne (I beleeve) are letters . . . which undoubtedlye have beene granted of God unto men for a soveraigne gift.—CASTIGLIONE, *Il Cortegiano* (Hoby).

WHEN we pass from Vittoria Colonna's early sonnets to her later ones, now collected under the title of *Rime sacre e morali*, to which is appended the capitolo, *Del Trionfo di Cristo*, we are conscious of a great advance in art, and an immense difference of atmosphere. The vein of artificiality and convention has wellnigh vanished, and with it the tedium that it induced. We are now in contact, not with what a woman wished to feel, or felt she ought to feel, but with what she did feel ; these are the records of experience, and such can hardly be dull ; moreover, they are the experiences won from contemplation, and from retirement into that cell of self-knowledge of which St. Catherine wrote : "Voi dovete sempre rinascere nella stalla del cognoscimento di voi."

We have already said that Vittoria had the power of making goodness attractive : she had the yet rarer faculty of making religion interesting. It would not be unprofitable to study how this comes about, for, undoubtedly, there is much genuine religion which repels, either by reason of its narrowness or its triviality, together with a certain aloofness from life. Christina Rossetti is an example of the contrary of this ; there is no stiffness or aloofness in her religion ; it is the thing that principally concerns and engrosses her ; we may take it or leave it as we like, but we cannot take her without it. This attitude is, perhaps, more characteristic of the Latin races than of the Northern ones ; less imaginative, less self-conscious, they are more alert, quicker to receive impressions, and they are at the same time dowered with that naive assurance which makes the chief charm of children— the certainty that whatever is important to them cannot be indifferent to others. Such minds, when they have assimilated religion, cannot help imparting it ; they live in the sunshine and the shadow and the mystery of it, and, if we approach them, we cannot escape from it, not because they are eager to teach, but because they are learning all the time.

In 1543, Rinaldo Corso published the *Trionfo di Cristo* with thirty-six of the *Rime sacre*, but not in the order in which they now stand. This little book contained a very long-winded commentary ; it was dedicated to the " very illustrious Madonna Veronica Gambara da Correggio : and to gentle Ladies," and began with the following introduction, " Alle amorose Donne " :—

" Since by your favour, most fair Ladies, I have come into an excellent harbour out of the first deep, I should willingly have avoided entering the second, as much because I do not find myself very well instructed in divine things, as because my intellect is not as capable of these conceptions as (thanks to you) it was of the others.

I should also have done so because it seems that subjects of this kind can only be described in a simple and clear manner. Nevertheless, because, on the other hand, our Vittoria is subtle and lofty in all her poems, I have not been able (however inadequate I feel myself) to refuse you my labour in any respect in which I think that it should prove of some utility or consolation to you. Therefore, howsoever it be, take this second part from me light-heartedly ; and, if my toil be at all dear to you, only permit me as a reward to love you, as I always did and shall do as long as I live."

The *Rime sacre e morali*, as they now stand, contain two hundred and eight sonnets, all of which are interesting as marking the author's development, the building up of her faith, and the strengthening of her mind. Some serve specially to confirm the fact that her doctrine was essentially Catholic—a fact that some Protestant writers have denied, one of whom goes so far as to state that " one thing is certain : none of her poems were addressed to saints or angels." What becomes then of the two beautiful sonnets to St. Francis (cxix, cxx), in one of which these lines occur :—

> " Francis, in whom like wax our Lord imprest
> His bitter wounds and sole elected thee,
> Sealed with the seal of love thus vividly,
> His image true to us to manifest.
>
> .　　.　　.　　.　　.
>
> Spirit in Paradise, I pray thee plead
> That I may follow thy fair, humble way,
> In thought, in wish, in every holy deed " :—[1]

---

[1] " Francesco, in cui, siccome in umil cera,
　　Con sigillo d' amor sì vive impresse

to say nothing of innumerable poems to the Blessed
Virgin ? Of the rest, Sonnet xvii is perhaps the finest.

" From joy to joy, from one to other band
    Of sweet and gentle thoughts, supernal Love
    From the hard winter and the cold thereof
    Guides me to springtide's warm and verdant land.
Haply the Lord—since He beholds me stand
    With breast like wax whereon the eternal seal
    Hath deeply cut a faith profound and real,
    Moulding my inmost heart beneath His hand—
Wills not with bitter cross and steep ascent,
    But with the easy yoke and burden light,
    To lead me into port by some smooth road.
Or it may be this little peace is lent
    By the wise goodness of my Father and God
    To arm and fit me for a weary fight."[1]

Gesù l' aspre sue piaghe, e sol t' elesse
A mostrarne di sè l' immagin vera.

.   .   .   .   .

. . . or prega in ciel, beato
Spirto, ch' io segua la bell' orma umíle,
I pensieri, i desiri, e l' opre sante."

[1] " Di gioia in gioia, d' una in altra schiera
    Di dolci e bei pensier, l' amor superno
    Mi guida fuor del freddo arido verno
    Alla sua verde e calda primavera.
Forse il Signor, fin che di molle cera
    Mi vegga il petto, onde 'l sigillo eterno
    M' imprima dentro nel più vivo interno
    Del cor la fede sua fondata e vera,
Non vuol con l' aspra croce al sentier erto,
    Ma col giogo soave e peso lieve
    Condurmi al porto per la via men dura :
O forse ancor, come benigno esperto
    Padre e maestro, in questa pace breve
    A lunga guerra m' arma e m' assecura."

And there is a long sequence of sonnets on the Passion, of which the following is one of the best.

" Stretched naked on the Cross the Lord I see,
    With piercèd side and nailèd hands and feet,
    Upon Whose head the thorny crown is set,
    By vilest men assailed with injury.
The heavy weight of the world's sin doth lie
    Upon His shoulders, and in such a plight
    The heart that only is with love alight
    O'ercometh death and every enemy.
Patience, obedience true, and humbleness,
    These were the stars, with other virtues high,
    That did adorn His sun of charity.
Therefore in that sharp fight did these appear
    After His lovely death to make more clear
    The glory of His everlasting grace."[1]

In the *Trionfo di Cristo*, written in terza rima, Vittoria reaches her highest level. The idea is evidently borrowed from Savonarola's *Trionfo della Croce*, with which we know the Marchesa to have been acquainted ; and

---

[1] " Veggio in croce il Signor nudo e disteso,
    Coi piedi e man chiodate e 'l destro lato
    Aperto, e 'l capo sol di spine ornato,
    E da vil gente d' ogni parte offeso ;
Avendo sulle spalle il grave peso
    Delle colpe del mondo ; e 'n tale stato
    La morte e l' avversario stuolo irato
    Vincer solo col cor d' amore acceso.
Pazienza, umiltà, vero ubbidire,
    Con l' altre alme virtù furon le stelle
    Ch' ornaro il sol della sua caritade :
Onde nell' aspra pugna e queste e quelle
    Fecer più chiara dopo 'l bel morire
    La gloria dell' eterna sua bontade."

both, no doubt, have taken something, not only from the much-imitated *Trionfi* of Petrarca, but also from the most glorious pageant ever imagined—Dante's veritable Trionfo, which is made sweet for all time with the "handfulls of lilies" that were showered upon Beatrice.

Savonarola, who set himself in this work to prove the truth of religion by reason, began by presenting a picture of the visible Church. "First then," he writes, "let us place before our eyes a four-wheeled chariot, and upon it Christ as a conqueror, all wounded and crowned with thorns, by which is shown forth all His Passion and Death, with which He overcame the whole world. And above His head there shall be a light like a sun with three faces, as a figure of the Blessed Trinity, from which a marvellous splendour shall proceed which shall illumine His Humanity together with the whole Church. In the left hand of Christ shall be the Cross with all the other instruments of His Passion, and in His right hand the Scriptures of the Old and New Testaments. Near His feet shall be placed the Chalice with the Host, and other vases of oils and balsams, with the other tokens of the Sacraments of the Church. Beneath this first step, on which is Christ, shall be the most holy Mother of God, the Virgin Mary, and, below her, vases of gold and of silver and of precious stones, full of ashes and of the bones of the dead, shall be arranged all round. In front of the chariot shall be Apostles and Preachers, so that it shall appear as though they drew the chariot, and these shall be preceded by Patriarchs and Prophets, with an innumerable number of men and women of the Old Testament. Round about the chariot, like a crown, there shall be an immense number of martyrs, among whom there shall be the Doctors of the Church with books open in their hands, and among them an innumerable multitude of virgins adorned with lilies. Then, behind the chariot, an infinite number of men and women of every condition . . . who are all with one heart praising Christ. . . . This chariot then, described and set in order before our eyes, will be like a new world from which we shall deduce a new philosophy. . . . And just as the philosophers say that, after the invisible substances, the Heavens are the principal cause of the things generated under them, so we say that, after the invisible divine Majesty, the principal cause of grace and of our salvation is the Cross and the Passion of Christ. . . . As then the philosophers, having before their eyes the order of the universe, and, by reason of their desire to learn, considering the marvellous effects of nature, seeking their causes, rising little by little from lower things to higher, attain to the knowledge of the invisible things and of the divine Majesty ; so we, if we diligently search into the things Christ has done and does continually in His Church, symbolised in this Triumph, shall begin to wonder at and earnestly to seek the causes of these things, and then we shall attain, little by little, to the knowledge of the invisible things and of the divine Majesty of Christ."

Part of Vittoria's vision, which begins with an allusion to the seven years during which she had bewailed her husband, runs thus :—

U

" Then I beheld a chariot of such fashion
　　It seemed to circle heaven and earth and sea
　　With its clear splendour and fair graciousness.

Upon it was the Emperor of Heaven,
　　He who descended here for our salvation
　　To save from bondage and from cruel death.

For many satiate their avarice
　　With goods of others, proudly triumphing,
　　Vile seekers after greedy, impious sway ;

But this One conquered and His kingdom gave
　　When as a sacrifice He gave Himself,
　　Washing away our fault with His pure Blood.

His was the victory and ours the prize ;
　　He wrought that life should follow from His death
　　To us who were the prey of the great foe.

　　·　　·　　·　　·　　·　　·

I saw the honoured and most sacred Head,
　　Which used to wear an ample crown of stars,
　　Wearing a crown inwoven of sharp thorns,

And wounded was the hand which metes out light,
　　Unto the heavens their course, to mortals life,
　　Here virtue, yonder lasting glory and good.

Upon the sacred shoulders, so that man
　　Of Heaven may be approved, I saw the wood
　　Which ever makes me weep for the first fault ;

That Cross which is our certain pledge of joy,
　　And which we ought to worship with clasped hands,
　　Since it supported Him, our true support.

Nor was the weight found grievous unto him,
　　By so much more the thought of our affliction,
　　Alas ! outweighed and made it seem but light.

Upon the right hand of the car was seated
  In royal state the Virgin, of all virtues
  Mirror, by whom we flee from endless doom.

She was, before all other temples, temple
  Sacred to God, and I beheld how she
  Through humbleness put down the proud and wicked.

And at the holy feet I also saw
  Her whom the same name honours, radiant
  With joyful love and crowned with golden hair.

A true compassion moved her to weep here ;
  Heaven therefore willeth that in equal measure
  Glory in place of grief she now should reap.

    .   .   .   .   .   .

Seeking her dead Lord at the sepulchre,
  He showed Himself alive, and gave her sea
  Of bitter tears their high and happy port.

Blessèd is she who, scorning fruit and root
  Of the world's good, now from her Lord receives
  Other and everlasting blessedness.

I, who beheld a more delightful dawn
  By other sun illumed, with other heat
  Than that which brings our flowers to bud and bloom,
Here fixed my eyes and made my thought stand firm."[1]

---

[1] " Io vidi allor un carro tal ch' a tondo
    Il ciel, la terra, il mar cinger parea
    Col suo chiaro splendor vago e giocondo ;

  Sovra, l' imperador del cielo avea,
    Quel che scese fra noi per noi scampare
    Del servir grave e della morte rea.

  E come molti empir l' invidie avare
    De' beni altrui, superbi trionfando,
    Vil voglie d' un ingordo empio regnare ;

Very little of Vittoria's prose has come down to us ; it can only be a very small proportion of her letters that have survived, and we do not know what besides may have been lost. All that remains is one prayer in Latin, a paraphrase of the *Ave Maria*, and the *Pianto sopra la Passione di Cristo*—a very beautiful meditation, which deals rather with the Compassion of Our Lady, and from which we give the following extracts :—

" It seems to me that the grief which all day long had been gathered up in the heart of the Virgin . . . .

Costui vinse e donò 'l suo regno, quando
 In sacrificio sè medesmo diede,
 Col puro sangue il nostro error lavando.

Sua la vittoria e nostra è la mercede :
 Fece che vita abbiam del suo morire,
 Noi ch' eravam del gran nemico prede.

  . . . . . .

Io vedea l' onorata e sacra testa
 Che suole aver di stelle ampia corona,
 Di spine averla acute ora contesta,

E piagata la man che toglie e dona
 Al ciel corso, al sol luce, ai mortal vita,
 Qui virtù, là su gloria eterna e buona.

Su gli omer santi, acciò ch' al ciel gradita
 Sia l' umil nostra spoglia, io vidi 'l legno
 Che a pianger sempre il primo error m' invita ;

Quel del nostro gioir securo pegno,
 Ch' adorar con le man giunte si deve,
 Perch' ei sostenne il nostro ver sostegno.

Non fu alle sante spalle il peso greve,
 Quanto dovrebbe, oimè, del nostro affanno
 Tal rimembranza farne il peso lieve !

now, in touching the sacred body of Christ, became infinitely greater, and issued from her eyes in more bitter tears, and from her lips in more ardent sighs . . . The Magdalen verily is here, serving Christ weeping ; she accompanies the Blessed Mother with such devotion and with such ardent love that she will be comforted before any other. . . . Now who could imagine with what tenderness the afflicted Mother thanked the celestial Father that He had put an end to that torment, and that he had made her the Mother of so

---

Sul carro, alla man destra, in real scanno
  La vergin era d' ogni virtù esempio,
  Per cui possiam fuggir l' eterno danno.

Costei fu innanzi a tutti i tempi tempio
  A Dio sacrato : e vidi e sapea come
  Con umiltà calcò 'l superbo e l' empio.

Ai santi piè colei, che simil nome
  Onora, vidi ardendo d' amor lieta
  Risplender cinta dell' aurate chiome.

La mosse a pianger qui ben degna pièta ;
  Onde 'l ciel vuol che con ugual misura,
  In vece del dolor, la gloria or mieta.

Al sepolcro cercando il Signor morto,
  L' apparve vivo e diede alto e felice
  Al gran mar delle sue lagrime porto.

Beata lei ch 'l frutto e la radice
  Sprezzò del mondo, e del suo Signor ora
  Altra dolcezza e sempiterna elice!

Io che da un altro sol più vaga aurora
  Illustrata vedea, con altro caldo
  Da quel che i nostri fiori apre e 'ncolora,
Tenni qui gli occhi fisi e 'l pensier saldo."

obedient a Son ; and with ardent charity she thanked
the Holy Spirit that, through excess of love, He had
made her rejoice in this pain ; and with what marvellous delight she thanked the Incarnate Wisdom and
her most beloved Christ, that with so much humble
obedience, He had consummated the sacrifice of Himself ! And with what great love she thanked the
angels that they were present to atone for the defection of man ! And I believe that, out of her profound
humility, stooping even to insensate things, she
thanked the sun that it became dark, the earth that it
trembled, the rocks that they were rent, the sky that it
was overcast . . . so that divers causes and many loves
tormented her, and it was only because of the immensity
of her love . . . that her spirit departed with the soul
of Christ, and her soul remained to honour the
Divinity and to weep over the dead body. . . . The
more she loved, the more she grieved . . . faith alone
kept her alive, and she kept faith alive to clothe therewith the whole world that was then despoiled of it.
So, since all the treasure that the Christian has springs
from the true faith, and he has received it from the
Virgin Mary (for, without her, it would have been dead),
we ought to consider under what an obligation we lie
to her, and certainly we shall find it so great that this
mortal life would not be sufficient to satisfy for the
thousandth part."

The following is a translation of the Marchesa's
Latin prayer :—

" Grant, I beseech Thee, O Lord, that I may always
adore Thee with that abasement of soul which befits my

humbleness, and with that exaltation of mind which Thy Majesty demands, and let me ever live in the fear which Thy justice inspires and in the hope which Thy mercy allows, and submit to Thee as Almighty, yield myself to Thee as All-wise, and turn to Thee as to supreme Perfection and Goodness. I beseech Thee, most tender Father, that Thy most living fire may purify me, that Thy most clear light may illumine me, and that Thy most pure love may so avail me that, without let or hindrance of mortal things, I may return to Thee in happiness and security." [1]

In spite of contemporary judgments, it would hardly be true to claim for Vittoria that she was a great poet, but it may fairly be said that, as a religious poet, she was both great and original, for the consecration of a talent to contemplative and mystical religion was a new thing at that time. Among our own poets, the one who most resembles her is Christina Rossetti, but she has a much freer flight ; yet they have to some extent the same limitations : they are both deep rather than wide, and they fall into the error of wearing their similes thin. To Vittoria the sun and the stars, to Christina the Lamb and the Dove, seem to exhaust all possible metaphor, and we grow weary of the reiteration. But these are trifles. The real significance of both writers is that they have sat at leisure in quiet places and have heard secret things ; they have learned some of the meaning of the Eternal Mystery, and they have something to unfold to us, if we too will sit at spiritual

---

[1] The text, from a MS. in the Biblioteca Casanatense, is given by Visconti, p. cxlv.

leisure ; and for this reason it is worth while not only to read them, but to return to them again and again.

A temple might be raised to Vittoria far exceeding in size and richness that which was erected to her beautiful sister-in-law, Giovanna d'Aragona, but, in an age when all wrote adulatory letters and complimentary sonnets, it is difficult to glean much from contemporary opinions. We like to know that those who were themselves possessors of the "soveraigne gift" gave her a foremost place in the world of letters, and that the arch-censor, Bembo, prized her taste in poetry above that of the most learned masters.

Ariosto, who praised so many, bestowed perhaps his noblest commendations on her :—

> " One shall I choose, who such an one shall be
> As above envy shall have soared so high
> That none could feel offence, if only she
> Of me were praised and all the rest passed by.
> She not alone wins immortality
> With that sweet style, the best that I descry,
> But makes whoe'er her speech or pen shall praise
> Rise from the grave and live eternal days.
>
> .   .   .   .   .
>
> Vittoria is her name." [1]

---

[1] " Sceglieronne una, e sceglierolla tale
    Che superato avrà l' invidia in modo,
    Che nessun' altra potrà avere a male,
    Se l' altre taccio, e se lei sola lodo.
    Quest' una ha non pur sè fatta immortale
    Col dolce stil, di che il miglior non odo;
    Ma può qualunque, di cui parli, o scriva,
    Trar del sepolcro, e far ch' eterno viva.

    .   .   .   .   .

    Vittoria è 'l nome."—*Orl. Fur.*, XXXVII. 16-18.

And very noble, too, is Annibale Caro's line,

"Victorious o'er the world and o'er herself,"[1]

but the noblest of all tributes paid to her was from the pen of him whose friendship was the crown and glory of her life, of whom it was said that she directed

"His course of life by loveliest ways to heaven."[2]

---

1 "Vinto avea 'l mondo e vinta avea sè stessa."

2 "Per voi si scrive, voi che 'l viver mio
   Volgeste al ciel per le più belle strade."

These two lines were added by the younger Michelangelo to his great-uncle's madrigal, "Ora su 'l destro, or su 'l sinistro piede." Cf. Guasti's edition of the *Rime* of Michelangelo, p. 30.

CHAPTER XII

OUT OF THE WORLD

We are not babes, but know the minute's worth,
And feel that life is large and the world small,
So wait till life have passed from out the world.

ROBERT BROWNING.

IT was towards the end of the year 1544 that the
Marchesa returned to Rome, much broken in health,
and took up her residence in the Benedictine Convent
of Sant' Anna de' Funari.[1] We cannot doubt from
what we know of her manner of life that, under any
circumstances, it would have been her choice to make
her home in a convent, but it must have been sad to
her to look round on the city in which nothing now
remained to her : her nearest relations were in exile,
their lands confiscated, their palaces in the hands of
strangers. The nearest relative left to her in Rome

---

[1] Sant' Anna de' Funari was in the quarter of Sant' Eustachio on
the site of the ruins of the Circus Flaminius, and was a district of rope-
makers, hence the cognomen of the convent. It was founded, under
the name of Santa Maria in Julia, as a Benedictine convent in 1297
by the Beata Santuccia Terrabotti di Gubbio; but in 1793, the number
of nuns having become greatly reduced, they were obliged to vacate
their convent and give it over to the Sisters of the Visitation, who
remained there until 1809. In 1815, the convent became an asylum
for poor orphans, and in 1887 the whole was demolished to make
room for modern improvements.

was her cousin, Giulia Colonna, who was married to
Giuliano Cesarini, and it was to the Cesarini palace
that, scarcely more than two years later, Vittoria was
carried to die.

Friends as well as kinsfolk were missing : the old
circle had been completely broken up, and death had
claimed many of them.   In 1543, Vittoria had lost her
very oldest friend, Giovan Matteo Giberti ; his loss,
following so closely on that of Contarini, must have
been a great sorrow for her.   Giberti was, perhaps,
the most interesting of all those for whom she cared,
combining as he did that mixture of sweetness, sanity,
and strength which is as rare as it is delightful.   We
have already noticed his way of life and his attitude
towards literature, but it is as a great reforming bishop
that he chiefly claims our admiration.   Contarini reported of him as far back as 1530 : "The bishop of
Verona surpasses all the others in cordial friendship
for his Holiness, but he has deliberately left the court
and attends to his bishoprick. . . . He seems to me
above all things supremely religious, and a true
bishop"; and, subsequently, San Carlo Borromeo
pointed to him as a perfect model.   Giberti's dealings
with Ochino were marked by good sense, charity, and
loyalty to the Church, Ochino himself testifying that
the bishop would counsel him to nothing but the most
absolute obedience.   He had no easy part to play, and,
while his strictness made him disliked by lax Catholics,
his gentleness laid him open to the suspicion of favour-
ing heretics.   Yet he seems one of the strong men of
those troublous times, and we feel that the Marchesa
was honoured by his friendship.

Giberti died at Verona on December 30, 1543, and on the first day of the new year his secretary, Francesco della Torre, wrote thus to Carlo Gualteruzzi : "I have taken up my pen to tell you some part of that which concerns you no less than me, but think in what state of mind I am, with the clanging of the bells, which are ringing for the funeral of his Lordship ; for although he left in his will that they should not spend more than ten scudi upon his burial, ordering that he should be carried without pomp from the bishop's palace to the church, the city nevertheless would not suffer this, but shows by every sign that she knows she has lost her father. I could not describe to you, nor would you believe (for I, who see and hear it, can hardly believe it myself) the public grief and lamentations, not only of the nobles, but of all the people. They flock from all parts of the city and of the contado to see the body, as a holy body of a true servant of God. Sunday and yesterday we kept him in the house, when it might have been the Jubilee. To-day, to be free from the noise, we have taken him to the church. I do not think there can be a single person in the city who has not come to see him. Some lament him, some praise him, some kiss his hands or his feet, some kneel down before him ; the sick come to touch him. I swear to you by our brotherly love that one could never find words to express the opinion which is here universal of his holiness, founded not only upon the innocence of his past life, but upon his most exemplary death, at which several beautiful incidents occurred, about some of which I will not keep silence. When he was near his end, he was asked if he would like to remain here if it were possible, and he answered quickly : 'No, no ; to die, to die, if it be the will of my Lord God.'   The Crucifix having been placed in his hands, it was impossible to remove it, for he held it in such a close embrace, in which act he showed a marvellous pleasure and sweetness.   At the end, having had the Blessed Sacrament brought to his room, with the greatest humility and devotion, with his eyes fixed upon It, immovable, without a quiver, he passed away with such quietness that it appeared exactly as if he were transformed into It."[1]

A few weeks later, della Torre writes again to the same friend : "To hear and see the things that we have heard and seen, and remain firm, is not possible without great help from divine grace, particularly for one who, like me, for eighteen years has continuously tasted the fruits of such sweet and holy company, treated more like a son or brother by that most noble soul.   Even if his nature had not always all that gentleness which mine would have desired, his imperfection in that regard was tempered with so many other perfections that that austerity could not offend.   I assure you, my most honoured brother, that now I wish to do nothing else but write and speak of him. . . . And to the most excellent Signora Marchesa I commend myself most devoutly, imploring her Excellence to deign to grant me a little portion of her favour; which gift, although it be great, cannot be denied me by her, begging it, as I do, by virtue of the merits of this most holy memory."[2]

---

[1] Pino, *Nuova Scelta di Lettere*, Lib. III, pp. 146–148.

[2] *Ibid.*, pp. 149, 150.   Letter of January 22, 1544.

From yet another letter of della Torre's to a fellow-secretary, Francesco Mazo, we should judge that the latter entered the Marchesa's service. "After the dissolution," writes della Torre, "of that tie, which held many of us bound together for a time in one same dwelling, each of us being obliged to take one one way and one another, you know that I was pleased above everything at the decision of those who, having the means to do so, elected not to seek the support of a new patron. . . . And what patron was ever worthy of so much love, honour, and respect as ours! But you must also remember that when, by letters from Rome, the course was proposed to you of entering the service of the most illustrious Signora Marchesa di Pescara, I was with all my mind of the opinion that you ought not to draw back from it ; for it seemed to me that it would not be departing from our first resolve to enter that house, where, as long as that most excellent Lady lives, the virtues of our patron, whom she loved so much, will remain always alive ; nay, that it would be rather a continuing as far as possible in the ancient service, and doing honour, and a thing most acceptable, to that most saintly soul, who, I am sure, will not hold himself less served by you after death because you will be faithful and diligent to that truly excellent Lady, whose genuine goodness and infinite worthiness he loved and esteemed so much."[1]

This letter is interesting as testifying to the high regard in which Giberti is known to have held Vittoria.

The year 1546 brought the Marchesa an intense grief

---

[1] Pino, *Nuova Scelta di Lettere*, Lib. I, pp. 289–291. Letter of June 25, 1544.

in the death of del Vasto. We get the following graphic
account of his end from the Life of Paola Antonia de'
Negri. "At length, finding himself sick unto death at
Vigevano, he wished that the Angelica should come to
visit him, and Count Francesco Landriano was among
those who made her come, and, when she had arrived,
she comforted him in such a manner that he made a
holy death, with so much readiness to suffer that he
offered to Our Lord to remain voluntarily in that
death-agony until the day of judgment, if that should
be His divine will ; and he showed a spirit of such great
joyousness that he seemed to rejoice in those pains,
always with such fervent prayers to Our Lord, that he
made everyone weep for tenderness. The Angelica
was always beside him, and he would not let her go
away, and talked with her to his last breath of the
manner in which Our Lord was dealing with his soul.
A great number of religious assembled to visit him
and to console him, and, not knowing his state of
mind, some said to him : Be of good cheer, most
illustrious son, for you will get back your health, and
you will be again famous and glorious in this world.
And he, albeit that he was almost at the point of death,
turned his eyes and face to the Mother Mistress,
smiling as though he ridiculed such words, and wished
to hear from her another fashion of speech, which was
to encourage him, as she did, to ask pardon for his sins,
to trust in the most precious Blood of Christ, to the
contempt of this life, and to resign himself wholly into
the hands of God, and to desire to be with Christ,
without prejudice, however, to that fervent desire to
suffer voluntarily every pain for love of Him. And

so he passed away most happily to a better life, dying in the arms of the Mother, to the great marvel of all the bystanders of every sort and condition, among whom many noble and illustrious persons understood that the desire of the Marchese had been to become a Capuchin, so great was his devotion."[1]

We know well that Vittoria would appreciate to the utmost all that was beautiful and consoling in this end ; and yet another friend was to pass away before her, though only by a few weeks ; Cardinal Bembo died in Rome in the January of 1547, while Cardinal Sadoleto survived her only by a few months.

Vittoria's great friendship with Michelangelo had suffered no diminution from separation. He himself records that she often sent him letters and poems from Orvieto and Viterbo, and that from the latter place she came frequently to see him ; but we may well imagine that her renewed intercourse with him was one of the chief interests of her last years, and that their relations with each other took on new lights and beauties. For love is at once most changing and most unchangeable. No great friendship ever stood still, but its differences are so subtle, its development so gradual, that we feel only a sense of growth, and never one of alteration : the Love of Friendship has its own Gospel ; its name-stone is an amethyst, its colour violet : its flowers are lilies of the valley.

Cardinal Pole returned to Rome in 1546, and, among these few who greatly loved her, we need not think of Vittoria as unhappy.

There are two attitudes which make life bearable.

---

[1] *Vita dell' Angelica Paola Antonia de' Negri*, pp. 29, 30.

One is the feeling we have in youth that life is before us—not necessarily happiness, but possibility, opportunity, above all, mystery. There is not anything that might not happen to us, and, where everything is out of sight, nothing is out of reach. Then, as the years pass by, another sense comes to us, no less satisfying, and far more restful: the feeling that life is behind us. And, as in youth we are lured on by life's potentialities and made eager, active, alert, in later life the point of view changes, and we let go anxiety and expectation; even as with Christian, the burden is loosed from our shoulders and falls from off our back, and we are the happier and the freer. This is the loveliness of age: it is a large freedom, a great deliverance. Middle-age, that uncertain period which is never really the middle of any man's life, but is an attitude which takes hold of people at quite different times, and which some seem to escape altogether, draws its grey gloom from the loss of the sense of mystery. When once we have recognised our limitations, have accepted the fact that there are some things we shall never attain, and that nothing very wonderful will ever happen to us, we may have said a true word, but we have not said a wise one; because there are certain senses in which no one need acknowledge limitations, certain hopes without which no one is called upon to live. Youth is personal, individual, egotistic, and that is the real limitation; it is the impersonal outlook which engages us to wide issues and prevents life narrowing and closing in around us.

To Vittoria that middle period never came; from the day of her husband's death, in her own estimation,

x

life was behind her ; all her personal hopes and dreams were over, and so she entered into her larger inheritance.

We are fortunate in having letters of this time which show where the Marchesa's interests and occupations lay. That her choice of a residence was happy, we learn from her own words to Morone : " I am much pleased with the solitude of Rome, and with the society of these pure and gentle spouses of Our Lord, who keep with Him, inwardly and outwardly, that faith which He has given them. And at the same time, my Lord, Christ has always shown me that I am not adapted to the affairs of the world, so that so much the more it seems to me that I am doing the best." [1] Also in a letter to her brother, Ascanio, written probably in the early days of her return to Rome, she says : " Of myself I can only say that I feel better every day ; the place is dry and convenient, and the Sisters have lived here for a long while past in a most edifying manner." [2] This letter contains much advice about his affairs, and in a still longer one written to her nephew, Fabrizio, Ascanio's son, she takes special trouble to explain to him the full history of the Colonna states, thereby showing that she still took the keenest interest in the fortunes of her family.

Three long letters to the Duchessa d'Amalfi probably date from these days ; this lady was her cousin, and had many points of resemblance with her, having been a friend and a follower of Valdès, while remaining loyal to the Church; she also shared the Marchesa's literary

[1] Letter dated May 27, 1545. *Carteggio*, CLXXII.
[2] *Carteggio*, Letter CLXXVI.

tastes, especially in the cultivation of poetry, and, like her, elected to pass her last years in a convent. These are rather religious meditations than letters, and, at any rate, serve to establish the fact that the writer's theology was distinctly Catholic. The first concludes with this passage : "Above all, I pray you, strive to see how Mary, our most singular Patroness and Queen, has incarnated in herself the wonderful Mystery of the most high Word, and how she melts with divine fervour to see her own flesh made a living eternal Sun, and how she lives blessed in the repose and sure peace of heaven, and how she rejoices to see that from her living Light are born the rays which make Paradise lovely, and which pass through His graciousness into the blessed, in order to unite them in the high eternal light of God, into which by His goodness may He lead us." [1]

In the second letter we have : "This morning my sweetest thought beheld with the mind's eye Heaven's Lady and ours, embracing her Son with intensest love and superabundant joy ; and, with purest light, I seemed to discern a thousand ties which bound them to each other with bonds of most ardent charity. In the first place, her clear and lucid intellect was united to Him, as much as the creature can be with the Creator, and her wise and most true soul was humbly joined to its sole divine object. The pure and resplendent Humanity not only reposed in her as in a dwelling, but my thought saw them so alike that one same flesh veiled this soul and that from us mortals. . . . And because He gave her the power of a mother, the

---

[1] *Carteggio*, Letter CLXVIII.

love of a spouse, the confidence of a daughter, He
made her able to soar far above all the heavenly choirs
on the wings of her great merit. . . . Now consider
devoutly this most high light, above all the angels,
united with her Beloved in the most profound peace,
and raise your mind a little to that One and Triune
Light, how It gazes on Its elect Lady, in whom appears
to be seen what was never seen before in any place.
The supreme, invisible Light sees Itself in this clear
and most pure crystal. It seems that here the great
Father is satisfied in having shown His invincible
power in this valiant daughter, and the Son rejoices to
have ordained for Himself with His wisdom so wise a
mother, and the Holy Spirit is gladdened by seeing His
supreme goodness glowing back in this most perfect
spouse.   And, in order that you may not be confused
by descending from such a height, return by the same
stair to meditate on her on earth. And think how she,
nourishing the Author of all life, was inwardly
nourished by Him, how sustaining Him she was sustained, and how, gently raising Him from the earth,
she was raised high in heaven, and how, for giving
Him brief repose in sleep, eternal peace was granted
her for a recompence." [1]

The third letter is a long, and very complicated,
comparison of the Magdalen and St. Catherine of
Alexandria, from which we only quote a few para-
graphs : "Of two glorious women, most beloved
sister, I should like to discourse with you ; of our
advocate and most faithful guide, Mary Magdalen,
and of her of whom we celebrate to-day the death, or

---

[1] *Carteggio*, Letter CLXIX.

rather the happy life, Catherine. . . . I see the most
fervent Magdalen hearing at the feet of Our Lord :
Dilexit multum ; and Catherine in the prison: *Agnosce,
Filia, Creatorem tuum.* The one appears to have soared
to the high degree of the seraphim by love, and the
other to be placed among the cherubim by intelligence.
. . . Let us pay then that true worship which befits
Him to Our Lord, at Whose feet I believe the one
eternally reposes with immense joy, in true and profound peace, and the other dwells on the right hand of
the Lady of Paradise, as spouse of her most blessed
Son. And therefore the former, as elect above every
other woman, and the latter as the first virgin render
thanks for God's grace to this glorious Queen, with
praise unceasing." [1]

In 1545, Cardinal Pole was sent to the Council of
Trent as legate, together with del Monte and Cervini.
Priuli and Flaminio also accompanied him. The
Marchesa felt great uneasiness on his account, as he
was known to have many enemies abroad, and it was
thought that attempts might be made to poison him.
It was because of these anxieties that she addressed the
following letter to Morone : "Knowing the confidence
that Monsignore has in your Lordship, and the
reverence that Monsignor Luisi and Monsignor
Marcantonio bear you, I implore you to remind
them constantly to attend to his safety with all possible
diligence, leaving to his Lordship in this the most
strict custody of his intrepid faith, thinking that
God has elected you out of so many others of His
servants to guard this member of His. I implore

---

[1] *Carteggio,* Letter clxx.

your Lordship for the sake of Christ, our only refuge, to deign to write to me sometimes, when you can conveniently do so."[1]

The other legates proceeded to Trent in March, but Pole deferred his departure owing to his suspicions of some plot having been made against him, and so did not arrive until May 4. In the June of the following year, he fell ill and retired to Padua. Some have said that Pole's illness was feigned in order that he might be absent during the discussions on the doctrine of Justification by Faith, as he differed widely from his colleagues ; but this is nowise borne out by the fact that, before giving any definitive sentence, the other legates sent to Pole to obtain his opinion, and incorporated his amendments into their resolution, so that the pronouncement then made has always been identified with the name of Pole. The Council, however, was broken up a few months later and adjourned to Bologna, but soon after prorogued, so that Pole, on the recovery of his health, obtained the Pope's leave to return to Rome. The Cardinal's illness had been a severe one, and during it he was attended by the famous Veronese doctor, Fracastoro, whom we have already met in connection with Vittoria. From Bembo's house at Padua he despatched this long letter to the Marchesa.

" Most illustrious Lady and honoured Mother,

"As soon as our Lilio had arrived here, he tired himself out in his first talk with me in vehemently trying to make me understand how heartily your Excellence wishes me well ; and, as if this were some-

---

[1] *Carteggio*, Letter CLXXI.

thing new and not known to me before, I let him go
on as long as he liked (which was a long time), awaiting
the conclusion he might draw from this. If this
had been, as it justly might, that, comparing my be-
haviour with such great and more than maternal love,
he convicted me of ingratitude, in that neither in deeds
nor words had I tried to respond to the least part of
such love, but had rather given signs to the contrary,
as would be easy to show, I certainly should have had
great pleasure in such a just reproof, given with that
simplicity which I have always loved in him. But, as he
did not conclude thus, I will myself draw this conclusion, and so much the more to my shame as I feel
myself to err greatly in this. And I never set myself
to correct this fault, although I cannot say that I have
not tried to do what I know I ought to do in this
matter, but, finding by experience that I cannot succeed
as I should wish, I let it stand, as though God deprived
me of this grace of being able to satisfy my mind in
this thing, which I so greatly desire to do. And this
really sometimes troubles me very much, and, when I
seek to comfort myself, I find no other sort of consolation save by persuading myself, as I have said and
written before to your Excellency, that the Divine
Will is so bent upon giving you the full reward
which it promises to such as are benefactors to those
from whom they look for no recompence (as Our Lord
declares in the parable of those who invite the poor to
their feasts), that it does not allow me to find a way to
render you courtesy in the way you use with me. And
with this hope I console myself, praying God that He
will make you ample restitution, with so much the

more affection of the soul, the more I feel that, on my part, I am infinitely wanting in it. And, at the same time, I enjoy in your great charity the image of the Divine Love, which does not tire of continuing its kindnesses, albeit the creature fails to correspond with them, but rather multiplies them the more, as does your Excellence with me. And for this I give infinite thanks to Our Lord, who gives me this experience, asking pardon for my shortcomings, first of His infinite goodness, and then of you. I need not tell you further of my condition, since our Lilio will be the bearer of this, and he will inform your Excellence of everything, and of the great comfort I have here in the house of the most reverend Bembo, where I am staying, first, with as much content and peace of mind as if I were in the house of my own father, and, secondly, with such ease that I could not desire anything better at this time : and with special enjoyment of two things in which I have always taken great delight, that is, a study and a garden, both of which I find so beautiful here, that I know not where I could find any more to my taste. And, in addition to this, the kind and delicate attention of his servants, who are so glad to see me here that that surpasses all other pleasures. And this I write to your Excellence as to my mother. . . . Do me the favour to recommend me to the prayers of that holy company with whom you are living at present. Since writing this, I heard, with much greater sorrow than I have ever felt at any of mine, of your Excellence's indisposition, beginning in the month of August and continuing to the present time. Nor have I anything to say of this, except that I will cry to the Physician of Heaven that

He will deign to be your physician, because I have no confidence that you will get any other remedy from this earthly one, except advice about diet and air, in which things I beg you to let yourself be governed. And I commend myself much to your devout prayers."[1]

In the next month Cardinal Pole returned to Rome, and probably never left it till after the Marchesa's death. He was with Bembo just before he died, and writes thus to Cardinal Cervini (the first words of the letter refer also to Pucci) : " May it please Our Lord God that both may have passed to the better life, which we may hope from His divine goodness, and from the excellent signs that we have seen of it. I speak specially of the most reverend Bembo, with whom, on account of our old friendship, at the invitation of his people, I was the day before his death, and I parted from him not without great consolation, seeing that, with a soul truly pious and Christian, he was ready and prepared for this passage."[2]

Vittoria was most likely too failing herself to have felt the loss of her old friend acutely. Becoming gravely ill, she was moved from the convent to the Cesarini palace in the Torre Argentina, where she occupied a room looking on to the garden, and here, on February 15, she made her will. She named her brother, Ascanio, her heir ; she remembered all her servants, and left much money for pious works, and she also left legacies of a thousand scudi each to four of the convents in which she had lived—San Paolo at Orvieto,

---

[1] Letter of October 4, 1546. *Carteggio*, Letter CLXXIV.
[2] Letter of February 5, 1547. *Epistolarum*, Pars IV, p. 206.

Santa Caterina in Viterbo, San Silvestro and Sant'
Anna in Rome. To Cardinal Pole she left nine thousand scudi, which, however, he would not keep, but
made the sum over to the Marchesa's favourite niece,
Vittoria, one of Ascanio's daughters, when she married
Don Garzia de Toledo—an instance of high-minded
generosity which, as Beccadelli naively suggests, most
of us would rather read about than imitate. As regards her burial, Vittoria recorded this wish : " She
wished and ordered that, when the soul should come to
leave the body, her body should be buried in a church
tomb to be selected by the venerable Abbess of the
Monastery in which the separation of soul and body
should take place, according to the style and custom of
that Monastery." Bartolommeo Stella and Lorenzo
Bonorio were named executors, and Cardinals Pole,
Sadoleto, and Morone trustees. The will is signed :
Ita testavi ego Victoria Columna.[1]

On February 25, 1547, Vittoria Colonna passed away,
giving in death, as in life, a lovely example of humility,
fortitude, and religion. Michelangelo was with her
when she was dying. On the same evening, by order
of Cardinal Pole, her body was removed to the Church
of Sant' Anna de' Funari.

Flaminio, writing to Caterina Cibo, says : " This
very day the Signora Marchesa has gone from the
world, with so much gladness of spirit and with so
much faith that we ought not to honour her death
with any other tears than those born of tenderness, and
pure and holy joy "; while Beccadelli, lamenting her loss,

---

[1] Visconti, p. cxxxix *n.* The will is printed in full by Bruto
Amante, *La Tomba di Vittoria Colonna,* pp. 48–64.

says of her that she was in poetry another Sappho, and in holy works and charity a St. Elizabeth.[1]

The ultimate resting-place of Vittoria has been, and still is, the subject of much controversy. Visconti and Reumont confidently affirm that she was buried in the common grave of the nuns, and with the same simple funeral ceremonial: this would be absolutely in accordance with the Marchesa's character and customs, and would furthermore account for the fact that no stone marks her tomb. But, while there is no manner of doubt that her body was deposited in the Church of Sant' Anna, there are letters extant which seem to show that this was only regarded as a temporary provision. These letters are from Lorenzo Bonorio, one of the Marchesa's executors, to Ascanio Colonna, and run thus :—

(February 25, 1547.) "This morning the Signora Marchesa passed away into the other life. To-night, after consultation with three most reverend Cardinals named in the will, and with all the relations of her Ladyship, male and female, the body was deposited in Sant' Anna, so that whatever your Excellence wishes may be done with it, and, if you do not wish anything different, it will remain here." (February 27.) "The body is still here in a pitched coffin ; it would be well if your Excellence would give your orders whether you wish it to remain here, and if you wish to have a velvet cover made for it, as is usual." (February 28.) "By the advice of the most reverend Cardinal of England, the case has been put in hand, and will be covered with velvet, as is usual, and it will be placed where

---

[1] Quoted by the editors of the *Carteggio*, pp. 367, 368.

they shall think fit in the Church of Sant' Anna, so
that it can be removed whenever it is desired to do
so." (March 15.) "Your orders about the body
have been carried out; it is in a pitched coffin; in three
days' time, it will be placed in the velvet case and
deposited above ground, and, if your Excellence de-
cides that it will be better to leave the body where it
is, it will be left here."[1]

From these extracts it is evident that the Marchesa's
body was deposited in the Church of Sant' Anna, but
not buried there, and it might seem likely that her
brother should have desired to place the coffin either
in one of the family vaults at the SS. Apostoli in
Rome, or at Sant' Andrea in Paliano, or beside that of
her husband in the Church of San Domenico at Naples.
There is, however, no record of such a removal. On
the other hand, in the annals of the Order, it is recorded that in 1651, owing to the papal decree, the
body of the Beata Santuccia, reformer of the Order
and foundress of the Convent of Sant' Anna, which had
up till then reposed under the high altar, was interred
in the convent burial-ground, and in this document it
is incidentally mentioned that the body of Vittoria
Colonna was interred at the same time. If this were
so, it is certainly strange that no monument of any
kind should have been set up to mark the resting-place
of one so illustrious, and, in the strict search which was
instituted at the time of the excavations in 1887, no
trace whatever could be found of her coffin.

In spite of the lack of support, there are not want-

---

[1] See Bruto Amante, *op. cit.*, pp. 28, 29. Cf. Domenico Tordi,
Carteggio, Appendix III.

ing those who believe that the Marchesa reposes in the sacristy of San Domenico Maggiore at Naples. Two coffins there bear the name of Ferdinandus Davalos, and one of them contains the skeleton of a woman with fair hair. This problem, therefore, appears to be one that will never be solved unless more documentary evidence should come to light. It would seem as though Vittoria had Providence on her side, and was to rest for ever in that humbleness and obscurity which she had always sought.

The records of the life of Vittoria Colonna are so slight, that year after year passes of which we have nothing to relate ; but, though her movements and her actions are often hidden from us, we surely know much of her character ; there is no change of intention, no divergence of ideal, only the purpose becomes more settled and the aim more true. Here was a woman perfectly equipped for the journey of life, fully developed on all sides, whose religion, being allied with intelligence, was at once more powerful and more interesting ; whose faith was as stimulating intellectually as it was spiritually satisfying ; whom a wide culture and a great charity delivered from all narrowness of mind and heart.

GENEALOGICAL TABLE OF THE HOUSE OF COLONNA

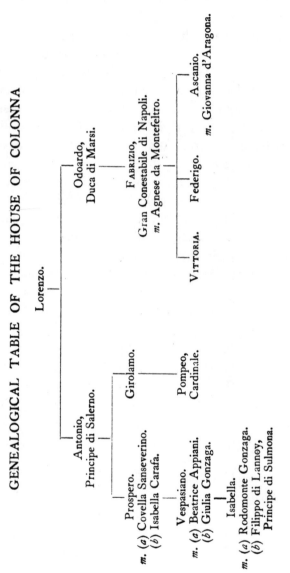

Lorenzo.

Antonio,
Principe di Salerno.

Odoardo,
Duca di Marsi.

Girolamo.

Prospero.
m. (*a*) Covella Sanseverino.
(*b*) Isabella Carafa.

Pompeo,
Cardinale.

Vespasiano.
m. (*a*) Beatrice Appiani.
(*b*) Giulia Gonzaga.

Isabella.
m. (*a*) Rodomonte Gonzaga.
(*b*) Filippo di Lannoy,
Principe di Sulmona.

Fabrizio,
Gran Conestabile di Napoli.
m. Agnese da Montefeltro.

Vittoria.

Federigo.

Ascanio.
m. Giovanna d'Aragona.

GENEALOGICAL TABLE, SHOWING HOW VITTORIA COLONNA WAS CONNECTED WITH THE HOUSE OF D'AVALOS

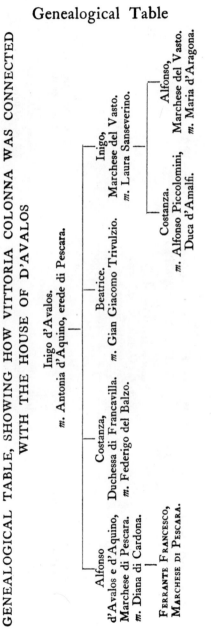

Inigo d'Avalos.
m. Antonia d'Aquino, erede di Pescara.

Costanza,
Duchessa di Francavilla.
m. Federigo del Balzo.

Beatrice.
m. Gian Giacomo Trivulzio.

Inigo,
Marchese del Vasto.
m. Laura Sanseverino.

Alfonso
d'Avalos e d'Aquino,
Marchese di Pescara.
m. Diana di Cardona.

FERRANTE FRANCESCO,
MARCHESE DI PESCARA.

Costanza.
m. Alfonso Piccolomini,
Duca d'Amalfi.

Alfonso,
Marchese del Vasto.
m. Maria d'Aragona.

GENEALOGICAL TABLE, SHOWING HOW VITTORIA COLONNA WAS CONNECTED
WITH THE HOUSE OF MONTEFELTRO

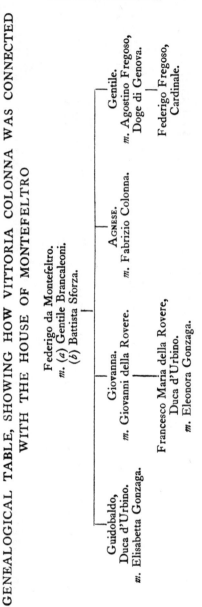

Federigo da Montefeltro.
m. (a) Gentile Brancaleoni.
(b) Battista Sforza.

Giovanna.
m. Giovanni della Rovere.

AGNESE.
m. Fabrizio Colonna.

Guidobaldo,
Duca d'Urbino.
m. Elisabetta Gonzaga.

Francesco Maria della Rovere,
Duca d'Urbino.
m. Eleonora Gonzaga.

Gentile.
m. Agostino Fregoso,
Doge di Genova.

Federigo Fregoso,
Cardinale.

GENEALOGICAL TABLE, SHOWING HOW VITTORIA COLONNA WAS CONNECTED
WITH THE HOUSE OF GONZAGA

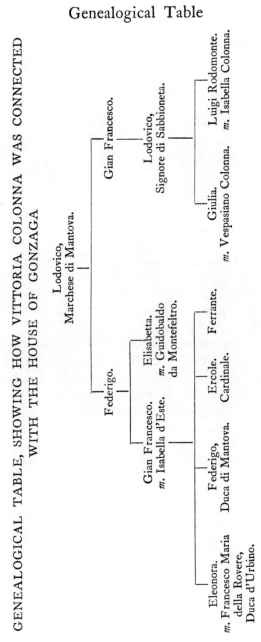

Lodovico,
Marchese di Mantova.

Federigo.

Gian Francesco.

Gian Francesco.
m. Isabella d'Este.

Elisabetta.
m. Guidobaldo
da Montefeltro.

Lodovico,
Signore di Sabbioneta.

Eleonora,
m. Francesco Maria
della Rovere,
Duca d'Urbino.

Federigo,
Duca di Mantova.

Ercole,
Cardinale.

Ferrante.

Giulia.
m. Vespasiano Colonna.

Luigi Rodomonte.
m. Isabella Colonna.

Y

BIBLIOGRAPHY

Adriani, G. B. *Istoria de' suoi Tempi.* Florence, 1583.

Agostino, A. *Pietro Carnesecchi e il movimento valdesiano.* Florence, 1899.

Amante, Bruto. *La Tomba di Vittoria Colonna e i testamenti finora inediti della Poetessa.* Bologna, 1896.

Bembo, Pietro. *Opere.* Milan, 1810.

Benrath, C. *Bernardino Ochino of Siena.* English translation by Helen Zimmern. London and Edinburgh, 1876.

Bernabei, N. *Vita del Cardinale Giovanni Morone.* Modena, 1885.

Boehmer, E. *Biblioteca Wiffeniana, Spanish Reformers of two centuries from 1520.* London, etc., 1874.

Borzelli, A. *Una poetessa italiana del secolo XVI.* Naples, 1885.

Brinton, Selwyn. *Correggio.* London, 1899.

Britonio, G. *Opera volgare, intitolata Gelosia del Sole.* Naples, 1519.

Burckhardt, J. *Die Cultur der Renaissance in Italien.* Basel, 1860.

Campori, G. *Vittoria Colonna.* (Atti e memorie delle RR. Deputazioni di Storia Patria per le Provincie dell' Emilia. New series, Vol. III, part II.) Modena, 1878.

Canello, U. *Storia della Letteratura Italiana nel secolo XVI.* Milan, 1881.

Cantù, C. *Gli eretici d'Italia.* 3 vols. Turin, 1865.

Caprile, L. *Due poetesse italiane nel secolo decimosesto.* Florence, 1902.

Carrer, L. *Amore infelice di Gaspara Stampa.* Venice, 1851.

Cartwright, Julia (Mrs. Henry Ady). *Isabella d'Este, Marchioness of Mantua.* 2 vols. London, 1903.

Castiglione, B. *Il Cortegiano,* annotato e illustrato da Vittorio Cian. Florence, 1894.

Castiglione, B. *Lettere.* 2 vols. Padua, 1769, 1771.

Cian, V. *Un decennio della vita di M. Pietro Bembo, 1521–1531.* Florence, 1885.

Colonna, Pompeo. *Pompeii Cardinalis Columnæ, S.R.E. Vicecancellarii, ad illustrem ac magnanimam Victoriam Columnam Marchionissam Piscariæ, Apologiæ Mulierum,* Lib. I et II. Biblioteca Vaticana, Cod. Lat. 3370.

Colonna, Vittoria. *Pianto . . . sopra la Passione di Cristo.* Bologna, 1557.

Colonna, Vittoria. *Rime di Vittoria Colonna corrette sui testi e pubblicate con la vita della medesima da* P. E. Visconti. Rome, 1840.

Colonna, Vittoria. *Carteggio raccolto e pubblicato da Ermanno Ferrero e Giuseppe Müller. Seconda edizione con Supplemento raccolto ed annotato da Domenico Tordi.* Florence, Rome, 1892.
See also under Amante, Corso, Guerrini, Luzio and Renier, Reumont, and Tordi.

Consorti, A. *Il Cardinale Pompeo Colonna.* Rome, 1902.

Contile, Luca. *Lettere di Luca Contile.* Pavia, 1564.

Corso, Rinaldo. *Dichiarazione fatta sopra la seconda parte delle Rime di Vittoria Colonna ; alla molta illustrissima Madonna Veronica Gambara da Correggio : et alle Donne gentili dedicata.* Bologna, 1543.

Corvisieri, C. *Compendio de' processi del S. Officio. (Archivio della Società Romana di Storia Patria,* Vol. III.) Rome, 1880.

Costa, E. *Sonetti amorosi inediti o rari di Veronica Gambara da Correggio.* Rome, 1890.

Doni, A. F. *La Libreria.* Venice, 1550.

Einstein, Lewis. *The Italian Renaissance in England.* New York, 1902.

Feliciangeli, B. *Notizie e documenti sulla vita di Caterina Cibo-Varano, Duchessa di Camerino.* Camerino, 1891.

Ferrero, Ermanno, e Müller, Giuseppe. *Vittoria Colonna, Marchesa di Pescara, Carteggio raccolto e pubblicato da Ermanno Ferrero e Giuseppe Müller. Seconda edizione con Supplemento raccolto ed annotato da Domenico Tordi.* Florence, Rome, 1892.

Flamini, F. *Il Cinquecento.* Milan, 1902.

Fontana, B. *Renata di Francia, Duchessa di Ferrara.* Rome, 1889–1899.

Gambara, Veronica. *Rime e lettere di Veronica Gambara* raccolte da Felice Rizzardi. Brescia, 1759.

Gambara, Veronica. *Rime e lettere di Veronica Gambara* novamente pubblicate per cura di Pia Mestica Chiappetti. Florence, 1879. *See* also under Costa, Corso, Guerrini, and Renier.

Gardner, E. G. *Dukes and Poets in Ferrara.* London, 1904.

Gaspary, A. *Storia della Letteratura Italiana. Volume secondo tradotto dal tedesco da* Vittorio Rossi. 2 parts. Turin, 1900, 1901.

Giovio, Paolo. *Le vite di diecinove huomini illustri.* Venice, 1561.

Graziani, A. *Gaspara Stampa e la lirica del Cinquecento.* Turin, 1899.

Guerrini, Olindo. *Rime di tre Gentildonne del secolo XVI. Vittoria Colonna ; Gaspara Stampa ; Veronica Gambara.* Milan, 1882.

Guicciardini, F. *Storia d' Italia.* Edited by G. Rossini. 5 vols. Turin, 1874, 1875.

Guidiccioni, Giovanni. *Opere nuovamente raccolte ed ordinate a cura di* Carlo Minutoli. Florence, 1867.

Holroyd, C. *Michael Angelo Buonarroti.* London, 1903.

Janitschek, H. *Die Gesellschaft der Renaissance in Italien und die Kunst.* Stuttgart, 1879.

Lawley, Hon. Alethea. *Vittoria Colonna, a study, with translations of some of her published and unpublished sonnets.* London, 1888.

Lettere di tredici huomini illustri. Venice, 1560.

Lettere volgari di diversi nobilissimi huomini. Venice, 1551.

Litta, Pompeo. *Le Famiglie celebri italiane.* Milan, 1819, etc.

Le Loyal Serviteur. *La très joyeuse et très plaisante Histoire composée par le Loyal Serviteur des Faits, Gestes, Triomphes et Prouesses du bon Chevalier sans Paour et sans Reprouche, le gentil Seigneur de Bayart.* Ed. Buchon. Paris, 1836.

Luzio, A. *Vittoria Colonna.* (Rivista storica mantovana, Vol. I.) Mantua, 1884.

Luzio, A, and Renier, R. *Mantova e Urbino : Isabella d' Este ed Elisabetta Gonzaga nelle relazioni famigliari e nelle vicende politiche.* Turin, 1893.

Luzio, A, and Renier, R. *La Coltura e le Relazioni Letterarie di Isabella d' Este Gonzaga.* (Giornale Storico della Letteratura Italiana, Vols. XXXIII–XL.) Turin, 1899–1902.

Manzoni, G. *Estratto del processo di Pietro Carnesecchi (Miscellanea di storia italiana* edita dalla R. Deputazione di Storia Patria, T. X.) Turin, 1870.

Michelangelo Buonarroti. *Le Lettere di Michelangelo Buonarroti pubblicate coi ricordi ed i contratti artistici per cura di* Gaetano Milanesi.
Florence, 1875.

Michelangelo Buonarroti. *Le Rime di Michelangelo Buonarroti, pubblicate da* Cesare Guasti. Florence, 1863.

Minozzi, E. *Gaspara Stampa.* 1893.

Müntz, E. *La Renaissance en Italie et en France à l'époque de
Charles VIII.* Paris, 1885.

Muzio, Girolamo. *Le mentite ochiniane.* Venice, 1551.

Negri, Angelica Paola Antonia. *Lettere spirituali.* Rome, 1576.

Ochino, Bernardino. *See* under Benrath and Muzio.

Pino, B. *Nuova scelta di Lettere di diversi nobilissimi huomini.* Venice,
1574.

Pole, Reginald. *Epistolarum Reginaldi Poli S.R.E. Cardinalis et aliorum
ad ipsum.* 5 vols. Brescia, 1744–1757.

Pungileoni, L. *Memorie istoriche di Antonio Allegri, detto il Correggio.*
3 vols. Parma, 1817–1821.

Renier, R. Review in the *Giornale Storico della Letteratura Italiana,*
Vol. XIV. Turin, 1889.
See also under Luzio.

Reumont, A. *Vittoria Colonna, Marchesa di Pescara, Vita, Fede e Poesia
nel secolo decimosesto, per* Alfredo Reumont. Versione di Giuseppe
Müller ed Ermanno Ferrero. Turin, 1892.

Sadoleto, J. *Jacobi Sadoleti Curtius et ejusdem Laocoon.* Bologna, 1532

Salza, A. *Luca Contile, uomo di lettere e di negozii del secolo XVI*
Florence, 1903.

Savonarola, Girolamo. *Il Trionfo della Croce.* Ed. P. Lodovico
Ferretti. Siena, 1899.

Schellhorn, J. G. *Amœnitates historiæ ecclesiasticæ et literariæ.* 2 tom.
Frankfort, 1537, 1538.

Stampa, Gaspara. *Rime di Madonna Gaspara Stampa.* Venice, 1554.
See under Borzelli, Caprile, Carrer, Graziani, Guerrini, and
Minozzi.

Symonds, J. A. *Life of Michelangelo Buonarroti.* 2 vols. London,
1893.

Symonds, J. A. *The Sonnets of Michelangelo Buonarroti,* translated by
J. A. Symonds. London, 1904.

Tansillo, L. *Poesie liriche.* Naples, 1882.

Tarsia, G. di. *Rime.* Naples, 1758.

Tasso, B. *Rime di Messer Bernardo Tasso.* Venice, 1560.

Thomas, William. *The historie of Italie, a boke exceedyng profitable to be redde.* London, 1549.

Tiraboschi, G. *Storia della Letteratura Italiana.* Milan, 1824, etc.

Tolomei, Claudio. *Lettere.* Naples, 1829.

Tordi, D. *Il codice delle rime di Vittoria Colonna appartenuto a Margherita d' Angoulême, regina di Navarra, scoperto ed illustrato.* 1900.

Tordi, D. *Vittoria Colonna in Orvieto durante la guerra del sale* (1541). Bollettino della Società Umbra di Storia Patria, Vol. I. Perugia, 1895.

See also under Ferrero e Müller.

Valdès, Juan de. *Due Dialoghi.* 1545.

Valdès, Juan de. *Alphabeto Christiano.* 1546.

Valdès, Juan de. *Dialogo de la Lengua.* Madrid, 1860.

Valdès, Juan de. *The Hundred and Ten Considerations of Signior J. Valdesso. Written in Spanish, and now translated out of the Italian copy into English with notes* (by G. Herbert). Oxford, 1638.

Wiffen, B. *Life and Writings of Juan de Valdès.* London, 1865.

Woodward, W. H. *Desiderius Erasmus, concerning the aim and method of education.* Cambridge, 1904.

INDEX

A

Adrian VI (Adrian of Utrecht) succeeds Leo X, 15, 93; Juan de Valdès one of his chamberlains, 199
Alamanni, Luigi, 115
Alexander VI (Rodrigo Borgia), 6
Alicarnassea, Filonico, his life of Vittoria, 70 n.
Allegri, Antonio (Correggio), decorates Veronica's Casino, 153; her friendship for him, 154; his relations with the house of Gonzaga, 154, 155; Vasari's account of him incorrect, 155
Angelica, the. *See* Negri, Paola Antonia de'
Anghiera, Pietro Martire, tutor of Alfonso and Juan de Valdès, 199
Aretino Pietro, his relations with Vittoria, 114; with Veronica, 162
Ariosto, Lodovico, the *Orlando* quoted, 11; his possible meeting with Vittoria, 13; his reception by Leo X, 14; his letter to Duke of Ferrara, 15; Latin epitaph on Pescara ascribed to him, 30; praises Giovanna d'Aragona, 61; canzone attributed to him, 71; visits Veronica, 153; celebrates Giulia Gonzaga, 204; his noble commendation of Vittoria, 296
Avalos, Alfonso d', Marchese del Vasto, brought up by Vittoria, 9; his sister's marriage, 13; accompanies Pescara to the war, 15; made Pescara's heir, 29; taken prisoner at Salerno, 53; persuades Doria to join the Emperor, 55; procures a picture for Vittoria, 60; in Rome with his wife, Maria d'Aragona, 61; dissuades Vittoria from going to the Holy Land, 209, 233; writes to her at Orvieto, 232; sketch of his life, 241-5; Ochino's letter to him,

245; the Angelica's letter to him, 247; assassination of French ambassadors, 250; defeat at Ceresole, 250; summoned before the Emperor, 251; dies at Vigevano, 251; Luca Contile's letter about his death, 251; account of his death from the life of the Angelica, 303, 304
Avalos, Beatrice d', aunt of Pescara, 64
Avalos, Costanza d', Duchessa, afterwards Principessa, of Francavilla, aunt of Pescara, 6, 9, 61, 116; one of Valdès' disciples, 205
Avalos, Costanza d', Duchessa of Amalfi, sister of the Marchese del Vasto, her marriage, 13; one of Valdès' disciples, 116, 203, 205; Vittoria's letters to her, 116, 306-309
Avalos, Ferrante Francesco d', Marchese di Pescara, betrothed to Vittoria, 5; their marriage, 6; early married life, 7; commands cavalry, 8; made prisoner at Ravenna, 11; set at liberty, 12; his *Dialogo d'Amore*, 12; goes to Ischia and Rome, 13; commands imperial infantry, 15; victory at Bicocca, 17; returns to Ischia, 17; goes to Spain, returns to Northern Italy, 18; death of Bayard, 19, 20; siege of Marseilles, 24; battle of Pavia, 25; his disappointment of reward, 25; intrigue with Morone, 25; betrays Morone, 28, 29; dies, 29; is buried at Milan and subsequently removed to Naples, 30; his character, 31; his commendation of Maramaldo, 56; love-affair with Delia, 63-5; his letters on Equicola's death, 65; Vittoria's *Epistola*, 67, 68
Avalos, Maria d' Aragona d', wife of the Marchese del Vasto, 61; sung by the poet, Tansillo, 62

B

Barbarossa, Khair-ed-din, African corsair, attempts to carry off Giulia Gonzaga, 204

Bayard, the Chevalier, on the battle of Ravenna, 11; account of his death quoted, 18–22

Beccadelli, Lodovico, describes Cardinal Pole's office at Viterbo, 117, 273; records instance of the Cardinal's generosity, 314; eulogizes Vittoria, 315

Bembo, Pietro, Cardinal, his friendship with Vittoria, 14, 98, 99; present at the finding of the Laocoon, 93; his position as a critic, 94, 95; his life at Ferrara, 95; the *Asolani*, 96; the *Prose della Volgar Lingua*, 96, 220; at Urbino, 96; papal secretary, 97; life at Noniano, 97, 98; Vittoria's sonnet to him, 99; his respect for her taste in poetry, 118, 296; his correspondence with Veronica, 141–5; friend of Carnesecchi, 205; letters to Vittoria, 214, 215; sends Cardinal Contarini's *Epistola* to Vittoria, 236; Cardinal Pole stays with him, 310–12; his death, 304, 313

Benedetto, Don, Benedictine monk of Mantua, supposed author of the book *Del Beneficio di Cristo*, 223

Bernardino, Fra, of Asti, made Vicar-General of the Cappuccini, 208

Boccaccio, Giovanni, 176

Bonaventura, Fra, presents Ochino with house and church in Venice, 214

Bonfadio, Jacopo, his letter lamenting Valdès' death, 223, 224

Bonorio, Lorenzo, one of Vittoria's executors, 314; his letters to Ascanio, 315, 316

Boverius, his account of Ochino's flight, 258, 259

Britonio, Girolamo, poet, dedication of his works to Vittoria, 70, 89, 90

C

Calvin, 212

Caraffa, Cardinal (afterwards Paul IV), member of the Oratory of Divine Love, 50; causes Ochino to be watched, 254; draws up a report on necessary reforms, 267; is instrumental in establishing the Inquisition in Rome, 268; prohibits some of Flaminio's works, 272

Cardona, Spanish Viceroy, commands Spaniards at Ravenna, 10

Carnesecchi, Pietro, disciple of Valdès, 203; introduced to him by Giulia Gonzaga, 205, 218; becomes intimate with Vittoria, 214; goes to Naples, 218; Bonfadio's letter to him, 223; Vittoria mentioned in the process against him, 268, 269, 273, 274, 276, 277; his uncertain attitude, 271; spends much time with Cardinal Pole, 274; Flaminio's letter to him, 275

Caro, Annibale, 115, 118; Guidiccioni's letter to him about Ochino, 214; line quoted from his sonnet in praise of Vittoria, 297

Carrer, Luigi, his romance of Gaspara Stampa, 178

Casa, Giovanni della, Archbishop of Benevento, friend of Gaspara and her sister, 177; author of the *Galateo*, 178 (quoted, 97); Cassandra's dedication of Gaspara's poems to him, 194–6

Castiglione, Baldassare, his character, 100; the *Cortegiano*, 100, 101; episode of Vittoria in the *Cortegiano*, 101–5; his death, 105; patron of Flaminio, 105; replies to Valdès' Dialogue on the Sack of Rome, 199

Catherine of Siena, St., belonged to the contrada of the *oca*, 206; Ferrarese Convent dedicated to her, 209, 210; Beata Lucia's visions of her, 210, 211; friend of Suora Daniella, 228; quoted, 283

Cavalieri, Tommaso, 122, 127

Cervini, Cardinal, Vittoria's letter to him, 262, 263; goes to the Council of Trent, 309; Cardinal Pole's letter to him, 313

Charles V, Roman Emperor, alliance with Leo X, 15; disappoints Pescara, 25; corresponds with Vittoria, 27; Pescara's conduct towards him, 29; Clement VII invites him to join the League, 36; Doria goes over to him, 55; his visits to Correggio, 154, 159, 160, 168; his coronation, 159; Alfonso de Valdès his Latin secretary, 199; hears Ochino preach, 208; visits Giovanna d'Aragona and

Vittoria in Rome, 208, 209; his alliance with the Farnese, 226, 227; his letter to Vittoria, 232; honours conferred by him on del Vasto, 242; del Vasto falls into disgrace with him, 250, 251

Charles VIII, King of France, 5

Cibo, Caterina, Duchessa of Camerino, her relations with Ochino and the Cappuccini, 203, 205, 206, 207; the *Seven Dialogues*, 217; suspected of heresy, 268; Flaminio writes to her of Vittoria's death, 314

Clement VII (Giulio de' Medici) made Pope, 15; letters about his accession from Ariosto and Vittoria, 15, 17; forbids Vittoria to take the veil, 34; his troubles with Spain and the Colonna, 36-9; sack of Rome, 40; delivers up seven hostages of whom Giberti is one, 40, 42; his esteem for Giberti, 49; intercedes with Doria on behalf of Ascanio and del Vasto, 53, 54; recalls Sadoleto to Rome, 93; his death mentioned by Veronica, 164; restores Giulia Gonzaga's domains to her, 203; makes Carnesecchi his secretary and loads him with honours, 205; his dealings with the Cappuccini, 205, 206

Collalto, Count of, 183; first meets Gaspara, 184; his coldness, 186; takes service with Henry II, King of France, 187; Gaspara's letter to him, 189, 190; he comes back, 191; returns to the French army, 193; marries, 194.

Colonna, Agnese (da Montefeltro), mother of Vittoria, 4; Ascanio's account of her death, 17

Colonna, Ascanio, brother of Vittoria, his letter, 17; goes to Vittoria, 32; withdraws from Rome, 36; Giberti's letter about him, 37; taken prisoner at Salerno, 53; the Pope intercedes on his behalf, 53, 54; set at liberty, 55; in Rome, 61, 62; disputes with Giulia Gonzaga, 203; entertains the Emperor at Marino, 208; marriage of his eldest son projected, 225; contests the salt-tax, 226; salt-war, 234, 235; helps Ochino, 257; letter from Vittoria to him, 306; is made Vittoria's heir, 313; Bonorio's letters to him, 315, 316

Colonna, Fabrizio, father of Vittoria, 4; Constable of Naples, 5; betrothes his daughter to Pescara, 5; fights for Federigo of Aragon and is taken prisoner, 5; joins Gonsalvo di Cordova, 6; is second in command of Spanish army in Italy, 8; commands the Italians at Ravenna, 10; taken prisoner by Duke of Ferrara and released, 11; Ariosto's mention of him, 11; interferes on behalf of the Duke, 12; receives Isabella d' Este at Ischia, 64

Colonna, Fabrizio, eldest son of Ascanio, 225, 306

Colonna, Federigo, brother of Vittoria, 13

Colonna, Giovanna d' Aragona, wife of Ascanio, 61; celebrated in Ruscelli's *Tempio*, 62; appeals to Paul III. during the Salt War, 234

Colonna, Giulia, married to Giuliano Cesarini, 299

Colonna, Isabella, 203

Colonna, Margherita, Beata, ancestress of Vittoria, 32; her history, 33; beatified by Pius IX, 34

Colonna, Pompeo, Cardinal, 36; sacks the Borgo, 38; his conduct during the sack of Rome, 40-2; Giovio's life of him, 42, 106; his book *Apologia Mulierum*, 44-8; Viceroy of Naples, 48; Bishop of Monreale, 49; his death, 49; Minturno wished to dedicate his poem to him, 106

Colonna, Prospero, 6

Colonna, Vespasiano, 36, 203

COLONNA, VITTORIA, MARCHESA DI PESCARA, her birth, 3; parentage, 4; betrothal, 5; marriage, 6; early married life, 7-9; adopts del Vasto, 9; battle of Ravenna, 10-12; at Ischia, 13; in Rome, 14; urges her husband to take del Vasto to the war, 15; her letter to Giberti, 16, 17; her mother's death, 17, 18; her letter to Federigo Gonzaga, 22, 23; at Marino, 24; correspondence with Charles V after Pavia, 26, 27; protest against accepting kingdom of Naples, 27, 28; her husband's death, 29; receives the news at Viterbo, 32; goes to San Silvestro in Rome, 32; goes South, 39; her work after the sack of Rome, 40;

her friendship with Cardinal Pompeo Colonna, 44-8 ; Ascanio and del Vasto taken prisoners at Salerno, 53 ; Sanga's letter to her, 53, 54 ; her letter on behalf of Maramaldo, 55-7 ; pictures executed for her, 58-60 ; returns to Rome, 61 ; her attitude towards her husband, 63, 66 ; the *Epistola*, 67, 68 ; her motto, 69 ; early editions of her poems, 70, 71 ; invites Guidiccioni to correct them, 71-4 ; lends a copy to della Torre, 74 ; sends one to Marguerite d'Angoulême, 75-7 ; and one to Michelangelo, 77 ; laments her husband seven years, 78-85 ; her friends, 86 ; her changes of residence, 88, 89 ; Britonio's dedication, 90 ; Tarsia's praises of her, 91 ; friendship with Sadoleto, 92, 94 ; her debt to Bembo, 94 ; her sonnet to him, 99 ; her connexion with the *Cortegiano*, 101-5 ; her acquaintance with Flaminio, 105 ; with Giovio, Minturno, and Tasso, 105-12 ; Guidiccioni's sonnet to her, 112 ; in Rome with Molza, 114 ; letters exchanged with Aretino, 114 ; her friendship with Claudio Tolomei, Contile, and Alamanni, 114, 115 ; her secretaries, 115 ; her women-friends, 116 ; her friends among the cardinals, 117 ; impression produced by her, 118, 252 ; her unique friendship with Michelangelo, 121 ; d'Ollanda's *Conversations*, 123-6 ; Michelangelo's drawings for her, 127 ; letters and poems exchanged, 127-35 ; character of their friendship, 136, 137, 304 ; Condivi's account of it quoted, 137, 138 ; Veronica's sonnets to her, 160, 161 ; letters compared, 162 ; life at Ischia, 198 ; relations with Giulia Gonzaga, 203 ; makes the acquaintance of Carnesecchi, 205 ; intercedes with the Pope for the Cappuccini, 205, 206 ; attends Ochino's sermons, 207 ; appeals again to the Pope for the Cappuccini, 208 ; receives visits from the Emperor, 208, 209 ; wishes to go to the Holy Land, 209 ; stays at Ferrara, 209-13 ; goes to the Bolognese, 214 ; to Florence and

Lucca, 214 ; Bembo's letters to her, 214-16 ; projects marriage for Ascanio's eldest son, 225 ; her negotiations during the salt-war, 226, 227 ; loses her secretary, Innocenza, 227 ; retires to Orvieto, 228 ; her reception, 229 ; closely watched by the governor, 229-34 ; her letters to the Duke of Ferrara, 235 ; writes the *Trionfo*, 236 ; Cardinal Pole's letter to her, 236 ; her letter to Eleonora Gonzaga, 237 ; Contile visits her, 238 ; Martinengo's letter about her, 241 ; her affection for del Vasto, 241, 242 ; proceeds to Viterbo, 251 ; Ochino's letter to her, 255-7 ; she gives it to Muzio, 261 ; letter to Cardinal Cervini, 262, 263 ; letter on Cardinal Contarini's death, 264-6 ; suspected by the Holy Office, 268, 270 ; letter to Giulia Gonzaga, 269 ; residence in Dominican convent, 273 ; visited by Flaminio and Priuli, 274 ; Cardinal Pole's influence over her, 276, 278 ; her illness, 278-82 ; her later poems, 283 ; edition brought out by Rinaldo Corso, 284 ; the *Rime sacre e morali*, 285-7 ; the *Trionfo*, 287-91 ; her prose, 292-5 ; her praises by Bembo, Ariosto, Caro, and Michelangelo, 296, 297 ; goes to Convent of Sant' Anna in Rome, 298 ; her friend, Giberti, dies, 299 ; his estimate of her, 302 ; her letter to Cardinal Morone, 306 ; three letters to the Duchessa d'Amalfi, 306-9 ; her letter to Cardinal Morone about Cardinal Pole, 309 ; Cardinal Pole's letter to her, 310-13 ; she is taken to the Cesarini palace, 313 ; her will, 313, 314 ; her death, 314 ; letters about her burial, 315, 316 ; place uncertain, 316, 317

Colonna, Vittoria, daughter of Ascanio, 62, 314

Condivi, A., quoted, 137, 138

Contarini, Cardinal, member of the Oratory of Divine Love, 50 ; defends Sadoleto's book, 94 ; addresses a treatise to Vittoria, 117 ; Vittoria writes to him, 206 ; Cardinal Pole's letter to him, 235 ; publishes *Epistola de Justificatione*, 236 ; on his death-bed is visited by Ochino, 255 ; his death, 263; was created Cardinal by Paul III, 267; his efforts for reform, 267; Pole's letters to him, 274, 275

Contile, Luca, admirer of Giovanna d'Aragona, 62; his devotion to Vittoria, 115, 237-9; his *Dialoghi Spirituali*, 239-41; Vittoria's influence on his book, 241; his letters about del Vasto, 243; letter about del Vasto's death, 251

Correggio. *See* Allegri

Correggio, Giberto X, lord of, marries Veronica Gambara, 148

Correggio, Chiara da, 166

Correggio, Girolamo da, 157, 158

Correggio, Ippolito da, 157, 158, 166

Corso, Rinaldo, 140; dedicates his commentary on Vittoria's *Rime* to Veronica, 166, 284, 285; details of his life, 166, 167

D

Daniella, Suora, Dominican nun, friend of St. Catherine, 228

Dante, quoted, 126; his pageant, 288

Delia, lady-in-waiting to Isabella d'Este, 63; accompanies her to Ischia, 64; love-affair with Pescara, 63-5

Della Torre. *See* Torre

Dolci, Lodovico, member of the Accademia dei Pellegrini, 176

Doni, A. F., Secretary of the Accademia dei Pellegrini, 172; his account of it, 172-4

Doria, Andrea, prisoners taken at Salerno sent to him, 53; the Pope intercedes on behalf of Ascanio and del Vasto, 53, 54; his relations with France and Spain, 54, 55

Doria, Filippino, cousin of Andrew, in command at the battle of Salerno, 51-3

E

Equicola, Mario, Secretary of Isabella d'Este, 22, 23 n.; the go-between in Pescara's love-affair, 64; his death, 65

Erasmus, friend of Alfonso and Juan de Valdés, 199; Juan compared with him, 201, 202

Ercolani, Agostino, correspondent of

Veronica, 162; two letters to him, 164

Este (da) Alfonso I, third Duke of Ferrara and Modena, supports the French in Italy, 8; takes Fabrizio Colonna prisoner at Ravenna, and releases him without ransom, 11; Fabrizio aids him to leave Rome, 12; Ariosto's letter to him about the election of Clement VII, 15, 16; Lucrezia Borgia his wife, 95

Este (da) Ercole I, second Duke of Ferrara and Modena, builds convent for the Beata Lucia, 209-11

Este (da) Ercole II, fourth Duke of Ferrara and Modena, invites learned men to meet Vittoria, 209; gives Ochino land and a house, 212; Vittoria's mention of him, 213; her letters to him, 213, 235, 273

Este (da) Leonello, thirteenth Marquis of Ferrara, pictures painted for him by Roger van der Weyden, 125

Este (da) Leonora, daughter of Alfonso and Renata, 212

Este (da) Lucrezia Borgia, Duchess of Ferrara, the *Asolani* dedicated to her, 96

Renata, Duchess of Ferrara. *See* Renata

Ettore, Conte di Carpegna, letter to him from Luca Contile, 237-39.

F

Farnese, Cardinal, Guidiccioni enters his service, 112; his esteem for Vittoria, 229; Governor of Orvieto's letter to him, 230-3; his letter about the capture of Ascanio's states, 235; Vittoria writes to him, 237; summons Ochino to Rome, 254; Ochino's accusations against him, 256

Farnese, Ottavio, marries Margaret of Austria, 226

Farnese, Vittoria, marriage projected for her with Ascanio's eldest son, 225

Ferdinand II, King of Naples, persuades Fabrizio to betroth his daughter to Pescara, 5

Federigo, King of Naples, gives himself up to France, 5

Ferrar, Nicholas, his translation of

the *Hundred and Ten Considerations* of Ochino, 220; George Herbert's letter to him about them, 220-2

Ferruccio, Francesco, story of the cats of Volterra, 57; dies at Gavignano, 57 n.

Filiberto, Prince of Orange, Vittoria's letter to him on behalf of Maramaldo, 55-7

Flaminio, Marcantonio, interview with Leo X, 105; Castiglioni invites him to Urbino, 105; goes to Naples, 105; friend of Carnesecchi, 205; his resemblance to Valdès, 218, 224; his relations with Pole, 271, 272; his life at Viterbo, 274, 275; his letter about the *Imitatione*, 276; accompanies Cardinal Pole to the Council of Trent, 309; his letter to Caterina Cibo about Vittoria's death, 314

Fogazzaro, A., quoted, 270

Foix, Gaston de, killed at Ravenna, 11; sacks Brescia, 156

Fossombrone, Fra Lodovico da, one of the founders of the Cappuccini, 206; refuses to convene the General Chapter, 208

Fracastoro, Girolamo, Veronese physician, friend of Giberti, his letter about Vittoria's illness, 280-2; attends Cardinal Pole, 310

Francis I, King of France, made prisoner at Pavia, 25; his relations with Andria Doria, 54, 55; orders Vittoria's poems to be given to his sister, 77; Sadoleto sent on a mission to him, 94

Fregoso, Federigo, Cardinal, friend of Castiglione, 101; corresponds with Vittoria at Orvieto, 230, 233; visits her there, 237; Vittoria's letter on his death, 237; chosen by Paul III to report on abuses, 267

G

Gabrielli, Trifone, 177

Gambara, Uberto, papal governor of Bologna, 157

Gambara, Veronica, birth and parentage, 139; education, 139, 140; correspondence with Bembo, 141-5; her letter to Isabella d'Este, 146;

to some nobleman, 147; her marriage, 148; her early poems, 148-52; madrigal, 152; her Casino, 153; Ariosto visits her, 153; her court painter, Allegri, 154, 155; her sons, 155; her escape from Brescia, 156; visit to Bologna, 156; grief for her husband's death, 156; left guardian of her sons, 157; goes to Bologna, 157; letter to Lodovico Rosso, 158; the Emperor's coronation, 159; Emperor goes to Correggio, 160; her two sonnets to Vittoria, 160, 161; her letters praised by Aretino, 162; her letters about public affairs, 162-5; Emperor's second visit to Correggio, 166; her defence of the town, 166; Corso dedicates his commentary on Vittoria's *Rime* to her, 166; her last years and death, 167; her character, 168

Gardner, Edmund G., 48 n., 211 n.

Giberti, Giovan Matteo, Datary and Bishop of Verona, Vittoria's letter to him, 16; sends her a blessed palm, 24; negotiates with Morone, 26; counsels Clement VII, 36; his letters to Vittoria, 37, 39; given as hostage, 40-2; his character, 49, 299; member of the Oratory of Divine Love, 50; retires to Verona, 50, 51; friend of Sanga, 53; and of Cardinal Pole, 117; dispatches della Torre to bring Vittoria to Verona, 209; his relations with Ochino, 254, 255, 299; chosen by Paul III to report on abuses and suggest reforms, 267; accounts of his death, 300, 301; his regard for Vittoria, 302

Giovanni, Britannico, 140

Giovio, Paolo, historian, 5; mentions Pescara's *Dialogo*, 12, 69; relates Vittoria's rejection of the Neapolitan scheme, 27, 28; his life of Cardinal Pompeo Colonna, 42, 49; his life of Pescara, 106

Giustiniani, Fabricio, 51, 53

Gonsalvo di Cordova, 7

Gonzaga, Agostino, 207

Gonzaga, Eleonora. *See* Rovere

Gonzaga, Ercole, Cardinal, Vittoria writes to him on behalf of the Cappuccini, 206; he wishes her to come to Mantua, 209 ; she writes to him about her life at Ferrara, 213 ; his letter about Vittoria and Paul III, 269

Gonzaga, Federigo, fifth Marquis and first Duke of Mantua, letter to him from Ascanio, 17, 18 ; letter from Vittoria, 22, 23 ; his letters to Vittoria, 58, 59 ; Allegri works for him, 154

Gonzaga, Francesco III, sixth Marquis and second Duke of Mantua, 167

Gonzaga, Giulia, marries Vespasiano Colonna, 116, 203 ; disciple of Valdès, 203, 205 ; Barbarossa's attempt to carry her off, 204 ; introduces Carneecchi to Valdès, 218 ; Valdès writes the *Alfabeto Cristiano* and other works for her, 219 ; suspected of heresy, 268 ; sends Valdès' *Commentary on S. Paul* to Vittoria, 269

Gonzaga, Isabella d'Este, her letter to del Vasto's secretary about the Magdalen, 60 ; Pescara in love with her lady-in-waiting, 63 ; her reception at Ischia by Fabrizio Colonna, 64 ; her daughter a friend of Vittoria, 116 ; Veronica's letter to her, 146 ; Allegri works for her, 154 ; goes to Bologna for the Emperor's coronation, 159 ; Agostino Gonzaga writes to her about Vittoria, 207 ; organizes a farewell festival for Vittoria at Ferrara, 213

Gonzaga, Luigi "Rodomonte", marries Isabella Colonna, 203

Gualteruzzi, Carlo, della Torre asks him for Vittoria's sonnets, 74 ; one of Vittoria's secretaries, 115 ; visits Vittoria at Bagnaja, 237 ; letter to him from Fracastoro about Vittoria's illness, 280–2 ; two letters to him from della Torre about Giberti's death, 300, 301

Gualteruzzi, Innocenza, daughter of Carlo, Vittoria's secretary, takes the veil at San Silvestro, 115, 227

Guidiccioni, Giovanni, friend of Vittoria's, invited to amend her sonnets, 71–4 ; account of his life, 112 ; his patriotic sonnet, 113 ; writes to Caro about Ochino, 214 ; Commissary-General for the Pope during the Salt War, 234

H

Herbert, George, Nicholas Ferrar sends him his translation of the *Hundred and Ten Considerations* of Valdès, 220 ; his letter about the book, 220–2

J

Julius II (Giuliano della Rovere), unites with the Spaniards against the French, 8 ; his treatment of the Duke of Ferrara, 12 ; orders excavation to be made in Rome, discovery of the Laocoon, 93

Jova, Giuseppe, one of Vittoria's secretaries, Guidiccioni's letter to him, 72 ; Caro and Varchi his admirers, 115

Justus of Ghent, 125

L

Lascaris, Costantino, Bembo learns Greek from him, 95

Leo X (Giovanni de' Medici) taken prisoner at Ravenna, 11 ; becomes Pope, 13 ; his reception of Ariosto, 14 ; his two secretaries, Sadoleto and Bembo, 14, 93 ; allies himself with the Emperor, 15 ; meets Francis I at Bologna, 156

Leyva, Antonio de, Spanish general in Italy, 25 ; Pescara arranges that he shall overhear Morone's plot, 28

Lodovico da Fossombrone, Fra, leaves the Osservanti, 206 ; refuses to convene the General Chapter of the Cappuccini, 208

Longa, Maria, founds a convent in Naples, 207

Lucia da Narni, Beata, 209–12

M

Manriquez, Isabella, disciple of Valdés, 203, 205

Maramaldo, Fabricio, serves under Pescara and del Vasto, 55 ; Vittoria's letter about him, 55–57 ; he kills Ferruccio, 57 n. ; is commissioned to apply to the Duke of Mantua for a picture, 58

Margaret of Austria, 226

Margherite d'Angonlême, Queen of Navarre, Vittoria sends her a copy

of her sonnets, 75 ; her character-
istics, 76 ; sonnets detained by
Montmorency, 77
Marino, Fra, 214
Martinengo, Fortunato, his letter quo-
ted, 241
Matteo da Bassi, Fra, founder of the
Cappuccini, 206
Medici, Ippolito de', Cardinal, 204
Memling, 125
Mignatelli, Fabio, Papal Nuncio in
Venice, 254
Minturno, Antonio, 48 ; his writings,
106
Mirtilla (Ippolita Roma), friend of
Gaspara, 178
Molino, poet, 175
Molza, Francesco Maria, poet, 70 ;
three of his sonnets erroneously in-
cluded among Vittoria's, 71 ; friend
of Vittoria in her later Roman days,
113, 114
Montefeltro, Elisabetta Gonzaga da,
wife of Guidobaldo I, second Duke
of Urbino, celebrated in the *Corteg-
iano*, 100, 102 n. ; aunt of Vittoria,
116
Montefeltro, Federigo da, Count, afterwards Duke of Urbino, 4 ; sends
for a Flemish painter, 125
Montefeltro, Guidobaldo da, second
Duke of Urbino, 4 ; celebrated in
the *Cortegiano*, 100
Moncada, Don Ugo de, Spanish
Viceroy in Naples, 36, 38, 51
Monte del, Cardinal, 309
Morone, Chancellor of Francesco
Sforza, Duke of Milan, 26 ; betrayed
by Pescara, 28, 29
Morone, Giovanni, Cardinal, Bishop
of Modena, 117 ; process against
him, 268 ; Vittoria tells him of her
obligations to Cardinal Pole, 277 ;
writes to him of the Convent of
Sant' Anna, 306 ; commends Car-
dinal Pole to him, 309 ; he is one
of her trustees, 314
Muzio, Girolamo, journeys with del
Varto, 242, 243 ; his letter to
Ochino, 261, 262

N

Navarro, Pedro, at the battle of
Ravenna, 10, 11

Negri, Paola Antonia de' (the Angelica), religious of San Paolo in Milan,
169, 170 ; her character, 178, 179 ;
her letter to Gaspara, 179-82 ; her
relations with del Vasto, 244 ; her
letter to him, 247-50 ; her prophecy
of Ochino's fall, 254 ; she is with
del Vasto when he dies, 303-4

O

Ochino, Fra Bernardino, one of Valdès'
circle, 203 ; erroneously said to have
been the founder of the Cappuccini,
205 ; his early life, 206, 207 ; joins
the Cappuccini, 207 ; appeals to
Vittoria on behalf of the Order, 208 ;
his fame as a preacher, 208, 214-16 ;
his *Seven Dialogues*, 217 ; goes to
Naples, 218 ; Vittoria speaks of him
with Luca Contile, 238 ; his letters
to Del Vasto, 245-7 ; his preaching,
245, 253 ; he is forbidden to preach
in Venice, 254 ; summoned to Rome,
254 ; goes to Bologna to consult
Cardinal Contarini, 255 ; Vermigli
counsels flight, 255 ; his letter to
Vittoria, 255-7 ; Ascanio assists
him, 257 ; account of his flight given
by Boverius, 258, 259 ; holds a
prebend in Canterbury Cathedral,
259 ; indications that he was on the
wrong road, 259 ; Tolomei's letter
to him, 260, 261 ; Muzio's letter of
remonstrance, 261, 262 ; Ochino's
answers, 262 ; Vittoria's letter about
him to Cardinal Cervini, 262, 263 ;
Caterina Cibo keeps up her connection with him, 268 ; Vittoria breaks
off all communicaion with him, 278 ;
his testimony as to Giberti's advice
to him, 299
Ollanda, Francisco d', Portuguese
miniature painter, his *Three Dialogues on Painting*, 123-6, 215

P

Parabosco, Girolamo, his *Lettere
amorose*, 175
Paul III (Alessandro Farnese), makes
Sadoleto a cardinal and sends him
on a diplomatic mission, 94 ; Veronica's satisfaction at his election,
164 ; recalls Vittoria to Rome, 214 ;
increases the duty on salt, 225 ; is

determined to possess the Colonna States, 234; his desire for reform, 267; establishes the Inquisition, 268; converses with Vittoria about his successor, 269; permits Pole to return to Rome, 310

Paul IV. *See* Caraffa, Cardinal

Petrucci, Pandolfo, a great power in Siena, 207.

Pico della Mirandola, Galeotto, invades Correggio, 166

Piombo, Sebastiano del, his portrait of Giulia Gonzaga, 204

Pole, Cardinal, member of the Oratory of Divine Love, 50; special friend of Vittoria, 117; friend of Carnesecchi, 205; attends Ochino's sermons, 214; his letters to Cardinal Contarini about Vittoria, 235; answer to her letter about his mother's death, 236; visits her at Bagnaja, 237; his advice to her about Ochino, 263; is chosen to report on existing abuses and to devise reforms, 267; his dealings with Flaminio, 271, 272; legate at Viterbo, 273; life at Viterbo, 274, 275; his influence with Vittoria, 276-8, 282; sent to the Council of Trent, 309; his illness, 310; his letters from Cardinal Bembo's house, 310-13; on Bembo's death, 313; Vittoria's legacy to him, 314; his orders about Vittoria's coffin, 315

Politi, Fra Ambrogio, 124 n.; his letter to, and treatise on, Ochino, 215, 262

Priuli, Luigi, member of the Oratory of Divine Love, 50; frequent visitor of Vittoria, 274; accompanies Cardinal Pole to Council of Trent, 309

Q

Querini, Cardinal, on Pole's relations with Flaminio, 271, 272

R

Renata, Duchess of Ferrara, Vittoria's visit to her, 212; she is said to have aided Ochino, 257

Reumont, A, 171, 237 n., 241 n., 315

Roma, Giovanni, 178

Roma, Ippolita, Paduan poetess. *See* Mirtilla

Romano, Mentebuona, 26

Rossi, Brunamonte de', Governor of Orvieto, his letters to Cardinal Farnese, 229-33

Rosso, Lodovico, friend of Veronica, 157; her letters to him, 158, 159, 162-5

Rovere (della), Eleonora Gonzaga, wife of Francesco Maria, 116; Vittoria's letter to her, 237

Rovere (della), Francesco Maria, Duke of Urbino, 101

Ruscelli, Girolamo, his *Tempio alla divina Signora Giovanna d'Aragona*, 61, 62

S

Sadoleto, Jacopo, papal secretary and Cardinal, friend of Vittoria, 14, 92, 117; member of the Oratory of Divine Love, 50; his Latin ode on the Laöcoon, 93; member of the Accademia Romana, 114; friend of Carnesecchi, 205; appointed to inquire into abuses and devise reforms, 267; one of Vittoria's trustees, 314

Sanga, Giovan Battista, papal secretary, his letters to Vittoria, 53

Sansovino, Ferranti, Prince of Salerno, 106

Sansovino, Francesco, friend of Gaspara, his letter and dedications to her, 176, 177

Savonarola, Fra Girolamo, his *Trionfo della Croce* quoted, 287-9

Sforza, Bona, her marriage, 11

Sforza, Francesco Maria, ninth Duke of Milan, 26, 29

Stampa, Baldassare, brother of Gaspara, 170, 176

Stampa, Cassandra, sister of Gaspara, 170; her letter to della Casa, 194-6

Stampa, Gaspara, birth, 169; her family, 170; her gifts and education, 170; life in Venice, 171; Parabosco's letter to her, 175; relations with Sansovino, 176, 177; friendship with della Casa, 177; her supposed letters to Mirtilla, 178; The Angelica's letter to her, 179-82; meets Collaltino, 183; her passion set forth in her poems, 184-8; her letter to him, 189, 190; further poems, 191, 192; separation from Collaltino, 193; religious sonnet, 193; her death, 194; dedication of her poems to della Casa, 194-7 ; character of her work, 196, 197

T

Tansillo, L., poet, sings in praise of Maria d'Aragona, 62

Tarsia, Galeazzo di, lover of Vittoria, 91 ; his sonnet to her, 92

Tasso, Bernardo, in the service of the Prince of Salerno, 106 ; his poems and letters to Vittoria, 107-12

Tasso, Torquato, 212

Terenziano, Giulio, 254

Terrabotti, Beata Santuccia, 298 n.

Titian (Tiziano Vecelli), commissioned to paint a Magdalen for Vittoria, 58, 59

Toledo, Don Pedro de, Juan de Valdès his secretary, 200

Tolomei, Claudio, founded the Accademia della Virtù, 114 ; his letters to Vittoria, 114. 115 ; on Contile's *Dialoghi Spirituali*, 240, 241 ; remonstrates with Ochino, 260-2 ; letters to Cincio on Vittoria's illness, 278-80

Tolomei, Lattantio, 74, 75 n., introduces d'Ollanda to Vittoria, 123 ; discussion between them, 124

Torre, Francesco della, Giberti's secretary, 74 ; sent to bring Vittoria to Verona, 209 ; his letters about Giberti's death, 300-2

Trissino, G., 140, 213.

Trivulzio, Teodoro, Venetian captain, 22, 23 n.

Trivulzio, Cardinal, 239

Trivulzio, Lodovica, Marchesa Pallavicino, 239

U

Urbino, servant and friend of Michelangelo, 130, 134

V

Valdès, Alfonso de, 198, 199

Valdès, Juan de, Spanish mystic, 198 ; the Dialogues, 199, 200 ; his characteristics, 201, 202 ; his disciples, 203-6 ; the *Alfabeto Cristiano*, 219 ; his other works, 220 ; the *Hundred and Ten Considerations* translated by Nicholas Ferrar, 220-23 ; his death, 223

Varchi, Benedetto, 70, 115

Vasari, Giorgio, 155, 204

Veniero, Domenico, 171

Vermigli, Pietro Martire, disciple of Valdès, 203, 218 ; counsels Ochino to fly, 255 ; becomes Dean of Christ Church, Oxford, 259

Visconti, P. E., his edition of Vittoria's poems, 67, 71

W

Wiffen, B., *Life and Writings of Juan de Valdès*, quoted, 220